city
Secrets

MANHATTAN
THE ESSENTIAL INSIDER'S GUIDE

ROBERT KAHN

SERIES EDITOR

FANG DUFF KAHN PUBLISHERS

NEW YORK

MANHATTAN

Queens

Fang Duff Kahn Publishers
611 Broadway, 4th Floor
New York, NY 10012
www.citysecrets.com

2011 2012 2013 2014 / 10 9 8 7 6 5 4 3 2 1

Printed in China through Asia Pacific Offset

ISBN: 978-0-9830795-4-5
Library of Congress Control Number: 2011929610
Library of Congress Cataloging-in-Publication Data
New York City / Robert Kahn, series editor.
1. Art, American—New York (State)—New York—Guidebooks.
2. Amusements—New York (State)—New York—Guidebooks.
3. New York
(N.Y.)—Guidebooks. I. Kahn, Robert   II. Series.

*Every care has been taken to ensure the accuracy of the information in this
book. However, the publisher is not able to accept responsibility for any
consequences arising from use of the guide or the information it contains.
If you do encounter a factual error, please let us know.*

*City Secrets books may be purchased at special quantity discounts for
business or promotional use. For information, please contact us at
info@fangduffkahn.com.*

Distributed by Publishers Group West

TABLE OF CONTENTS

"One belongs to New York instantly, one belongs to it as much in five minutes as in five years."
—THOMAS WOLFE

PREFACE

E. B. White wrote that New Yorkers have "the sense of belonging to something unique, cosmopolitan, mighty and unparalleled." Although much has changed since he wrote these words over fifty years ago, the heart of the message remains as true now as it was then.

Whether entering this great city for the first time or the hundredth time, it is difficult not to be awed by the possibility of New York. From afar, there is the exhilaration and grandeur of the great metropolis, yet within, there is the comfort and familiarity of one's own neighborhood. The city is made up of hundreds of small villages connected by streets and avenues, parks and playgrounds, bridges and tunnels. For many, no neighborhood is more important or interesting than their own. New Yorkers take great pride in knowing their particular corner of the city and, as this book demonstrates, in telling others about it. This willingness to share personal "secrets" does not surprise me, for I have found New Yorkers to be generous and gracious people. I know of no other city that so quickly accepts anyone choosing to be a part of it—perhaps because it is a city that rarely forgets that it was built by and for immigrants. New York can be inconvenient, preoccupied with commerce and success, at times overwhelming . . . yet we New Yorkers cannot imagine living anywhere else. This sense of belonging was never more evident than in the days and months following the tragedy of September 11th, 2001. On that day, New York became everyone's city. This book is a reminder that the city exists as a continuum of the people who live here and the places they inhabit. What follows are the personal insights of our extraordinary contributors—a love letter to New York.

ROBERT KAHN
New York City

HOW TO USE THIS BOOK

This is a highly subjective guidebook that reflects the personal tastes and insights of its contributors. We asked architects, painters, writers, and other cultural figures to recommend an overlooked or under-appreciated site or artwork, or, alternatively, one that is well-known but about which they could offer fresh insights, personal observations, or specialized information. Respondents were also invited to describe strolls, neighborhoods, events, shops, and all manner of idiosyncratic and traditional ways of spending time in Manhattan.

These recommendations have been organized into fourteen chapters. Each chapter has an accompanying map, keyed to the text by numbers. Two icons appear throughout the book to reference restaurants and shops.

The editors are delighted with the high number of unusual and delightful recommendations included here. At the same time, we acknowledge that Manhattan provides an endless number of rich experiences. It is our hope that you will be inspired by the enthusiasm of our contributors to explore even further and discover secrets of your own.

USEFUL WEBSITES

Central Park (www.centralparknyc.org) The official website for Central Park. Includes maps, schedule of events, as well as information about bike rentals, guided tours, sites, the zoo, sports programs, the history of the park, etc.

Lincoln Center for the Performing Arts (www.lincolncenter.org) The official Lincoln Center website provides up-to-date information about the New York City Ballet, Metropolitan Opera, New York Philharmonic, and Lincoln Center theater.

Go City Kids (www.gocitykids.com) All sorts of information about children's activities, kid-friendly restaurants, events, etc.

New York Magazine (www.nymag.com/visitorsguide) Restaurant reviews, recommendations for shopping, sightseeing, hotels, etc. Organized by topic and neighborhood.

Manhattan User's Guide (www.manhattanusersguide.com) Up-to-date information about food, shopping, art, cultural events, etc.

Context Travel (www.contexttravel.com) A network of scholars and specialists who design and lead in-depth walking seminars for small groups of intellectually curious travelers.

Nosh Walks (www.noshwalks.com) Walking tours in ethnic neighborhoods primarily to the markets, bakeries, and eateries.

NYC The Official Guide (www.nycgo.com) Offers information about events, restaurants, tickets, restaurants, etc.

Hop Stop (www.hopstop.com) For directions by subway or bus in the five boroughs.

Metropolitan Transportation Authority (www. tripplanner.mta.info, www.mta.info) Maps, schedules, directions via public transportation, and train schedules.

CHAPTER 1

Ellis Island, Statue of Liberty, Financial District & Battery Park City

ELLIS ISLAND & STATUE OF LIBERTY

1.1   **Ellis Island National Monument and Ellis Island Immigration Museum**
1900, Boring & Tilton; 1991, restoration by Beyer Blinder Belle and Notter Finegold & Alexander
Ellis Island information: ☎ 212 363 3200; www.nps.gov
Ferry: ☎ 877 523 9848; www.statuecruises.com

Not exactly a "city secret" this, but a visit to Ellis Island is so rewarding that it should not be missed by anyone curious about the history of New York or, indeed, the United States. About a hundred million Americans, roughly forty percent of the population, are related to someone who entered the country through Ellis Island. The museum presents the history of this extraordinary story, good and bad, in an intelligent, moving, and entertaining way.

You enter through the Baggage Hall. Suitcases and bundles stacked onto original baggage carts set the scene. You climb the stairs that, had you been an immigrant, would (unbeknownst to you) have been your first medical test. Any sign of distress and your coat would have been marked with a chalk code to alert the doctors to investigate further. America wanted immigrants, but she wanted them healthy.

At the top of the stairs is the impressive Registration Room with its vaulted tiled ceiling. The museum designers have been clever here: the room is restored, but left more or less empty, save some of the original inspectors's desks and some benches the immigrants would have waited on.

Looking down on this space from the balcony, one imagines today's tourists almost in the role of extras; as they shuffle around, it's easy to imagine them as immigrants waiting their turn to be registered.

The historical information is presented upstairs in a series of small former inspection rooms. Here you can hear audio recordings of Ellis Island immigrants.

Not only is a visit to Ellis Island informative, it is also a great day out. The view back to the island of Manhattan is alone worth the trip.

CHARLES MARSDEN-SMEDLEY
Museum and exhibition designer

1.2 ## Statue of Liberty National Monument

1871–1886, Frédéric Auguste Bartholdi, sculptor; Alexandre Gustave Eiffel, engineer; Richard Morris Hunt, architect of the base
Liberty Island information: ☎ 212 363 3200; www.nps.gov

Although it is often thought of as a tourist trap, the Statue of Liberty is also a magnificent monument to dichotomy in architecture. It is at once both metal and masonry, frame and load bearing, literal and abstract. As a representation of old and new, the lady has better folds and warped surfaces than anything in current architectural fashion, and is in contrast to the finely composed base by Richard Morris Hunt. The star fortress below is just an added attraction. With contributions by Hunt, Eiffel, and Bartholdi, "base-middle-top" has never been played better and there is no finer example of "firmness, commodity and delight."—Vitruvius

ROBERT LIVESEY
Architect

Yes, you'll be on a boat with a thousand tourists, surrounded by seagulls that won't leave you alone. Yes, it's kind of corny. Still, I'm always surprisingly moved by the entire experience.

ERIC STOLTZ
Actor

FINANCIAL DISTRICT & VICINITY

1.4 ### Staten Island Ferry
South Street at foot of Whitehall Street
☎ 718 815 2628; www.siferry.com
Ferry runs 24 hours.

> *We were very tired, we were very merry—*
> *We had gone back and forth all night on the ferry.*
> —Edna St. Vincent Millay

The best free ride in the world, a round trip on the Staten Island Ferry offers unparalleled views of the Statue of Liberty, Governors Island, Ellis Island, the New York Harbor, and the downtown skyline. The ferry connects lower Manhattan with St. George in Staten Island for seventy-thousand commuters and tourists twenty-four hours a day: during rush hour at fifteen-minute intervals, at thirty-minute intervals most of the day, and hourly late at night. It was the sole lifeline to Staten Island until 1964, when the Verrazano-Narrows Bridge opened. For decades the fare was just a nickel; now it's free. Peter Minuit Park, named to honor the man and the twenty-four-dollar deal that enabled the Dutch to buy (steal) Manhattan from the Indians, fronts the Staten Island Ferry Terminal. The terminal was designed by Walker & Morris in 1907, but a series of subsequent additions and renovations has all but obliterated the original structure. Imagine that it once looked exactly like its magnificent neighbor, the landmarked Battery Maritime Building. Board the ferry after work with your sweetheart and uncork a bottle of champagne. On the way over, watch the sun set behind the Statue of Liberty. On the way back, you'll see the downtown skyline and a thousand twinkling lights.
FREDERIC SCHWARTZ
Architect

Floating the Apple

Check website for locations.

☎ 212 564 5412; www.floatingtheapple.org

This organization rows in beautiful old-time rowboats, not little chunky modern things, but twenty-five feet long, the kind of boats that raced out to bring passengers in from the latest sailboat over from Europe in 1820.

PETE SEEGER
Songwriter

Melville's Manhattan

Herman Melville may have written *Moby Dick* while looking at a mountain out his window in the Berkshires, but he was born and lived most of his life in New York City. Melville liked islands (England, Tahiti) and never got too far from "the insular city of Manhattoes." His best friend Ishmael wonders why people, island people in particular, are so attracted to water, and why it is that on a Sunday you will find countless citizens congregating at the Battery simply staring at the water. This water-gazing is as true now as it was in 1851, when Melville wrote *Moby Dick*, or back in 1819 when he was born only yards away from the Battery, on Pearl Street, so named because of the glistening oyster shells strewn upon it. People are water-gazers, and the Battery is still the place to stroll along the breezy promenade, lean against the rail, and watch people looking beyond the Statue of Liberty (in full view) for the opening to New York's bay (just out of view) and the rolling Atlantic beyond.

Of course, the rail you lean against rests on landfill. As a toddler Melville never witnessed the grass and trees that now intervene between the house of his nativity and the promenade; it was all water then. But the view is much the same: ships, pleasure craft, birds, and people bumping into each other because they are gazing at the water. The home at 6 Pearl Street where Herman learned to walk has vanished and is now the site for an insurance company's skyscraper and a modest museum for city archaeology.

Melville died farther uptown, at 104 East 26th Street, in the Gramercy Park area. That home is also gone. He had returned to Manhattan after his Berkshire years (thirteen in all), and spent close to three decades ignored and virtually unknown, writing poetry and *Billy Budd*. Before his death in 1891, he would take the trolley with his granddaughter to Central Park to watch her run on the meadows and jump from rocks, and to listen to the flapping of her skirts. They sounded much like sails.

JOHN BRYANT
Writer, editor, and professor

1.6 Battery Park
Southernmost tip of Manhattan

This is the place in lower Manhattan that makes one forget all about that other, bigger, more central park to the north, especially if you are drawn to the water and especially if you happen to be a runner. Battery Park combines sweeping green lawns, lush flowerbeds, and a whiff of the city's energy from nearby Wall Street with a continuous view of the mighty Hudson. If you squeeze your eyes and look out between Roosevelt Island and Staten Island and the Statue of Liberty, you can almost convince yourself that you are alone in New York City, staring at your own private section of the Hudson River.

KATHLEEN DEMARCO VAN CLEVE
Author, screenwriter, and film producer

The Wilds of New York Nature Tour

In Manhattan:

1.7 **National Museum of the American Indian**
Alexander Hamilton U.S. Custom House
1 Bowling Green between Whitehall and State Streets
☎ 212 514 3700; www.nmai.si.edu

5.37 **Merchant's House Museum**
29 East 4th Street between Lafayette Street and Bowery
☎ 212 777 1089; www.merchantshouse.com

12.16 **Belvedere Castle**
Central Park, mid-park at 79th Street
www.centralpark.com

14.14 **Inwood Hill Park**
Northwest corner of Manhattan above Dyckman Street
www.nycgovparks.org

In the Bronx:

Orchard Beach
Pelham Bay Park (not on map)
www.nycgovparks.org

In Brooklyn:

Prospect Park
1873, Frederick Law Olmsted & Calvert Vaux
Between Prospect Park West and Flatbush, Parkside and
Ocean Avenues (not on map)
www.nycgovparks.org

Old Stone House
Originally built, 1699; rebuilt, 1935
336 3rd Street between Fourth and Fifth Avenues,
in James J. Byrne Memorial Playground (not on map)
☎ 718 768 3195; www.theoldstonehouse.org

The Salt Marsh Nature Center
Marine Park
Between Flatbush, Gerritsen, and Fillmore Avenues,
and Jamaica Bay to the south (not on map)
📞 718 421 2021; www.saltmarshalliance.org
Closed Wednesdays.

While many come to New York City to see its granite
grandeur and the splashy commercialism for which it is
so widely known, one shouldn't overlook the city's natural
side. New York lies at the intersection of several migratory
pathways and the juncture of several ecotypes. The city
holds treasures and relics reflecting nearly a thousand years
of human occupation; secreted within its emerald necklace
of parks are various jewels containing fragments of its
distinguished natural history.

   Be brave and, in a car, trace the city's cultural and
natural heritage. Start at the National Museum of the
American Indian. Located at Bowling Green Park in lower
Manhattan, the museum holds an incredible collection of
artifacts from the various people who originally occupied
this area. Then head north. If it's autumn, stop at Belvedere
Castle in Central Park to see the hawk migration. Thousands
of raptors pass over the park on cold fronts in September
and October, and there is a ranger available to help you
identify in-flight raptors, as well as eagles, falcons, harriers,
and accipiters. Then, on to Inwood Hill Park (see p. 328)
in upper Manhattan, where you will find the island's last
great forest, surrounding a series of caves used for eons by
Native Americans. Cross the Bronx and stop at Orchard
Beach. If you walk all the way eastward on the boardwalk,
you will come to a nature center that opens out onto a
splendid beach, a back-bay salt marsh, and a beautiful
upland forest that still contains vestige populations of
American chestnuts. The beach sand was barged in from

southern Long Island by Robert Moses, just so northern New Yorkers could have a beach as nice as any in Brooklyn or Queens. Have a seafood lunch on City Island and you'll think you're in Mystic. Head south across the Whitestone Bridge, take the BQE to Prospect Park, enjoying the park's sylvan scenery. It's worth your while to pause at the Old Stone House nearby for a taste of New York during the Revolutionary War. See where General Alexander badgered George Washington into a hasty retreat and listen to how four hundred Marylanders saved the Colonial Army so it could fight another day. Off again now, farther south to the shore. Stop in at the Salt Marsh Nature Center in Marine Park. Here is one of the great hidden treasures of the city: a nature center facing a vast marsh that turns bronze each fall and is always teeming with wildlife. It also hosts unique exhibits and creative programs prepared by park rangers and the National Geographic Society. Once you're back in Manhattan, wrap up this epic journey by stopping off at East 4th Street to visit the Merchant's House Museum (see p. 98). This cozy brown stone contains whale oil lamps, secret passages for the Underground Railroad, and great furnishings from the late nineteenth century.

ALEXANDER R. BRASH
Chairman, Habitat Committee in the EPA's Harbor Estuary Program

1.8 **Bank of New York (originally Irving Trust Company)**
1932, Voorhees, Gmelin & Walker
1 Wall Street at Broadway
www.nyc-architecture.com

The building is well known, but the "red room" banking hall, a superb blend of red terrazzo, dark purple marble, and sparkling red-to-orange-to-gold mosaic tiles, is one of the best surprises in New York. This masterpiece deserves

a special trip, especially if you're looking for New York
Art Deco.
DAVID M. CHILDS
Architect

1.9   Wall Street Wall

Steeped in city, national, and international history for nearly
four centuries, the world's best-known address was actually
once a wall. In 1653, the city's slaves were ordered to build
a protective barricade with logs "twelve feet long, eighteen
inches in circumference, sharpened at the upper end" from
river (Hudson) to river (East) across Manhattan Island.
Demolished in 1699, its first official market was an East
River depot constructed in 1711 for the sale of slaves. In
1791, brokers and investors began meeting under a button-
wood (sycamore) tree at Broad and Wall Streets, and a
year later founded a market for the buying and selling of
stocks and securities.
CHRISTOPHER PAUL MOORE
Historian, author, and research coordinator for exhibitions,
New York Public Library's Schomburg Center for Research on
Black Culture

1.10   Trinity Church

1846, Richard Upjohn
Broadway at Wall Street
📞 212 602 0800; www.trinitywallstreet.org

Trinity Church, the principal church of New York's first
Episcopal parish, is worth a visit as much for its Wall Street
context as for its extraordinary architecture. The most
impressive nineteenth-century Gothic monument in New
York, Trinity was completed in 1846 to the design of
Richard Upjohn. The brownstone church and its graveyard
seem to hold their own in the canyon of vintage skyscrapers
at Broadway and Wall Street. The inside of the church, with

its marble altar and reredos memorializing William B. Astor, completes this Gothic vision from the age of Melville.
PETER PENNOYER
Architect

A Perfect Evening

2.21 **The Peking Duck House**
28 Mott Street between Pell Street and Chatham Square
📞 212 227 1810; www.pekingduckhousenyc.com

2.9 **City Hall**
1811, Joseph François Mangin and John McComb Jr.
City Hall Park between Broadway and Park Row
www.nyc-architecture.com

1.10 **Trinity Church**
1846, Richard Upjohn
Broadway at Wall Street
📞 212 602 0800; www.trinitywallstreet.org

1.11 **George Washington Statue**
1883, James Quincy Adams Ward, pedestal by Richard Morris Hunt
26 Wall Street, in front of Federal Hall
www.nyharborparks.org

1.5 **Wall Street Bull (*Charging Bull*)**
1989, Arturo di Modica
Broadway at Bowling Green

1.4 **Staten Island Ferry**
South Street at the foot of Whitehall Street
📞 718 815 2628; www.siferry.com
Ferry runs 24 hours.

Whenever friends come to town and go to see the Statue of Liberty, I feel deeply ashamed. I know New York the way I know my oldest friends, all the secret back corners and all the bad stuff, too, but the places I know least are the ones that visitors usually see. The closest I've been to the General Assembly of the United Nations is the pressroom, and the last time I took the Circle Line boat around Manhattan was twenty years ago, and then only because of a reporting assignment.

The New York I know and love is less eventful and more unremarked, less monument and boulevard and more row house and alleyway. And here is how I used to spend a perfect evening with my husband before we had children.

We would go to dinner at a place on Mott Street in Chinatown called the Peking Duck House, where you can eat Peking duck without ordering it in advance. We would browse in the little shops that sell cheap Chinese dishes, sandals, and fans.

We would walk south past the courts and the municipal buildings and into the pocket park that stands in front of the prettiest city hall in America, a graceful, oddly diminutive building with a beautiful floating staircase inside.

We'd continue toward the end of the island, passing through the area that was called Five Points when Manhattan was young, a neighborhood that two hundred and fifty years ago was a den of thieves, prostitutes, and streetgangs, all of whom have now moved largely uptown. We would pass the spire of Trinity Church (see p. 20), the neo-Gothic house of worship that was once the tallest point in the city, and cross over Wall Street, which is named after a wall the earliest immigrant New Yorkers, the Dutch, built to keep out the earliest New Yorkers, the Indians.

We would arrive at the giant statue of George Washington that commemorates his inauguration in New York and the giant statue of a bull that commemorates Wall Street's most recent incarnation. And suddenly we would run out of land at the point of Manhattan, where the ferry terminal stands.

So of course we would take the ferry to Staten Island.

We never stayed on Staten Island, just used its best-known, most romantic form of mass transit to see the city strung around us like a hive of hyperactive fireflies. (Staten Island actually has its own little aboveground subway system called the SIRT, which is as different from the rest of the subway as Staten Island is from the rest of the city. But that's another story.) Then we would take the ferry back again.

This constitutes a practically perfect experience, even better than taking the subway to Coney Island, looking at the beluga whales in the New York Aquarium, and having a hot dog and fries at Nathan's.

ANNA QUINDLEN
Author, journalist, and opinions columnist

1.13 Bridge Cafe

279 Water Street at Dover Street
212 227 3344; www.bridgecafenyc.com

There's nothing that will make you feel more like a real New Yorker than being one of the lucky few who know to head down to the Bridge Cafe the moment the first snow-flakes of winter start to cover Manhattan's streets. Cozy up with an Irish coffee in the tin-ceilinged room and watch out the big windows as the snow dusts the two-hundred-plus-year-old cobblestone streets, and the lights on the Brooklyn Bridge, practically within touching distance, twinkle through the flakes. And think about what it was like when Water Street really fronted the East River and Prohibition-era guests slipped Irish whiskey into their coffees, right where you sit.

MARYELLEN GORDON
Founder, Stable of Content

1.14 Brooklyn Bridge

1867–1883, John A. Roebling & Washington Roebling
Park Row (Manhattan) to Adams Street (Brooklyn)

The Brooklyn Bridge celebrates the simple act of passage, elevating the commonplace to a ritual. Always a threshold to the city that is an island, the bridge normally is traversed by car, and during rush hours it is as rushed and full and bustling as any other downtown street. On the pedestrian walk, however, traffic is slowed to an almost stillness. The wooden platform stretches between two remarkable Gothic piers, pacing and dividing the excursion into three parts. The true privilege is in being able to use it this way, not as a special event but as an everyday occurrence.
FREDERICK BIEHLE
Architect

There is a component of Roebling's engineering design that I find so emphatically lyrical and marvelously beautiful that I almost prefer to keep it to myself. I have in mind a major structural feature that presents itself most dramatically from the Manhattan approach—namely, the great low-slung follow-through whereby the main cable, descending from the towers, sweeps down below the roadway only to sweep back up again without missing a beat, securing itself in the stone abutment. It strikes me as utterly modern—not pre-modern, but absolutely modern. I have long been convinced that this mathematical chord-like structural form inspired the governing motive of Albert Gleizes's curiously hearty 1915 Cubist painting, *Brooklyn Bridge*, now in the Guggenheim Museum.
JOSEPH MASHECK
Art historian

1.15 Former American Telephone & Telegraph Company
1923, William Welles Bosworth
195 Broadway between Dey and Fulton Streets

The lobby is a forest of Doric columns, in true hypostyle
fashion, on an approximate fifteen-foot grid—an exquisite
room, the way one should enter a grand and proud corpo-
ration. Beautiful craftsmanship and detailing, even though
four panels created for this space by Paul Manship are no
longer there. (Evelyn Beatrice Longman's *Genius of the
Telegraph*, popularly known as "Golden Boy," once perched
on the building's pinnacle, later was moved to AT&T's
lobby in Philip Johnson's "Chippendale" tower at 550
Madison Avenue, and is now regretfully sentenced to their
suburban New Jersey complex.)
DAVID M. CHILDS
Architect

1.16 Woolworth Building
1913, Cass Gilbert
233 Broadway between Park Place and Barclay Street
www.nyc-architecture.com

At seven hundred and ninety two feet, the Woolworth
was the tallest building in the world until 1930, when the
Chrysler Building surpassed it. The massing became a model
for skyscrapers—a soaring, slender campanile of glazed
terra cotta. Gilbert remarked, "a skyscraper, by its height,
makes its upper parts appear lost in the clouds, whose
masses must become more and more inspired as it rises."
The lobby of this Gothic "cathedral to commerce" vibrates
with mosaics, murals, and marble. Brendan Gill waxed that
it was "one of the most sumptuous in the country...a bedaz-
zlement of marble walls and gilt bronze doors with a vaulted
ceiling of blue and gold mosaics." One whimsical carving

includes caricatures of Gilbert with a model of the building and five-and-dime founder F. W. Woolworth counting his nickels.

FREDERIC SCHWARTZ AND TRACEY HUMMER
Architect and Writer

American Modernism

2.9   **City Hall**
1811, Joseph François Mangin and John McComb Jr.
City Hall Park between Broadway and Park Row
www.nyc-architecture.com

1.16   **Woolworth Building**
1913, Cass Gilbert
233 Broadway between Park Place and Barclay Street

It's 1913. Put together John Marin, the Woolworth Building, and City Hall, and you're right at the divide between safe Gothic skyscraper style and an insurgent American Modernism. Then jump twenty years to see Alfred Stieglitz, Modernism's major progenitor, promoting these insurgent impulses in Depression-era America.

First, go down to City Hall with a book of John Marin's city drawings. Stand on the steps of City Hall and look across Broadway to the ornamented Woolworth Building, then to Marin's drawings of the building, made in 1913, just after the then tallest building in the world opened.

The building itself has a regal look, quite proud of its height, design, and dripping ornament. But the drawings, a kind of abstraction, show the building bending, swerving, dancing. Marin said he made the building move because people move and people give it life, in itself a distinctly humanist expression of the Modernist impulse. Alfred Stieglitz hailed these drawings and immediately hung them at his gallery, 291 (located at 291 Fifth Avenue). One day

Cass Gilbert, the building's architect, came to see them.
He walked in, looked around, and was so horrified that
he stomped out—a perfect example of the clash between
architecture's formalist entry into the twentieth century
and painting's break-loose Modernist spirit.

Add twenty-one years to the same scene and you see
Stieglitz, usually pigeonholed as elitist and formalist, striving
to deepen Modernism's place in the American consciousness.
It's May 8, 1934, sunny and spring-like. A crowd of two
thousand looks up at the steps of City Hall, where Stieglitz,
the main speaker, is standing with Lewis Mumford and John
Dewey. The three, spokespersons for Artists for Democratic
Action, a communist front, demanded of Mayor La Guardia
a municipal center of art where artists and the people of
New York might exhibit, teach, learn, socialize—and feed
America's creative soul. The center never happened. But the
next day Mumford and Stieglitz congratulated each other
for the crowd's vision—and for their own performances.
JUDITH MARA GUTMAN
Writer

**1.17 New York Telephone Company
(Barclay-Vesey Building)**
1927, McKenzie, Voorhees & Gmelin
140 West Street between Barclay and Vesey Streets
www.nyc-architecture.com

A favorite of Le Corbusier's and the frontispiece for his *Vers
une architecture*, this trendsetting building, designed by a
leading early Modernist, Ralph Walker, concretely illustrates
the bold massing of the 1916 zoning laws as best rendered
by Hugh Ferris in 1922. Massive, uplifting, uninterrupted
skyward brick piers alternate with recessed vertical stripes
of windows and spandrels capped by stone Art Deco motifs.
Walker's preliminary massing studies predate the design of

Rockefeller Center. As the architect who introduced the "urban twist," he acknowledged the city's powerful grid by anchoring the parallelogram base to the local streets while twisting its tower for a citywide reading. Don't miss the Guastavino vaults under one of the city's only public sidewalk arcades.

FREDERIC SCHWARTZ
Architect

BATTERY PARK CITY

Battery Park City Esplanade
Battery Park City along the Hudson River from
Chambers Street to Battery Place
📞 212 267 9700; www.bpcparks.org; www.batteryparkcity.org

1.18 **The Real World**
1992, Tom Otterness

1.19 **Inscribed Writings**
1994, Mark Strand and Seamus Heaney

1.20 **North Cove Yacht Harbor Railing**
1986, Walt Whitman and Frank O'Hara
West of the World Financial Center
www.batteryparkcity.org

1.21 **Museum of Jewish Heritage**
18 First Place, Battery Park City
📞 212 509 6130; www.mjhnyc.org

Run down Hudson River Park to the Battery Park City Esplanade along the river. Besides all the joggers and bicyclists, there's much to see. In the northeast corner of

Governor Nelson A. Rockefeller Park (at Chambers Street), there is the wonderful world of sculptures by Tom Otterness called *The Real World*. Groupings of funny Lilliputian animal-humans reflect our own world of work with humor and parody. Just above North Cove is the Lily Pool, with inscriptions by Mark Strand from *The Continuous Life*, and Seamus Heaney from *Death of a Naturalist*. Farther south at North Cove Yacht Harbor is a metal rail fence with the words of Frank O'Hara and Walt Whitman, and right past the Japanese gardens, where Robert F. Wagner Jr. Park begins, is the Museum of Jewish Heritage.

GAIL KRIEGEL
Playwright, librettist, and composer

1.20 North Cove Yacht Harbor Railing
1986, Walt Whitman and Frank O'Hara
West of the World Financial Center
www.batteryparkcity.org

At the beginning of a group of marble benches at the marina, you will see a rail resplendent with gold letters. Follow these words as you view the docked yachts and sailboats with Ellis Island as a backdrop. In these evocative phrases you may discover two of the most apt descriptions of New York City.

> *City of the world (for all races are here,*
> *All the lands of the earth make contributions here;)*
> *City of the sea!*
> *City of wharves and stores—city of tall façades*
>   *of marble and iron!*
> *Proud and passionate city—mettlesome, mad,*
>   *extravagant, city!*
> —Walt Whitman

For a different take on the city's charms, follow the words

on the other side of the marble stairs.

> *One need never leave the confines of New York to get all the greenery one wishes—I can't even enjoy a blade of grass unless I know there's a subway handy, or a record store or some other sign that people do not totally regret life.*
> —Frank O'Hara

THERESA CRAIG
Writer

1.22 Robert F. Wagner Jr. Park
1989, Olin Partnership; Machado & Silvetti; Lynden Miller
At the foot of Battery Park City
www.batteryparkcity.org

Robert F. Wagner Jr. Park is just steps from one of the city's oldest tourist locations, Castle Clinton in Battery Park, and one of its newest museums, the Museum of Jewish Heritage, which includes the Living Memorial to the Holocaust. Featuring a beautifully landscaped setting of well-tended flower gardens, lawns, and walkways, the waterfront Robert F. Wagner Park offers spectacular views of the harbor. At its center is Gigino (20 Battery Place, ☎ 212 528 2228), the perfect place for an al fresco lunch or dinner, where the loudest noise is not the backfire of a truck but the low rumble of passing tugboats. Joggers, skaters, and a few sunbathers complete the tranquil outdoor scene.

ROBERT COOK
Attorney

Ape & Cat (At the Dance)
1993, Jim Dine
www.batteryparkcity.org

In the middle of Robert F. Wagner Jr. Park is a circular English garden, a patch of beauty and serenity with a majestic brick pavilion and wide walkways that look out onto the river. In the winter, the frozen peaks of the waves are sublime. On the lawn, in front of the pavilion, is my favorite piece: two human-size, graceful bronze figures called *Ape & Cat (At the Dance)* by Jim Dine. I never tire of looking at the details of their clasped hands, their regal clothes, their kind faces. One can't help feeling tenderly toward this elegant "mixed" couple standing in the grass at the edge of the city.

GAIL KRIEGEL
Playwright, librettist, and composer

1.24 The Skyscraper Museum

2004, Skidmore, Owings & Merrill
39 Battery Place
☎ 212 968 1961; www.skyscraper.org
Closed Mondays and Tuesdays.

Founded in 1996, this can-do museum has put on exhibitions whose subject matter ranges from downtown New York to an international survey of the world's largest buildings. Thankfully, it has found a new high-concept permanent home, designed by Skidmore, Owings & Merrill, in the Ritz-Carlton Downtown located in lower Manhattan—the birth-place of the skyscraper.

WALTER CHATHAM
Architect

CHAPTER 2

Tribeca, Civic Center & Chinatown

TRIBECA

2.1 **Hudson River Park**
Along the Hudson River from 59th Street to Battery Park City
www.hudsonriverpark.org

At one time, downtowners wishing to run, skate, bike, or power walk had to go uptown to Central Park. Now the Hudson River Park, a long strip of interconnected parks and gardens from West 59th Street to Battery Park (and growing), provides traffic-free space and relatively fresh air filtered off the Hudson. Watch the ferries shuttling people between New Jersey and the Financial District while the Statue of Liberty looks on. Plantings along the path are in full bloom during the spring and summer, and in the winter Canada geese graze. Along the way are the famous Stuyvesant High School, an open field to rival Central Park's Great Lawn, a children's park, a pier where boats of the rich and famous dock, a wooden boardwalk where fishermen cast their lines year-round, and, right before Battery Park, the Museum of Jewish Heritage. A nearby set of steps provides a great view of the river and Ellis Island. Walk the steps slowly or run up like Rocky Balboa, on top of the world.

ADAM BERLIN
Writer

2.2 **Former American Express Stables**
1867
157 Hudson Street between Laight and Hubert Streets

The American Express Company was originally an express company; that is, it hauled things. Its headquarters were located in the then newly commercial part of New York west of Broadway and south of Canal, which today is once again residential. The company built a handsome marble-faced building at the southwest corner of Hudson and Jay Streets, now gone, though the present building on that site was also built by American Express in the 1880s. But American Express has left a small remnant where the keen-eyed observer can see it, at the northeast corner of Hubert and Collister Streets, and likewise at the southeast corner of Collister and Laight Streets. The handsome building that runs along Collister Street was the stable for its superb horses, and at either end of the building, high up in the steep gable, are circular reliefs with what are supposed to be dogs (the emblem of the company before that vapid centurion), surrounded by the words "American Express Co." The dog on Hubert Street looks more like a bear or a large cat with odd jaws; the dog on Laight is far more doglike, but oddly like a Chihuahua. They were supposed to be bulldogs, sources say, but neither one achieves proper bulldogginess. What's even odder is that they don't match. The building itself is a lovely brick composition, massive and confident, with splendid Palladian windows on the second floor.

ROBIN CLEMENTS
Teacher

Summer in New York

2.1 **Hudson River Park**
Along the Hudson River from 59th Street to Battery Park City
www.hudsonriverpark.org

3.11 **Kayak Rental**
The New York City Downtown Boathouse at Pier 40
On the Hudson River at West Houston Street
www.downtownboathouse.org

1.20   **North Cove Yacht Harbor**
West of World Financial Center, on the Hudson River
www.batteryparkcity.org

1.21   **Museum of Jewish Heritage**
18 First Place, Battery Park City
☎ 212 509 6130; www.mjhnyc.org

1.22   **Robert F. Wagner Jr. Park**
At the foot of Battery Park City
www.bpcparks.org

1.23   **Gigino**
In Robert F. Wagner Jr. Park
20 Battery Place
☎ 212 528 2228; www.gigino-wagnerpark.com

Take a bike and ride to the lower west side of Manhattan
along the path that hugs the Hudson River and runs to the
tip of Battery Park City. While this esplanade is still evolving and is by no means any competition for Frederick Law
Olmsted, it attempts to open a new area of the city for
exploration, allowing New Yorkers and visitors access to
the Hudson River.

Starting at 23rd Street, this ride runs along the old piers
of the lower Hudson River. It passes a variety of attractions
along the way, including a boathouse for kayak rental, the
ferry dock for rides to New Jersey, cafes and restaurants
surrounding the yacht harbor at the World Financial Center,
and the Museum of Jewish Heritage, before arriving at the
jewel-like Robert F. Wagner Jr. Park at the foot of Battery
Park City. Here one is thrilled by a magnificent view of
New York Harbor and one of the great sculptural achievements of the nineteenth century—the captivating Statue of
Liberty. This tiny park, designed by the firm of Machado
& Silvetti, works beautifully.

2

🍴 A little cafe, Gigino, open in the summer months, with tables and umbrellas, is tucked gently into the base of the brick observation deck. Below stretches a plane of perfect green grass.

CAROLYN CARTWRIGHT
Feature-film set decorator and interior designer

2.3 Walker's
16 North Moore Street at Varick Street
☎ 212 941 0142

🍴 This is the requisite no-frills bar/restaurant in Tribeca. Walker's has three rooms, big windows, great fries, and a decently expanded menu that makes this the place to go when sophisticated restaurants with sophisticated pricing seem just too much of a hassle and what you really want is to be in a comfortable place with relaxed people and good food.

KATHLEEN DEMARCO VAN CLEVE
Author, screenwriter, and film producer

2.4 Ted Muehling
52 White Street between Broadway and Church Street
☎ 212 431 3825; www.tedmuehling.com

🎁 Although almost every fashionable woman I know owns at least one pair of beautiful earrings from Ted Muehling's elegant workshop on Howard Street, the origin of these treasures remains somehow mysterious. Maybe it's because ownership of a pair is like membership in an exclusive club. Or maybe because, like me, husbands refuse to tell their wives the location of this never-fail "get-out-of-jail-free" card. Whatever the reason, Ted Muehling has resisted the temptation to go "wide," and the quality and design remain unsurpassed. Though mostly abstract, these earrings, necklaces, bracelets, and pins find their inspiration in organic forms such as berries, rice, shells, nuts, and eggs.

The shop also carries beautiful ceramic pieces designed by Mr. Muehling and manufactured by the great Nymphenburg porcelain factory in Germany. Highly recommended as a source of simple beauty.

ROBERT KAHN
Architect

2.5   **Taste of Tribeca**
Duane Street between Greenwich and Hudson Streets
www.tasteoftribeca.com

¶� In this annual event, world-class local restaurants and catering firms provide a mouth-watering outdoor buffet luncheon. Dozens of Tribeca's finest chefs prepare their signature dishes so that, on a late May Sunday from end of morning until mid-afternoon, they may be sampled by diners who stroll down Duane Street. Participating restaurants have included Boule, Nobu, Capsouto Frères, and Tribeca Grill, to name just a few. In terms of cuisine, no ordinary street fest. First held in 1996 in an effort to raise money for art in the neighborhood's public schools, Taste of Tribeca was conceived by its founders as a moment and place where, on a beautiful day in spring, their passion for great food and art and their children's education would converge.

JANE FISHER
Marketing consultant

2.8   **Odeon**
145 West Broadway between Duane and Thomas Streets
☎ 212 233 0507; www.theodeonrestaurant.com

¶� Once the trendiest restaurant in the city (think long ago, like the '80s), this place has become a classic because they just do everything right: big dining area, great food, an atmosphere that remains comfortably chic but not off-putting. Odeon will probably continue to thrive for good reason.

KATHLEEN DEMARCO VAN CLEVE
Author, screenwriter, and film producer

Kayaking on the Hudson

☎ 646 613 0740; www.downtownboathouse.org
Seasonal and weather permitting.

3.11 **The New York City Downtown Boathouse at Pier 40**
On the Hudson River at West Houston Street

9.22 **The New York City Downtown Boathouse at Pier 96**
On the Hudson River at West 56th Street

Well off the beaten path psychologically, but easily accessible, is the Downtown Boathouse, which offers free kayaking in two locations in a city more known for crowded subways, noisy buses, rushing taxis, and busy sidewalks. Just show up on a summer weekend and you'll find a free kayak to use, basic instruction, and access to a relatively protected portion of the Hudson River. For more advanced kayakers, show up before 9 a.m. on the weekend (Pier 40 only) for a three-hour paddle to the Statue of Liberty or the *U.S.S. Intrepid*. Although there are often more people than boats for these longer trips, it's a great chance to get back to nature in a dramatically man-made city.
THORIN TRITTER
Historian

CIVIC CENTER

Civic Center Stroll
www.nyc.gov

2.9 **City Hall**
1812, Joseph François Mangin and John McComb Jr.
City Hall Park between Broadway and Park Row
www.nyc-architecture.com

2.10 **Old New York County Courthouse ("Tweed" Courthouse)**
1872, John Kellum and Thomas Little
52 Chambers Street between Broadway and Centre Street
www.nyc.gov

2.11 **Former Emigrant Industrial Savings Bank Building**
1912, Raymond F. Almirall
51 Chambers Street between Broadway and Elk Street
www.nyc-architecture.com

2.12 **Surrogate's Courthouse**
1907, John R. Thomas
31 Chambers Street at Centre Street
www.nyc.gov

2.13 **Manhattan Municipal Building**
1914, McKim, Mead & White
1 Centre Street opposite Chambers Street
www.nyc.gov

2.15 **U.S. Courthouse**
1936, Cass Gilbert and Cass Gilbert Jr.
40 Centre Street at Pearl Street
www.nyc-architecture.com

2.16 **New York County Courthouse (New York State Supreme Court)**
1925, Guy Lowell
60 Centre Street between Pearl and Worth Streets,
in Foley Square
www.nyc.gov

2.17 **Criminal Courts Building and Men's House of Detention**
1941, Harvey Corbett and Charles B. Meyers
100 Centre Street between Leonard and White Streets
www.nyc.gov

1.14 **Brooklyn Bridge**
1867–83, John A. Roebling & Washington Roebling
Park Row in Manhattan to Adams Street in Brooklyn

1.16 **Woolworth Building**
1913, Cass Gilbert
233 Broadway between Park Place and Barclay Street
www.nyc-architecture.com

I recommend an incredible group of buildings that I have often taken friends and students to visit. The tour can be completed in an hour unless one is detained by the many interesting aspects of this visit. It's best to go during business hours, as the interiors are of as much interest as the exteriors and are not open on the weekend.

I like to start at the front of City Hall, in the newly renovated City Hall Park. City Hall has an elegant 1812 French Renaissance façade by Joseph F. Mangin and John McComb Jr. and a dramatic interior hall with a twin circular stair and dome.

One used to be able to go out the back door to the "Tweed" Courthouse, on axis behind City Hall. In 1876, C. L. W. Eidlitz added a Romanesque cast-iron hall with glass walkways and a steel truss skylight that once held stained glass. You can leave Tweed Hall by the basement door in the front.

Across the street, on axis, is the former Emigrant Industrial Savings Bank Building, designed by Raymond F. Almirall in 1912. One can enter this interesting double tower building to see an impressive banking hall.

Just east on Chambers Street is the Surrogate's Court building (see p. 43). This Beaux Arts building has entries from both Chambers and Elk Streets. From Chambers, one passes through a double colonnaded entry to the center skylighted hall. There is an elegant and complex stair at the end of the hall that appears to be independent of its container. It begins with a symmetrical center entry and becomes asymmetrical as it rises above the skylit center court.

From here, one is confronted with the Arch of Constantine screen in front of the U-shaped Municipal Building. The Municipal Building is split by Chambers Street, with a vaulted space in the form of the entry to the Palazzo Farnese in Rome. This urban solution forced two lobbies and two elevator banks rising to the colonnaded top where stands the statue *Civic Fame*.

Now walk north on Centre Street; at Foley Square is the U.S. Courthouse, with its pyramided tower by Cass Gilbert and Cass Gilbert Jr. North of that is the New York County Courthouse, designed in 1912, but built fifteen years later. The hexagonal plan has a great interior hall surrounded by a colonnade.

Continue north to the Art Deco Criminal Courts Building and Men's House of Detention—"The Tombs" (see p. 44). Peek into the formidable center hall, then turn back to City Hall Park. This time, passing the screen of the Municipal Building under the south arm of Guastavino tile work, one can look down the axis of the Brooklyn Bridge.

Saving a walk over the bridge for another time, cross the park with eyes on the Woolworth Building (see p. 25). The delicate exterior is complemented by the glass mosaic

lobby, which seems like a cross between a Byzantine street system and the proclaimed "cathedral of commerce."
JON MICHAEL SCHWARTING
Director of the graduate program in Urban and Regional Design, New York Institute of Technology

2.12 Surrogate's Court

1907, John R. Thomas
31 Chambers Street between Centre and Elk Streets
www.nyc.gov

The next best thing to seeing the Paris Opera House is a visit to the lobby of the Surrogate's Court. Open to the public during regular court hours, this spectacular granite building was begun in 1899 and completed in 1907. The courtrooms on the fifth floor, made of mahogany and English oak, are well worth the elevator ride. The building also houses the archives of the City of New York.
JAMES J. BRUCIA
Justice (retired), New York State Supreme Court

2.14 African Burial Ground Memorial

c. 1690
Corner of Duane and African Burial Ground Way (Elk Street)
Visitor Center: 290 Broadway, close to Foley Square and just north of City Hall
www.nps.gov/afbg

Unearthed during construction of the federal office building at 290 Broadway in 1991, the Colonial-era cemetery once spanned more than five acres or about five city blocks. Archaeologists estimate more than twenty thousand men, women, and children were once buried at the site, which included the preserved portion at the corner of Duane and Elk Streets.
CHRISTOPHER PAUL MOORE
Historian, author, and research coordinator, New York Public Library's Schomburg Center for Research on Black Culture

2.17 Criminal Courts Building and Men's House of Detention ("The Tombs")

1939, Harvey Wiley Corbett and Charles B. Meyers
100 Centre Street between Leonard and White Streets

Go to night court and listen to the pleas of a parade of pimps, prostitutes, petty thieves, and, every once in a while, a murderer. It's gritty and it's real. The Art Moderne design by Harvey Wiley Corbett is a poor man's Rockefeller Center. Named "The Tombs" after its Egyptian Revival predecessor across the street, it lived up to its name for decades as symbol of the deplorable condition of correctional institutions.
FREDERIC SCHWARTZ
Architect

CHINATOWN

2.18 Canal Street

This bustling, traffic-riddled crosstown thoroughfare originally functioned as a canal and is now virtually a linear flea market starting east at the Manhattan Bridge, running through the Lower East Side, Chinatown, Little Italy, SoHo, and Tribeca and ending west at the Hudson River. You can buy anything under the sun (and more), it seems, as vendors spill out on the sidewalks hawking their wares from sunrise to sundown. Brush up on your bartering skills before buying the knockoff handbags and watches that abound, and also watch your pockets. A great place to score the requisite NYC T-shirts and baseball caps at way below Midtown prices. Treat yourself to the best *café con leche* in New York at the West Side Coffee Shop (corner of Church and Lispenard).
FREDERIC SCHWARTZ AND TRACEY HUMMER
Architect and writer

Chinatown Walk

2.19 **Tunnel**
5 Doyers Street between Pell Street and Bowery
www.scoutingny.com/?p=1757; www.nychinatown.org

2.20 **Nom Wah Tea Parlor**
13 Doyers Street between Pell Street and Bowery
☎ 212 962 6047; www.nomwah.com

Head for Pell Street, where at No. 16 you'll find a bronze placard reading "Hip Sing Association." Pell Street has been home to the Hip Sing Tong, or association, since the 1880s. The Hip Sing were fierce rivals of the On Leong Tong (who were headquartered in the Pagoda on the southwest corner of Mott and Canal). From the late nineteenth century through the 1930s, the tongs would regularly erupt in battles over gambling turf and other interests of the day. These conflicts, referred to legendarily as the Tong Wars, were full of shootings and stabbings that spilled over from Pell Street onto adjoining Doyers Street. No. 5 Doyers, site of the Old Chinese Opera House, was the scene of an especially gruesome power play in 1906, when Hip Singers fired into an audience of On Leongers. The attackers made their getaway through Chinatown's network of ancient tunnels, and you can enter one of them at 5 Doyers Street today.

Take the staircase below ground and follow the tunnel until you exit at Chatham Square, farther to the south. What you'll encounter en route is a dingy arcade of small businesses. Still, it doesn't take too much fantasizing to conjure up images of blood, battle, and flight in this corridor a century ago. If you double back and exit on Doyers Street, you can stop for tea at Nom Wah (No. 13)—New York's oldest (1927) dim sum parlor.

JANE FISHER
Marketing consultant

2.20 Nom Wah Tea Parlor

13 Doyers Street between Pell Street and Bowery
212 962 6047; www.nomwah.com

Located on Doyers Street since 1920, Nom Wah is the
oldest tea parlor in Chinatown. This is the real deal. The
food is terrific, and extremely reasonable. Try the shrimp
shumai—said to be the best in the city.

CLARISSA BLOCK
Fashion stylist and children's jewelry designer

2.22 Kam Kuo Food Corp.

17A Mott Street between Mosco and Worth Streets
212 233 5387

New York's Chinatown has grown tremendously in recent
times, taking over the old Little Italy and reaching into
the Lower East Side. In some ways, it is a city within a city
and exploring it can be daunting. One good place to get
started is the Kam Kuo Food Corp. From the street this
looks like an ordinary small store, but once inside you'll
realize that it's as large as a suburban supermarket and it
has a second floor as well.

It's definitely not a tourist spot. Most people there are
just doing their regular grocery shopping, and unless you
ask for help, you will be left alone. Begin at the collection
of bins in front. Mixed in with the usual bulk goods is
more unusual fare, such as shredded squid, pickled tanger-
ines, and preserved dry olives. One row offers six different
kinds of ginseng, ranging from sixteen to sixty-three dollars
a pound. There are some familiar brands on the shelves
—Carnation, Nestlé—but these are products made for the
Asian market, not the ones you see in America. Then
there are the brands manufactured and sold in Asia, with
Western names chosen to sound exotic in their target
markets: Kewpie mayonnaise, Mickey Mouse haw candy,
Bull-Dog Worcestershire sauce, Beefeater pukka tea.

Kam Kuo is a good source for hard-to-find foods from many Asian countries. They have a wonderful selection of ready-made foods; especially worth trying are the frozen steam buns. Try to leave with at least one product that you've never heard of before. It shouldn't be too difficult. On a recent visit some items to be considered were white fungus with pineapple, grass jelly drink, toddy palm seeds, shrink-wrapped preserved quail eggs, canned rambutan, sapote, jackfruit, "odour frying fish with chili," peanut gluten, salted croaker (a kind of fish), medlar-chrysanthemum drink crystal, honey-fritillary-and-loquat beverage, pickled *mayom*, as well as some foods whose names are translated only into Latin because there isn't an English equivalent.

Upstairs they sell mostly cookware and a few household appliances. You can find cheap, high-quality pots and utensils and beautiful dishes here. If you're having a banquet for fifty people, their banquet room has all sorts of little tables and chairs. And if you need an industrial-sized soybean drink press or a melon-seed cracker, you will find one here.

JANET B. PASCAL
Writer and production editor, Viking Children's Books

Mott Street Stroll

2.23 **Ten Ren's Tea Time**
75 Mott Street between Canal and Bayard Streets
☎ 212 732 7178; www.tenrenusa.com

2.24 **Chinatown Ice Cream Factory**
65 Bayard Street between Mott and Elizabeth Streets
☎ 212 608 4170; www.chinatownicecreamfactory.com

2.25 **Columbus Park**
Between Baxter, Mulberry, Bayard, and Worth Streets
www.nyc.gov

🍴 Most people think of Chinatown as a noisy, sprawling
🏮 market of trinkets, gadgets, street vendors, and odd-
looking food. But if you know where to go, you can enjoy
the neighborhood at a slow pace, taking in its quiet
moments in unexpected ways.

Enter the gateway to old Chinatown at the southern
intersection of Mott and Canal Streets. Head south on
Mott, where you'll soon see a cluster of new teahouses
boasting the latest drink innovation: flavored tapioca teas
or "bubble tea." These candy-colored teahouses are the new
social clubs for young Asians, who are a few generations
removed from the old benevolent societies their grandparents
patronized. You may choose from a number of fruits and
flavors, but all the drinks have giant black pearls of tapioca
(hence the nickname, "bubble tea") bobbing on the bottom.
Sucked up through a giant straw, the gummy beads pop
into your mouth and require considerable chewing before
you can swallow them (kids love this part).

Continuing south, just to the left on Bayard Street, is a
tried-and-true institution, the Chinatown Ice Cream Factory.
Forget about thirty-one flavors, the nearby Häagen-Dazs,
or those two guys from Vermont; the ice cream here is made
fresh daily, and many flavors, such as almond cookie,
chrysanthemum tea, and lychee, are from ancestral Chinese
recipes. Try these flavors you won't find in the supermarket
freezer: ginger, taro, red bean, and green tea. Get a cone,
or a dish, and continue your stroll down Mott Street until
you reach Mosco Street. Follow Mosco to Columbus Park,
an outdoor living room and salon for the community. The
sounds of the city disappear here, not for the peace, but for
the loud chirps of birds, the buzz of hundreds of people
talking, and the clapping of mahjong tiles on the tables.
Throngs of Chinese sitting on cardboard boxes and milk
crates socialize here all year round, testing their skills and
fortunes. They're young and old, male and female, but the

activities seem to be segregated: the women play cards, the men play dominoes. Along the wire fence, fortune-tellers hang their red banners and point to mysterious battered books and long, thin reeds, devices used to divine the future. As few of the "wise women" speak English, having your destiny revealed may not come easy.

LANA BORTOLOT
Writer

WEST VILLAGE

3.2 **Corner Bistro**

331 West 4th Street at Jane Street

📞 212 242 9502; www.cornerbistrony.com

🍴🍷 Located on the corner of one of the most maddeningly
tangled sections of the West Village: the intersection of
Eighth Avenue and West 4th and Jane Streets. It is, however, quite easy to find "the Bistro." Inevitably, there will
be people pouring out of it, walking into it, and, depending
on the weather, lounging outside of it. Forget everything
you've heard about fancy service and sleek decor (there is a
reason everything is so cheap) and order one of the Bistro's
legendary hamburgers, fries, and a beer. A particular
American species, Frat Boy, mistakenly believes it owns this
place, but just push right by him and head for the back
tables. You may look up one night (it doesn't close until
the wee hours of the morning) and see Bruce Springsteen
having dinner, right next to a bunch of businessmen, next
to an in-love couple, next to a man who won't stop smiling.
If it weren't always so crowded, it would be perfect.
KATHLEEN DEMARCO VAN CLEVE
Author, screenwriter, and film producer

3.3 **The Village Vanguard**

178 Seventh Avenue South between West 11th and
Perry Streets

📞 212 255 4037; www.villagevanguard.com

The legendary club that Miles Davis used to play in is
dark, a little uncomfortable, and absolutely delightful.
ERIC STOLTZ
Actor

3.4 Smalls Jazz Club

183 West 10th Street between West 4th Street and
Seventh Avenue South

☎ 212 929 7565; www.smallsjazzclub.com

3

If Charles Mingus were ever to call me on the telephone and
ask me to go to Minton's Playhouse up in Harlem, I would
say, "But Charlie, Minton's is closed," and I would take him
to Smalls. Smalls is a jazz club pinched between Seventh
Avenue and West 4th Street, at the bottom of a stairwell
that twists into the basement. The music at Smalls almost
never stops. It starts every night at about 7:30 or 8 p.m.,
and flows like a glowing current of electricity until musicians
can no longer honk, bleat, or swing, and sunlight cracks
your eyes as you climb the stairwell and stumble back out
into the street.

Sometimes on cold winter evenings, people will stand for
hours holding plastic bags filled with imported beer or wine
bottles, in a line so long that it wraps around the corner
onto West 4th Street. They'll wait and wait until it's their
turn to pay the ten-dollar cover charge to Mr. Borden, the
man at the door, who is probably reading poetry or playing
his violin. The inside of Smalls is smoky and very dark, and
there's room for about fifty people. There's no stage, and
musicians perform in the front of the club, in an area about
the size of a phone booth. The club's brick walls are covered
by black-and-white photos of jazz legends. Patrons sit at
small, round, candlelit tables, on padded benches, or at the
bar, which serves only fruit juice and iced tea. Musicians
are paid entirely from the sale of CDs, but applause is also
a valid form of currency. Mounted on the wall, behind
where the drums are usually set up, is an old photograph
of Louis Armstrong, sitting cross-legged on the ground,
smiling gloriously because his ears are delighted.

ALEX FRENCH
Writer and journalist

West Village à la Carte

3.5 **Mary's Fish Camp**
64 Charles Street at West 4th Street
☎ 646 486 2185; www.marysfishcamp.com

5.11 **Pearl Oyster Bar**
18 Cornelia Street between Bleecker and West 4th Streets
☎ 212 691 8211; www.pearloysterbar.com

5.18 **Murray's Cheese Shop**
257 Bleecker Street at Cornelia Street
☎ 212 243 3289; www.murrayscheese.com

3.8 **Garden of the Church of St. Luke-in-the-Fields**
487 Hudson Street between Barrow and Christopher Streets,
entrance on Barrow Street
☎ 212 924 0562; www.stlukeinthefields.org

5.12 **Blue Hill**
75 Washington Place between Sixth Avenue and
Washington Square West
☎ 212 539 1776; www.bluehillfarm.com

5.13 **Washington Square Park**
At the foot of Fifth Avenue
www.nycgovparks.org

3.9 **Cherry Lane Theatre**
38 Commerce Street at Barrow Street
☎ 212 989 2020; www.cherrylanetheatre.org

3.1 **Pastis**
9 Ninth Avenue at Little 12th Street
☎ 212 929 4844; www.pastisny.com

¶⚲ Greenwich Village: the best place in Manhattan! Grab a
lobster roll at Mary's or Pearl or a *panini* at my place,
Murray's, and savor it in St. Luke's Garden. Have a late
dinner on a summer evening at Blue Hill restaurant, then
sit on a bench and watch the people go by in Washington
Square Park (see p. 85). Catch a Sunday matinee at the
Cherry Lane Theatre, and marvel at the most beautiful residential architecture in Manhattan. Stay up really late and
have a bite to eat at Pastis in the meat market, then hit the
local nightclubs.

ROBERT KAUFELT
Proprietor, Murray's Cheese Shop

3.8 ## Garden of the Church of St. Luke-in-the-Fields
487 Hudson Street between Barrow and Christopher Streets,
entrance on Barrow Street
212 924 0562; www.stlukeinthefields.org

Walk through the street gate and follow the path to the
walled garden. A walled garden—the kind so many of us
imagined as children! In the center, a flowering tree, paths
through lilac and tulips and roses (tended by bands of
invisible volunteers), a few benches, squirrels, singing birds.
It feels safe and sacred—a broken-off piece of paradise.

   The garden is lovely in all seasons—in winter with snow
falling, in spring when the first crocus comes up. People
seem to talk softly and to smile and nod to one another as
people do in churches, but it's also a good place for a kiss.
I've seen commuters striding to the PATH train in the early
morning stop and stare from the sidewalk, as if looking back
into paradise from the fallen world.

MARIE HOWE
Poet

3.10 Former Home of Edna St. Vincent Millay

1873
75 1/2 Bedford Street between Morton and Commerce Streets
Not open to the public.

This house on Bedford Street is the smallest row house in Greenwich Village, once known as the "Edna St. Vincent Millay Doll's House" because the famous poet lived there with her husband Eugen Boissevain during the 1920s. It is said that the original house consisted of one narrow room on each of its floors, but it had the advantage of a closed-in backyard that gave easy access to a neighboring house occupied by Edna's one-time lover and lifelong friend, the poet Arthur Davison Ficke, then married to another dear friend, Gladys Brown.

EDMUND KEELEY
Author, critic, and translator

Stargazing

After several decades, the brick façades of many row houses built in New York during the Federal period began to fatigue and buckle, and it became necessary to "tie" the brick back to the joists with metal rods, which were then capped by iron plates on the outside walls. Early versions of these plates, which functioned like large washers, were made in straightforward utilitarian shapes—a couple of crossed iron strips, or perhaps a simple rondel. By the end of the Civil War, however, ironworkers began making them from melted-down cannonballs and casting them in the shape of stars to honor the enduring Republic. You'll find these utilitarian but beautiful symbols on brick walls throughout lower Manhattan and the Village—affecting examples of turning swords into plowshares.

ANGELA HEDERMAN
Publisher

Celebrated Women

6.21 **Home of Emma Goldman**
210 East 13th Street between Second and Third Avenues
Not open to the public.

3

3.10 **Home of Edna St. Vincent Millay**
75 1/2 Bedford Street between Morton and Commerce Streets
www.nyc-architecture.com
Not open to the public.

Two houses—one a tenement in the East Village, one a tiny town house in the West Village—still stand in lower Manhattan, much as they were in the early decades of the twentieth century, despite occasional renovations. Each memorializes the vibrant labors of a celebrated woman, each of whose creative accomplishments contributed to the exuberant spirit of an era.

At 210 East 13th Street, Emma Goldman (1869–1940), the anarchist organizer, feminist agitator, birth-control and free-love advocate who was tagged by FBI chief J. Edgar Hoover "the most dangerous woman in the world," lived for a decade. She moved to her "oasis in the desert," as she called it, in 1903, soon after she emerged from hiding, following President William McKinley's assassination in 1901 by a deranged anarchist whom Goldman was falsely accused of abetting. In the living room/bedroom, which also became her office, she launched her anarchist journal of art and politics, *Mother Earth*, in 1906; it appeared monthly for twelve years, interrupted only by occasional police interference. In that dashing era of the New Woman, Goldman's cold-water flat quickly became one of the city's liveliest centers of feminist agitation and radical thought. "There was always someone sleeping in the front, someone who had stayed too late and lived too far away or who was too shaky on their feet or needed cold compresses or who had no home to go to," wrote Goldman in her autobiography, *Living My Life.* The apartment was described by one friend as "a home for lost dogs," and lauded by another (Wobbly labor leader Big Bill Haywood) for its coffee "black asnight, strong as the revolutionary ideal, sweet as love."

Across town and some blocks south stands the house of Edna St. Vincent Millay (1892–1950), another New Woman. Her 1922 poem,

> *My candle burns at both ends;*
> *It will not last the night;*
> *But ah, my foes, and oh, my friends—*
> *It gives a lovely light!*

was taken up as the anthem of a generation. This celebrated poet, playwright, and advocate of women's sexual freedom was one of three famously beautiful sisters who took bohemian Greenwich Village by storm. They acted at the Provincetown Playhouse on MacDougal Street, sometimes in Millay's own plays. A decade after gaining national attention for a long poem she published at age twenty, Millay won a Pulitzer Prize in poetry in 1922, the first awarded to a woman. Her one-time lover, the influential critic Edmund Wilson, described her as "almost supernaturally beautiful" and her readings as "thrilling," noting ruefully that she was more interested in poetry than in men. After half a dozen years spent in various Village apartments with her sisters and sometimes their mother, Millay married in 1923 and moved for a while to the one-room-wide, three-story house—reputedly the city's narrowest—at 75½ Bedford Street. In her eighties, Millay's sister Norma told me that back during Prohibition the sisters would sometimes tend bar as a favor to their friend Lee Chumley, owner of Chumley's, a then popular speakeasy at 86 Bedford, diagonally across the street from Millay's house. If Lee Chumley was away, Norma confided, they invited their friends in for an evening of free drinks.

ALIX KATES SHULMAN
Writer

CHAPTER 4

SoHo, Nolita & Little Italy

SOHO

4.1 **The Film Forum**

209 West Houston between Sixth Avenue and Varick Street

☏ 212 727 8110; www.filmforum.org

Don't worry about what's on the bill at this intimate three-theater complex. Just trust the programmer's taste and go. Whether it's a quirky low-budget job, a pristine new print of an American classic, or a contemporary foreign film, these folks find and screen the best. The atmosphere is unpretentious, the crowd is smart and appreciative, and they have the best popcorn in New York.

GREGORY MOSHER
Theater director and producer

4.2 **Joe's Dairy**

156 Sullivan Street between Prince and West Houston Streets

☏ 212 677 8780

Closed Sundays and Mondays.

🍴 If you're a mozzarella snob or just like a good Italian sandwich, you will do well to make a stop at Joe's Dairy. It's a tiny, old-fashioned storefront, a vestige from the days when this neighborhood was the western half of Little Italy (split by what is now SoHo). Inside you'll find an ample cheese selection along with other dairy staples such as milk, mascarpone, and ricotta. Filling the shelves are a sampling of olive oils and dried pastas. But the real reason to make the pilgrimage is the mozzarella—unsalted, salted, and smoked. You may never taste better outside Italy. If you're lucky, you'll catch the cheese makers in action in the back, stirring and stretching the gooey white stuff in enormous soup pots. If you happen to walk by and see smoke billowing out of the place and the entire staff hanging around outside, don't bother calling the fire department . . . it's only the smoked mozzarella being made. Grab a half of a smoked for a tasty snack, or take an unsalted home for the perfect, rich, velvety accompaniment to a fresh tomato and sprig of basil. Joe's sells a nice mozzarella sandwich and also will grate your just-cut piece of Parmigiano Reggiano.

SARAH CAPLAN
Designer, graphic artist, and writer

4

Sullivan Street Stroll

4.3 **St. Anthony of Padua Roman Catholic Church**
c. 1888
155 Sullivan Street at West Houston Street
☎ 212 777 2755; www.stanthonynyc.org

4.4 **Pepe Rosso to Go**
149 Sullivan Street between West Houston and Prince Streets
☎ 212 677 4555; www.peperossotogo.com

4.5 **Pino's Prime Meats**
149 Sullivan Street between West Houston and Prince Streets
☎ 212 475 8134

4.8 **Anonymous Hair Salon**
105 Sullivan Street between Prince and Spring Streets
☎ 212 966 6806

🍴🍷 There's a street, Sullivan Street, that was the spine of an Italian-American neighborhood now devoured by the advance of SoHo. But if you start at Houston and walk the three blocks south to Broome, a few places that remain can give you the flavor of what was.

Start at the church of St. Anthony of Padua. On a good Saturday you can catch an old-fashioned Italian-American wedding, with the chance of a horse and buggy or at least the longest white stretch limo you've ever seen. Walk past 150 Sullivan, which used to be Canapa's Bakery. Across the street is Pepe Rosso to Go, which used to be Rocky's Vegetable Store. The butcher shop's another leftover, with sawdust on the floor and a butcher block from years ago. Pino took over for Mario, but the flavor's the same. There used to be another butcher on this street, as well as two bakeries, two grocery stores, a club, some storefronts, and some stores that were just for rent to keep baby carriages and bicycles.

Cross Prince Street and keep walking and you'll come to a sign that reads "Anonymous Hair Salon." Go in on a Saturday morning and you'll be back in the old neighborhood. All the seniors come to get their hair washed and set and teased into bouffants that will hold all week. You'll get all the gossip: who died, who's sick, who's been naughty and who's been nice, plus you'll get a good haircut. Ask for Pat. She'll order you coffee and a sandwich at lunch-time. But be nice...you gotta be nice in the neighborhood. Then shop all you want in the SoHo everybody knows.

LOUISA ERMELINO
Writer and chief of reporters, InStyle

4.6   Dia Center for the Arts: *The New York Earth Room*
1977, Walter De Maria
141 Wooster Street between West Houston and Prince Streets
☎ 212 989 5566; www.earthroom.org
Closed Mondays and Tuesdays.

If the urban shuffle is making you pine for pastoral environs or if you just want a place to reflect, the Earth Room—a sanctuary in a SoHo loft—is the answer. Created in 1977 by American artist Walter De Maria, it is filled with two hundred and fifty cubic yards of rich, dark topsoil weighing two hundred and eighty thousand pounds and standing twenty-two inches high. Originally one of three Earth Rooms—the other two created by De Maria in Germany—this is the only one still remaining, sponsored and maintained by the Dia Center for the Arts. Prepare to be transported by an incredibly unique experience.

CHRISTINE MOOG
Graphic designer

4

4.7 **Raoul's**
180 Prince Street between Sullivan and Thompson Streets
☎ 212 966 3518; www.raouls.com

🍴 For someone who finds comfort in the gloriously faded past while being entirely immersed in the present, Raoul's is a godsend. I remember pulling up to the bar when I was a young writer and feeling as though I'd arrived home. Countless evenings have been spent enjoying long, winding discussions with friends, surrounded by straight talkers and abstract expressionists, gumshoes, and rock stars. Fifteen years after my first steak au poivre at Raoul's, I still look forward to every visit—every greeting from Eddie, maître d' and dear friend; every walk through the hectic kitchen to the back room; every journey up the precarious circular staircase leading to the restrooms. I've enjoyed dinners for fifteen in the front room settled comfortably into the seemingly ancient long banquette, as well as simple dinners for two, hidden away at a table under the skylight. Raoul's seems to get better every year, even though it hasn't changed a bit.

ANDY SPADE
Co-founder of Kate Spade New York, Partners & Spade, and Jack Spade,

Vintage Bars

4.9 **The Ear Inn**
326 Spring Street between Greenwich and Washington Streets
☎ 212 226 9060; www.earinn.com

4.16 **Fanelli's Cafe**
94 Prince Street at Mercer Street
☎ 212 226 9412
(see p. 122)

3.6 **The White Horse Tavern**
567 Hudson Street at West 11th Street
☎ 212 243 9260

¶♀ Originally located on the banks of the Hudson River and originally known as the James Brown House, the Ear is one of the few remaining two-story, wood-framed, Federal-style buildings in Manhattan. One of the oldest taverns in the city (c. 1817), the Ear served as a halfway house for runaway slaves during the Civil War. Not only a beautiful and historic landmark, it's also the best meal for your money below Houston Street. The daily fresh fish special cannot be beat. A friendly, loud, and eclectic downtown neighborhood crowd that includes workers, bikers, artists, and musicians spills out on the sidewalk on summer evenings.

Though there is much debate about which is the oldest bar in the city (Fraunces Tavern, 1762; Bridge Cafe, 1794; Ear Inn, 1817; Pete's Tavern, 1864; McSorley's Ale House, 1854), Fanelli's is surely one of the oldest and best. Serving food and drink continuously since 1847, it operated as a speakeasy during Prohibition from 1920 to 1933. Perhaps the most beautiful back bar in the city, it faces a wall of original boxing photos and portraits dating from the turn of the century. Fanelli's was once my friendly local neighborhood watering hole, but as SoHo has changed, unfortunately so has the crowd (and boy, is it crowded). So, go very late at night after the tourists, shoppers, and the bridge-and-tunnel gang have gone to bed and try hard to engage Bob the bartender in conversation. A retired former prizefighter, he once fought Bob Chavalo for the Canadian heavyweight championship and was smart enough to turn down a fight with mean Sonny Liston. If you get

Bob going, then you're in for an education loaded with
vicious one-liners and lots of laughs.

Once a speakeasy, the White Horse Tavern has been a
favorite of locals, workers, artists, and writers since 1880
(including such neighborhood notables as Jack Kerouac,
Norman Mailer, and Bob Dylan). Fact: in 1953, Dylan
Thomas, on a two-day binge, drank himself to death here.
("I've had eighteen straight whiskeys and I believe that's the
record.") Sit outside at the corner table on a lazy Saturday
afternoon and watch Jane Jacobs's neighborhood stroll by.
Stick to the beer, a good bacon burger, or my favorite, the
tuna melt.

FREDERIC SCHWARTZ
Architect

4.10 Dia Center for the Arts: *The Broken Kilometer*

1979, Walter De Maria
393 West Broadway between Spring and Broome Streets
☎ 212 989 5566; www.brokenkilometer.org

Walter De Maria's five hundred-piece work is both the
bright golden reflection you see and the silence you hear in
the white room it inhabits: a weightless, drifting space.
Looking left to right, the building's row of cast-iron
columns gives comparison to scale, and divides the work
into two rows of bars on one side, and three on the other.
From foreground to background, all weight, dimension, and
shape disappear into light. The rear bars float off the floor
and the wall drops behind the horizon. The work's calm,
mystical euphoria owes everything to its simple perspective
in pictorial space. It feels huge and timeless and exists in a
pure state of relativity. Seeing and understanding its specific
physicality becomes a way of thinking while you are there,
which is then claimed quickly by memory once you exit
through the short maze and return to the outside.

JAMES L. BODNAR
Architect

4.11   Broome Street Bar
363 West Broadway at Broome Street
☎ 212 925 2086; www.broomestreetbar.ypguides.net

🍴🍸 A wonderful no-frills restaurant located smack in the center
of SoHo. After too much shopping at Prada and and too
much walking and people-gazing and all the rest of the
things people do in SoHo, go to the Broome Street Bar, sit
back, order a beer, look out the window, and be so happy
that there are places like this in the city where comfort
reigns and pretension is permanently barred.
KATHLEEN DEMARCO VAN CLEVE
Author, screenwriter, and film producer

Howard Street

4.12   E. Vogel Inc.
19 Howard Street between Broadway and Lafayette Street
☎ 212 925 2460; www.vogelboots.com

4.13   Putnam Rolling Ladder Co. Inc.
32 Howard Street between Broadway and Crosby Street
☎ 212 226 5147; www.putnamrollingladder.com

🪲 While on Howard Street, look in on two establishments
devoted to Old World craftsmanship. At No. 19, visit the
three-story brick townhouse, home to E. Vogel, and order
a pair of made-to-measure jodhpurs or a pair of custom
dress shoes. You will be in good company; this fourth-
generation establishment (thirty-two years in its present
location, to which it moved from its 1879 Warren Street
home) has made riding boots and shoes for General
Pershing, Charles Lindbergh, Paul Newman, and Jacqueline
Onassis, as well as for Olympic equestrian teams, and
kings and queens.
   At No. 32, you will find the Putnam Rolling Ladder
Company. Their model Number 1—think library ladder

sliding along a brass rail—has been in continuous production since 1905. The ownership is in its third generation,
having taken possession of the company in 1946 when Mr.
Putnam sold it to his longtime employee. The shop has
been on Howard Street at its current whereabouts since the
1930s and nothing appears to have changed much. Even
the sign above the shop is from Mr. Putnam's horse-drawn
carriage. Current clients range from Diane von Furstenberg
to Barnes & Noble.

ROBERT KAHN
Architect

NOTE: Ted Muehling's jewelry store, located on Howard Street for
many years, has moved to 52 White Street (see p. 37).

4.14 Patina

451 Broome Street between Broadway and Mercer Street
☎ 212 625 3375; www.patinavintage.com

This unique SoHo shop features items that reflect the passions
of its energetic owner, Lenore Newman. Hand-selected
vintage clothing and accessories, unusual jewelry, ceramics,
tableware, and glassware (both old and new) are available.
Displays, in the form of amusing vignettes, are constantly
changing, and new merchandise enters the store regularly.
Perfect for that hard-to-find gift.

SUSAN TUNICK
Artist and writer

4.15 Singer Building

1904, Ernest Flagg
561 Broadway between Prince and Spring Streets

The two façades of Ernest Flagg's 1902–1904 Singer
Building (the second façade pops out on Prince Street) rank
among the most innovative structural and material expressions of New York architecture. Combining glazed and buff
terra-cotta tiles, florid wrought iron and structural steel,

and large panes of glass in different planes, the building is one of the most sophisticated responses to a strain of French architecture usually overshadowed by the Beaux Arts. It provided a richly suggestive direction for New York's high-rise architecture, yet had a disappointingly small progeny. Ten years later, Flagg offered a more refined variant on the theme in his building for Scribner's Bookstore (now a Sephora) on Fifth Avenue at 48th Street.

BARRY BERGDOLL
Philip Johnson Chief Curator of Architecture and Design, Museum of Modern Art

Savoir Fare

4.17 **Balthazar**
80 Spring Street between Broadway and Crosby Street
📞 212 965 1414; www.balthazarny.com

4.18 **Savoy**
70 Prince Street at Crosby Street
📞 212 219 8570; www.savoynyc.com

🍴 There are two restaurants that I rely on for sustenance. The busy, often crowded Balthazar is a terrific place for breakfast. When you walk in you can pick up *The New York Times*, bring it to your table, and read it over a cappuccino or a bowl of café au lait. You can also, if you wish, have delicious rolls—plain or sweet—or eggs Benedict or whatever pleases you. It is easily the most relaxed breakfast that I know. I sometimes go to Balthazar for dinner, and I like to be seated near the entrance. If I am early, I can catch the stylish and often outrageously attired guests making their entrance.

Perhaps my favorite place in which to eat, at least in downtown Manhattan, is the very intimate and not overly expensive Savoy. One has a choice of eating downstairs in

a comfortable atmosphere, selecting a meal from a varied menu, or upstairs, in a smallish room with logs burning in the fireplace, where one eats from a prix-fixe menu. Whether one chooses downstairs or upstairs, the food will be delicious. The wine list is small but brilliantly selected. In all the years I have been eating there, I have not been disappointed with any meal. The people who work at Savoy are without question the friendliest yet least obtrusive of restaurant personnel. It is a great place to finish off the day.
MARK STRAND
Poet

4.19 **E. R. Butler & Co.**
53–55 Prince Street between Mulberry and Lafayette Streets
☎ 212 925 3565; www.erbutler.com
By appointment only.

Shopping at this hardware showroom is like a visit to Berry Brothers & Rudd Ltd., wine merchants to the Queen—you sit at a lovely mahogany table (in Butler's case, designed by the fine-furniture maker Chris Lehrecke) and the hardware is brought to you. It feels more like a museum of architectural hardware than a place to buy a latch set and a pair of hinges. Whether you are looking for a traditional, authentic early-American door handle or one designed by the philosopher Ludwig Wittgenstein, the Bauhaus master Walter Gropius, or the contemporary architect Richard Meier, you will find it here. If it exists, they have it; if it doesn't, they will make it for you, in any of seventy-five hand-finished metal patination formulas, including sterling silver. (And should you need to jot down a thought, the notepads are engraved.)

Behind this quiet and elegant showroom is a high-tech and sophisticated enterprise, including state-of-the-art CNC machines, prototype development, as well as antique conservation and restoration. There is even a library with five thousand rare trade catalogs, six thousand original drawings, and thousands of original hardware patterns.

The only catch (so to speak) is that the showroom is open to design professionals and their clients by appointment, and to the rest of you by pleading.

ROBERT KAHN
Architect

WNYC

820 AM or 93.9 FM

The best way to wake up and get your news—never too harsh or hyped, a gentle nudge into your day.

ERIC STOLTZ
Actor

NOLITA & LITTLE ITALY

4.20 St. Patrick's Old Cathedral

1815, Joseph Mangin
260–264 Mulberry Street between East Houston and Prince Streets
www.oldcathedral.org

Old St. Patrick's is a very charming brick church with a lot of greenery around it, an unexpected piece of the nineteenth century. Formally opened in 1815 to a crowd of more than four thousand worshippers and dignitaries, it was New York's first cathedral, the second Roman Catholic church in America, and the first house of worship in the United States to be dedicated to Ireland's patron saint, Patrick. The building was engulfed by a fire in 1866, which destroyed all but the outer walls, but was reconstructed in two years' time. It is surrounded on Mott, Prince, and

Mulberry Streets by a beautiful brick wall, built to protect the cathedral from the frequent brawls and street riots between Protestants and Catholics. When the Cardinal's seat was moved uptown to the new St. Patrick's Cathedral on Fifth Avenue, dedicated in 1879, the historic St. Patrick's downtown became a parish church.

JOAN SILBER
Writer

4.21 Storefront for Art and Architecture

1993, Steven Holl and Vito Acconci
97 Kenmare Street at Cleveland Place
☎ 212 431 5795; www.storefrontnews.org

On a small plot of land at the crossroads of SoHo, Little Italy, and Chinatown, a storefront façade uniquely defines its turf. In renovating a space to be dedicated to showing architectural schemes and urban plans, utopian or dystopian, Holl and Acconci conceived a wall that transforms itself from a blank surface into a geometric plane, hinged within to allow for bold opening sections that pivot out into the street. Windows and a door appear, then disappear, reverting to the planar surface from which they emerged. But the intellectual excitement of all this is in the realization of a kind of paper architecture in the very materials of the façade itself.

MARJORIE WELISH
Poet, artist, and art critic

The design of this gallery provides New York with a genuine stage for urban theater. The unfolding wall establishes a threshold that takes art into the street and brings people close to the exhibits.

IAIN LOW
Architect, and professor of architecture, University of Cape Town

CHAPTER 5

GREENWICH VILLAGE

5.1 Strand Book Store
828 Broadway at East 12th Street
☎ 212 473 1452; www.strandbooks.com

For more than twenty years I've lived within a three minute
walk to the Strand Book Store, which means I've had to
contend with more than two decades of sheer temptation.
The Strand's celebrated claim of "over eighteen miles of
used books" certainly can no longer be true; I've purchased
at least a mile's worth myself.

Now almost the last remnant in what used to be a
thriving district of used-book and print shops, the Strand
boasts a splendid selection of used books in all fields,
along with extensive discounted offerings of review books.
In addition, I will confess to enjoying a vicarious kick by
purchasing discarded volumes from distinguished owners;
my shelves contain books once owned by Elizabeth
Hardwick, Aileen Ward, John Simon, and Joseph Alsop,
among others.

Big, dusty, sometimes a bit confusing, often crowded, and
resolutely unair-conditioned, the Strand remains a stalwart
institution dedicated to the hopelessly addicted bibliophile.
RICHARD LAVENSTEIN
Architect

5.2 Forbes Magazine Building and Galleries
1925, Carrère & Hastings and Shreve & Lamb
62 Fifth Avenue at 12th Street
☎ 212 206 5548; www.forbesgalleries.com
The galleries are closed Sundays and Mondays.

The Forbes Building was built as the American headquarters for the British publisher, Macmillan. Architect Thomas Hastings of Carrère & Hastings (The New York Public Library) died before completion; the successor architects were Shreve & Lamb (Empire State Building). Elements of both firms' styles are visible here. The member of the Macmillan family who selected architects and oversaw construction was Harold Macmillan, who left publishing to go into politics when he returned to the U.K. and ended up Prime Minister. The building and adjacent 1840s brownstone were acquired by Forbes Inc. in 1964; the ground floor now houses the Forbes Magazine Galleries.

5

Shortly after the entire ground floor of the building opened as the Forbes Magazine Galleries in 1986, a friend of my father turned to him and laughingly observed, "Malcolm, that's the happiest sequence of non sequiturs I've ever experienced." Featuring a staggering archive of American historical documents, the earliest surviving renderings of the game Monopoly, an armada of toy boats, platoons of toy soldiers, inscribed trophies, and rotating exhibitions of paintings and photographs, the galleries are an evolving manifestation of the diverse collecting enthusiasms of three generations of Forbeses.

CHRISTOPHER FORBES
Vice chairman, Forbes Inc.

My vote for the best little jewel of a museum (and free to boot) is the Forbes Galleries in the lobby of the Forbes Magazine Building on Fifth Avenue. Apparently Malcolm Forbes's interests in collecting crossed many borders. Until recently, it featured the world's largest collection of Fabergé eggs. There is a fabulous collection of historical memorabilia, including the bill for Paul Revere's ride (who knew he was a consultant?) and Lincoln's opera glasses. The collection of toy tin soldiers and boats and the prototypes for the original Monopoly game are also wonderful.

MARIA MANHATTAN
Artist

5.4   Second Cemetery of the Spanish and Portuguese Synagogue

1805–1829
72–76 West 11th Street between Fifth and Sixth Avenues

In the middle of frenetic Manhattan, along one of the loveliest tree-lined streets in Greenwich Village, it is possible to miss one of the city's most unusual little gems if you walk too quickly. There, nestled along the south side of 11th Street, just a few feet from the streaming traffic along Sixth Avenue, is a tiny triangle that comprises one of the city's few Spanish-Portuguese-Jewish cemeteries. Scattered haphazardly on the small plot are a handful of simple weathered tombstones—somehow, in the midst of Manhattan's mad rush for development, this sacred corner of the dead survived intact. Today, occupying a tiny slice of real estate, this is a completely different stop for any city visitor. When finished, go to French Roast on the corner of West 11th Street and Sixth Avenue, and toast the dead with a good glass of house wine.

GERALD POSNER
Journalist and author

It is typical of New York that, unlike any other major city in the world, it does not have a recognizable and accessible cemetery. No Highbury, no Père-Lachaise, no San Michele. Maybe this lack of graveyard gravitas comes from the famous Gotham mercenary attitude; the lust for power and wealth have little to do with bones moldering six feet under.

There is, however, a tiny Jewish cemetery on West 11th. The men and women buried there came to New York in the early nineteenth century as refugees from South America in the wake of upheavals surrounding independence. There are a couple dozen headstones with Hebrew writing, two tombs, and an ivy-strewn brick walkway that meanders through the plots. But the walkway has nowhere to go. The cemetery is a triangle, no more than thirty feet in any direction, appallingly hemmed in on all sides by the city—by an apartment building, a brick wall, and a sidewalk. The hemming-in was so violent that more than one gravestone is a part of the brick wall that lies on its western and southern edge. The forces of real estate were so powerful that someone simply built walls through the gravestones.

The cemetery has a sad appearance, especially in a downpour, this forgotten place, no one to come to tend to the graves, and no one alive who knows any of the people resting there.

JAMES ZUG
Historian, journalist, and author

Greenwich Village Stroll

5.5 **Milligan Place**
1852
Sixth Avenue between West 10th and West 11th Streets

5.6 **Patchin Place**
1849
Off West 10th Street between Greenwich and Sixth Avenues

3.7 **Grove Court**
1854
Grove Street between Bedford and Hudson Streets

3.10 **Home of Edna St. Vincent Millay**
1873
75 1/2 Bedford Street between Morton and Commerce Streets
Not open to the public.

5.10 Home of W. H. Auden
7 Cornelia Street between Bleecker and West 4th Streets
Not open to the public.

6.23 Home of W. H. Auden
77 St. Mark's Place between First and Second Avenues
Not open to the public.

Let me take you away from the hurly-burly of Broadway,
the elegant shops of Madison Avenue, and the dazzling
corridors of art offered by the Metropolitan Museum.
And where shall I lead you? Downtown on a ten-minute
walk to some of the smallest and most poetic streets in
Manhattan's Greenwich Village. Each is a gated cul-de-sac,
tucked away from the furors of urban life and festooned
in a quiet otherworldliness. The first and smallest is
Milligan Place; you will need to look really sharp to espy
it on the west side of the avenue, opposite Jefferson
Market. There, inside the marked gate, a wee cluster of
homes appears to belong to a private world. Built in the
1850s, they were conceived as boarding houses for Basque
waiters and workers employed nearby. Farther west, off
10th Street, is Patchin Place—with two rows of diminutive
dwellings dating from 1848; they, too, were built as
boarding houses for toiling New Yorkers. At No. 4, near the
gate, lived the poet E. E. Cummings, and at various times
Patchin Place was the home of Djuna Barnes, Theodore
Dreiser, and Padraic Colum. Continue west on 10th Street,
turn south on Seventh Avenue, and west on Grove Street,
mindful to keep looking sharp. Between Bedford and
Hudson Streets you will come to Grove Court with its row
of Victorian houses built in the mid-1850s, again for the
working class. Compared with the heft of skyscrapers
profiling the city, you will surely find the houses in each of
these charmed groves doll-like in their proportions. You
are also likely to comment on the irregularity of the early

property lines that define them—no right angles here. Leon Trotsky, who arrived as an exile in New York in 1917 looking for working-class quarters and found them in the Bronx, characterized the dominant geometric pattern of New York's layout as "a triumph of Cubism." In an earlier century, Thomas Paine, the ex-corset maker from England turned eloquent revolutionary, found refuge during the final years of his life at various addresses amidst the wavering property lines of the West Village area. A brilliant proponent of American independence and author of *Common Sense* (1776), Paine died sad and lonely in the year 1809 in the back room of a frame dwelling on the site of what is now 59 Grove Street. But sadness will not be yours in the beckoning, small-street intimacy that defines the Village. There are colorful crowds, lively art galleries, and shops throughout, as well as cafés aplenty for a lingering cappuccino and conversation. Artists and writers who made—and still make—the Village their home are too numerous to mention, but you should take a look while you are in this area at the narrowest house in the Village located at 75$^1/_2$ Bedford Street (see p. 56). In the early 1920s, it was the home of the poet Edna St. Vincent Millay, who was moved to write that

> *The trees along this city street . . .*
> *Would make a sound as thin and sweet*
> *As trees in country lanes.*

W. H. Auden chose the Village as the locus of his several dwellings here and abroad, living at 7 Cornelia Street and then at 77 St. Mark's Place. In 1969 he declared,

> *My Eden landscapes and their climes*
> *Are constructs from Edwardian times.*

GLORIA DEAK
Writer

5.7   **Jefferson Market Library and Garden**

1877, Frederick Clark Withers and Calvert Vaux

425 Sixth Avenue at West 10th Street

☏ 212 243 4334; www.jeffersonmarketgarden.org

Smack in the middle of bustling, downtown Sixth Avenue, you will find a magnificent and elaborate concoction of a building, the Jefferson Market Library. Originally a courthouse (1876–1945) with an adjacent prison and market (both torn down in 1929 and replaced by a Women's House of Detention), this neighborhood library is a wonder of arches and turrets and stained-glass windows. It looks, as my daughter says, like a castle in a fairy tale. There is even a clock tower. In rare, quiet moments, you can hear the bell, which once summoned volunteer firemen, chime out the time.

The country's attention was focused on the original courthouse in 1906, when Harry K. Thaw was tried here for the murder of architect Stanford White. White's affair with chorus girl/model Evelyn Nesbit before her marriage to Thaw was the motive in this crime of passion, an episode captured by E. L. Doctorow in *Ragtime*.

Behind the library, largely hidden from view on Sixth Avenue, is the Jefferson Market Garden—a beautiful oasis in the middle of city gridlock. In the early 1970s, the Women's House of Detention on this site was closed, then demolished, creating the opportunity for this garden, now a beloved feature of the Greenwich Village Historic District. You will find wooden benches hidden among flowers, a small pond with fish and a fountain, and an arch with climbing vines marking the garden's perimeter path. Flowerbeds, dripping with color and scent, continue to change throughout the seasons. A luscious green lawn fills the middle—not to walk on, just to gaze upon.

The entrance to the garden is on Greenwich Avenue, and when the gates are open, there is a table with a volunteer or two, and a donation box, out front. Walk slowly along the garden path, and note the labels identifying the wide variety of flowers. If you are lucky, you may snag a bench for a little while. The city and its traffic never completely disappear, but they are held at bay in this garden, behind its lovely wrought-iron fence, a bequest of the Astor Foundation.

ELISSA STEIN
Graphic designer, illustrator, and writer

5.8 Three Lives & Co.
154 West 10th Street at Waverly Place
☎ 212 741 2069; www.threelives.com

Three Lives & Co. is one of the great small bookstores in the world. It is staffed by avid, eccentric readers, any one of whom, if asked, will recommend books on any subject. They are often books of which you have never heard; they are always revelations. Three Lives stocks a catholic selection of new books and a smattering of old ones, but trying to describe it in terms of its stock and even its remarkable staff is a little like trying to describe a face by offering the precise locations of the mouth, nose, and eyes. Three Lives is magical, utterly mysterious; it is enormously hospitable; it shines. I go there not only to buy books but sometimes simply to be reminded of why one writes books. I once asked the former owners if I could someday be buried there, under the floorboards in the southwest corner, but they told me they weren't zoned for that.

MICHAEL CUNNINGHAM
Writer

5.9 Patisserie Claude

187 West 4th Street between Sixth and Seventh Avenues
☎ 212 255 5911

🍴🍽 Patisserie Claude is coincidentally owned and operated
by a permanently taciturn man named Claude. Patisserie
is the key word here: walk in and innocently ask for bread
and Claude or one of his minions, if they are feeling kindly
that day, will inform you that they know how to spell
boulangerie and do you see *boulangerie* in the name of the
store, you *américain stupide*? No bread, only pastry and
maybe you should go away for a while.

First impressions can be telling. When I first met Claude
some fifteen or so years ago, I was intimidated by his gruff
manner and thought him to be cold, aloof, and disdainful.
I now know that he *is* cold, aloof, and disdainful. Which
doesn't mean a thing because Claude does make the best
croissant, brioche, and *pain au chocolat* in the city. His
fruit tarts are near equals to the tarts my wife's great aunt,
Marie-Rose, used to cook up in Cannes, and to get them
you don't have to sleep on that lumpy mattress and listen
endlessly to Charles Trenet.

Claude has a simple rule. Less is more may fly in
certain architectural circles, but not for Claude. Claude,
like Albert Einstein, sought a central unifying theme to
the universe. Unlike Albert, Claude found it, and it is
called butter. More is better. Each croissant has at least a
stick of butter in it and is the better for it. My visiting
French relatives and friends generally drop their bags at
the house and make a beeline for Claude's because they
claim it is very difficult to get croissants, etc. that good
in Paris anymore.

Claude's has a couple of perfunctory tables up front

where you can sip your coffee, look pensive in your beret, and eat the best patisserie in the city. But whatever you do, don't ask for bread.

ANDREW S. PAUL
Attorney

NOTE: Patisserie Claude is now owned and run by one of Claude's longtime employees; however, the patisseries are just as good as they were when Claude was in charge.

5

5.13 Washington Square Park
At the foot of Fifth Avenue
www.nycgovparks.org

"The Secret Worlds of Washington Square" would be an essay describing the multiple societies that coexist yet seldom interact in this treasured public space. Here are dog owners (large and small, separated by different exercise yards), chess players, musicians, amateur gardeners, students, lonely squirrel and pigeon feeders (each jealously guarding her bit of pavement), photographers, runners, bocce players...all dutifully recorded by busloads of tourists. As an N.Y.U. professor who has lived in the West Village for forty years, I pass through the park almost daily and love it as one who has seen—and participated in—its struggle against oblivion. Practically every book about the city repeats the facts and myths that have accumulated since the area was, first, a graveyard for slaves, then a drill ground for Revolutionary troops.

GEORGE C. STONEY
Filmmaker and Professor Emeritus, Tisch School of the Arts

When the city sizzles, and it's impossible to find a spot of concrete at any public pool, the Washington Square Park fountain offers a downtown oasis. With its wide seating

area and five mighty water jets, it's one of the few fountains where jumping in and getting soaked is customary. The spot is never overcrowded (nearly empty before noon), and a midday splash is akin to a Midwestern run through the front yard sprinkler (though at a hundred times the power).
SCOTT HESS
Screenwiter, performer, and writer

Theater al Fresco

5.13 **Washington Square Park**
At the foot of Fifth Avenue

5.14 **Provincetown Playhouse**
133 MacDougal Street at West 3rd Street
www.nyu.edu/construction/provincetown

Washington Square Park is always alive, especially on the weekends, with music, acrobats, clowns, stand-up comics, people hanging out, every breed of dog being walked, kids on swings. In the summer nights you might stumble across a group of young actors doing a Shakespeare play by flashlight. And there's the statue of Garibaldi, reminding us that the leader of the Risorgimento, the revolutionary movement that united Italy, lived right here in New York and worked in Staten Island at a candle factory. Cut down MacDougal Street and look in at the Provincetown Playhouse, where modern American theater was born, thanks to Eugene O'Neill. (Until a couple of years ago the original set for *The Emperor Jones* was still part of the permanent structure of the stage.) Now you're in the Village, and it's still the best part of town.
JOHN GUARE
Playwright

Village Breadbasket

5.15 **Ottomanelli & Sons**
285 Bleecker Street between Seventh Avenue South
and Jones Street
☎ 212 675 4217

5.16 **John's Pizzeria**
278 Bleecker Street between Jones and Morton Streets
☎ 212 243 1680; www.johnsbrickovenpizza.com

5.17 **Cones**
272 Bleecker Street between Jones and Morton Streets
☎ 212 414 1795

5.18 **Murray's Cheese Shop**
254 Bleecker Street at Cornelia Street
☎ 212 243 3289; www.murrayscheese.com

5.19 **Faicco's Pork Shop**
260 Bleecker Street between Morton and Cornelia Streets
☎ 212 243 1974

5.20 **Rocco's Pastry Shop**
243 Bleecker Street between Leroy and Carmine Streets
☎ 212 242 6031; www.roccospastry.com

5.21 **Sir Winston Churchill Square**
West side of Sixth Avenue where Downing Street
meets Bleecker Street
www.nycgovparks.org

5.22 **Minetta Triangle**
Northeast corner of Sixth Avenue and Minetta Street
www.nycgovparks.org

5.23 **Father Demo Square**
Intersection of Carmine and Bleecker Streets and Sixth Avenue

5

In the area popularly considered Little Italy, the Italian inhabitants are now only a memory. Except for a couple of tenacious survivors and a row of tourist restaurants, the area is now, for all practical purposes, part of Chinatown. If you want a sense of Little Italy as it used to be, go to Bleecker Street between Sixth Avenue and Seventh Avenue. From the turn of the century to the 1940s, this block, which has been called the "breadbasket of the Village," was choked with pushcarts selling provisions to the primarily southern Italian population. Following the passage of stricter sanitary laws, much of this commerce moved indoors; several stores established at that time still survive.

Beginning at Sixth Avenue, on the north side of Bleecker, is Ottomanelli & Sons, the butcher shop. The Ottomanelli family immigrated to New York from Bari in 1900 and established itself in the wholesale meat business. Their store opened on Bleecker Street in the 1940s. Since that time, it is substantially unchanged—it remains a real, old-fashioned butcher shop, with a long counter, huge hams and sides of beef hanging in the window, and personal service.

Across the street is John's Pizzeria. Founded in 1929 by John Sasso, John's famously does not sell single slices. But that's okay—the pizza is so good you'll want a whole one. The restaurant is now run by the nephew of the original John, and it's a good celebrity-spotting site, frequented by Woody Allen, Johnny Depp, Danny DeVito, Jack Nicholson, Mary Tyler Moore, and Matt Dillon, among others.

Next door is Cones. Self-described "ice-cream artisans" Oscar and Raul D'Aloisio make what is arguably not only the most authentically Italian gelato but the best ice cream of any kind in the city. The brothers come from Buenos Aires, where there is a large Italian community. Oscar says that when he tasted Häagen-Dazs ice cream, he thought, "This is the best America has to offer?" and decided to come over and show us what ice cream should be. The flavors, especially the fruit flavors, are startlingly intense and authentic. I also recommend the zabaglione.

Founded in 1940 as a wholesale vendor of butter and eggs, Murray's Cheese Shop used to be around the corner on Cornelia Street. The new, larger shop may not be as quaint as the old one, but it no longer has a perpetual line of waiting customers spilling out the door. They stock more than two-hundred-and-fifty different kinds of cheese from countries all over the world; if you've heard of a cheese, they have it. They also sell delicatessen fare such as olives, salami, prosciutto, and prepared foods.

Back on the south side of the street is another deli, Faicco's Pork Shop. As the blue pig on the storefront sign proudly announces, this store was founded in 1900, making it the oldest on the block (although it only moved from Thompson Street to its present location in the 1940s). Originally they sold only pork, and although they now sell a range of other Italian foods, too, their glory is still their pork sausage, which you can watch them make right in the shop.

For about eighty years, the Sixth Avenue end of the block was distinguished by its two side-by-side pastry shops—Bleecker Street Pastry and Rocco's. Bleecker Street Pastry was recently replaced by Pasticceria Bruno, and is now very elegant and upscale, although it retains the old decor. But Rocco's continues the same as ever. If you've ever been to Italy, the smell of anise as you walk in the door will take you right back. Everything in Rocco's is extraordinarily cheap and unself-consciously Italian, from the nuclear-blue and hot-pink decorations on some of the cakes to the hand-filled cannoli to the pink-and-green neon decor. Particularly noteworthy is their freshly baked, authentic tasting panettone—a hard-to-find treasure outside of Italy except during the Christmas season. In the summer they offer refreshing Italian ices, of which the hazelnut is especially good.

If you live near Bleecker Street, you can still do your shopping the old-fashioned way, with daily trips to the butcher, the baker, the dairy, and the greengrocer. If you're from farther away, try coming down on a nice day and assembling a picnic lunch as you walk down the block. Where Bleecker intersects Sixth Avenue, several tiny parks have recently been redesigned and offer restful places to eat. In the triangle formed by Downing and Bleecker Streets, Winston Churchill Square offers winding paths and benches around a sundial in the form of an armillary sphere. On the other side of the avenue, the even smaller Minetta Triangle has a few shady, secluded seats. Or if you prefer a more urban atmosphere, the older Father Demo Square between the two is an open brick plaza with trees, benches, and lots of street life and pigeons.

JANET B. PASCAL
Writer and production editor, Viking Children's Books

Father Demo Square

5.23 **Father Demo Square**
Intersection of Carmine and Bleecker Streets and Sixth Avenue
www.nycgovparks.org

5.21 **Sir Winston Churchill Square**
West side of Sixth Avenue where Downing Street meets Bleecker Street
www.nycgovparks.org

5.24 **Minetta Lane**
South of West 3rd Street, between Sixth Avenue and MacDougal Street

5.25 **Joe's Pizza**
7 Carmine Street at Bleecker Street
☎ 212 366 1182; www.joespizzanyc.com

5.26 **Bagels on the Square**
7 Carmine Street between Bleecker Street and Sixth Avenue
☎ 212 691 3041

5.27 **Trattoria Spaghetto**
232 Bleecker Street at Carmine Street
☎ 212 255-6752; www.trattoriaspaghetto.com

5.28 **Da Silvano**
260 Sixth Avenue between Bleecker and West Houston Streets
☎ 212 982 2343; www.dasilvano.com

5.29 **Bar Pitti**
268 Sixth Avenue between Bleecker and West Houston Streets
☎ 212 982 3300

🍴 Arrive hungry: you are at the threshold of great treats.

🎁 But before you indulge, pause a few moments in this
charming piazza. More triangle than not, this étoile stands
at the crossroads of Sixth Avenue, Bleecker, Carmine,
Downing, and Minetta Streets. Father Demo, the Italian-
born pastor of nearby Our Lady of Pompeii Church, was
lauded for his Herculean efforts during the famed Triangle
Shirtwaist Company Fire of 1911 (see p. 100). In thanks,
the Borough of Manhattan commemorated his life's work
with this brick-paved homage.

Bordered to the southwest by the majestic single-domed
church, the square spills onto Downing Street, at whose feet
sits tiny, impeccable Churchill Square—a reference to the
London abode of the only Prime Minister with a New Yorker
mother. Folded into an adjacent corner of the park is a
typical neighborhood playground, complete with whimsical

frog and seal sculptures for climbing. (Discover, in a few paces's stroll along Downing Street, some of lower Manhattan's most interesting single-family residences.) Your bench on the east side of the piazza will provide an inimitable view north of both Jefferson Market Library and the Empire State Building. Also of note: Minetta Street, where Al Pacino's Serpico lived; and on the southeast corner of Bleecker Street and Sixth Avenue, the Little Red School House, an enduring neighborhood private school made famous by both Auntie Mame and the Rosenbergs.

And now you may eat, for Father Demo Square is home not only to Joe's Pizza and Bagels on the Square—both Village classics—but also Trattoria Spaghetto, where the finest bowl of minestrone soup on the island can be consumed. And if there's time for a proper meal, then by all means cross Sixth Avenue to the south and invest a couple of hours sitting outside at either Da Silvano or Bar Pitti. Known fondly to regulars as "first-class and coach," the relationship is as magnetically charged as that of Paris' Café de Flore and Les Deux Magots. Silvano costs more and takes major credit cards; Pitti is cheap and takes only cash. Both are delicious. Whichever you choose, you will not be sorry.

RACHAEL HOROVITZ
Film producer and co-founder of the Cinema School

Best Tuna

5.30 'ino
21 Bedford Street between Sixth Avenue and Downing Street
☎ 212 989 5769; www.cafeino.com

2.7 Morgan's Market
13 Hudson Street at Reade Street
☎ 212 964 4283

2.6   **Washington Market Park**
Greenwich Street between Chambers and Duane Streets

5.31   **The Grey Dog's Coffee**
33 Carmine Street between Bleecker and Bedford Streets
📞 212 462 0041; www.thegreydog.com

5

🍴 As one who loves the city deeply, I offer you this favorite thing (of many) about New York: the tuna sandwich.

I want to omit any mention of tuna "steak," the slabs of rare tuna on toast (the Odeon! my favorite; see p. 38). What I prefer to recommend are tuna salad sandwiches, those that originate in a can and are easy to eat with one hand while turning pages of a book or properly folded newspaper. Here are three personal favorites:

1. The tuna *tramezzini* at 'ino. Tuna in a bit of oil with caperberries and black olive pesto on Pullman bread with the crust removed. Two subway cars side by side could just fit into this little room with a scuffed floor on an aging side street. Have wine and coffee with your sandwich and, after lunch, stumble left to the Village or right into SoHo.

2. Tuna with lettuce on a pita at Morgan's Market in TriBeCa. Kind of creamy, kind of plain, kind of perfect tuna salad. There's no place to sit down here (it's a market). You can carry your lunch bag a block down Reade Street to Washington Market Park, a nice patch of tree-lined grass with a playground and benches. Hudson River Park (see p. 34), only two long blocks west, is right on the water.

3. The No. 8 at Grey Dog. Dense, happy tuna with lettuce and tomato and one secret ingredient—relish—on sponge-sized slabs of big fresh bread. Order your sandwich at the counter and find a little table. FM music and doggie biscuits; it's loud and dimly lit, in a good way, with moms

and writers and the occasional EMS girl or well-known actress, a little-known painter, a suit, a teacher, a couple of kids. Ain't life grand; it's that kind of place.

STACY COCHRAN
Filmmaker

5.32 Village Comics

214 Sullivan Street between Bleecker and West 3rd Streets
☎ 212 777 2770

There are comics stores in New York such as Forbidden Planet that cater to the superhero, alternative, and weirdo-comics aficionado, and then there's Village Comics, which appeals to the rest of us. Though not a big comic-book fan myself, I have a voyeuristic interest in the countercultures that comprise this fan base.

Village Comics is something of an epicenter for the underground, overground, and middle earth of comics. It sells the usual fare of DC and Marvel, the unusual oddities by the likes of Chris Ware, and for this voyeur, comic models—plastic, resin, and dolls galore. But don't let the *habitués* hear you say the word "dolls": they prefer the state-of-the-art term "action figures."

The store is fully stocked with action figures that you'll never see at Toys "R" Us, representing troops from the Civil War, World War II (German and American), Vietnam, members of SWAT teams, special forces, and more. The avid recreationist who builds large dioramas and vignettes in which these figures play will find a wall covered with doll clothes and miniature weaponry. Also in stock for the art enthusiast are resin models, samples of which are precisely constructed and displayed in glass reliquaries. Models on hand run the gamut from classic Revel snap-togethers of cars, ships, and planes to variations of odd comics characters in revealing, if not kinky, garb. There is also the requisite Adults Only section, which I have never dared enter, given the fact that whenever I'm in the store, I feel just like a kid.

STEVEN HELLER
Art director, writer, and co-chair of MFA/Design, The School of Visual Arts

5.33 ## University Village
1966, I.M. Pei & Partners
From Bleecker Street to West Houston Street, between LaGuardia Place and Mercer Street

Escape the hodgepodge of Greenwich Village into I. M. Pei's urban utopia. The three simple concrete towers stretch above the neighboring horizon, injecting light, air, and space into the otherwise crowded cityscape. Follow the rough-cut stone drive from Bleecker Street to a central square. Here you will be greeted by an enormous, thirty-six-foot-high cast-stone-and-concrete *Portrait of Sylvette* by Pablo Picasso. (This enlargement of Picasso's much smaller sculpture is the 1970 work of Carl Nesjar.) The combination of massive forms, idealism, and simplicity is truly impressive. A visit to this austere oasis never fails to leave me at peace.

GEORGIA O'NEAL
Owner, Tree and Leaf Farm

5.34 ## Bayard Building (originally Condict Building)
1899, Louis Sullivan
65 Bleecker Street between Broadway and Lafayette Street

This is the only Louis Sullivan building in New York and is pretty and calming to look at. I have always thought of it as the wedding-cake building. When it was built, architectural critic Carl Condit (not to be confused with the building's first owner, Silas Condict), supposedly said, "Who would expect an aesthetic experience on Bleecker Street?"

JOAN SILBER
Writer

The only building in New York designed by Louis H. Sullivan is best viewed from the corner of Houston and Crosby on a sunny day when the filigreed terra-cotta-clad façade beams white. On the skyscraper of his time, Sullivan wrote: "It must be tall, every inch of it tall. The force and power of altitude must be in it." Commanding all of thirteen stories, the supporting columns indeed shoot skyward, giving way to arches, porthole windows, and heavy-handed ornamentation. Bring your binoculars to catch the dragonfly women—with arms and wings outstretched. They're the high altitude caryatids that carry the cornice and were reportedly added to the design against Sullivan's wishes.

FREDERIC SCHWARTZ AND TRACEY HUMMER
Architect and Writer

5.35 Il Buco

47 Bond Street between Lafayette Street and Bowery
☎ 212 533 1932; www.ilbuco.com

🍴🍷 One of the most gracious dining experiences in Manhattan is, without doubt, Il Buco. In the capable hands of its proprietor, Donna Lennard, I have eaten many of my most memorable New York dinners. This unassuming gem serves an Italian cuisine in a cozy, yet lively setting. Ask for tips on the wine menu, as their steward is most knowledgeable and insightful. Octopus carpaccio is nicely paired with a glass of *prosecco* to start, moving on to roasted baby beets and goat cheese followed by any number of fish or pasta dishes accompanied by a beautiful, hot, crusty fresh bread soaked in deep green, first-press olive oil. Ask to eat in the wine cellar, which served as the inspiration for Edgar Allen Poe's *The Cask of Amontillado*. Call early for reservations, as this treasure has been discovered.

CAROLYN CARTWRIGHT
Feature-film set decorator and interior designer

5

5.36 The Cooper Union for the Advancement of Science and Art Foundation Building

1859, Frederick A. Peterson
7 East 7th Street at Cooper Square
☎ 212 353 4100; www.cooper.edu

Cooper Union is steeped in history. On February 27, 1860, Abraham Lincoln spoke in the Great Hall, effectively beginning his first presidential campaign. Abolitionist and women's rights activist Frederick Douglass spoke several times in the same hall. As a child, my maternal grandmother walked in yellow lamplight through a snowstorm with her parents, from her house on West 10th Street to Cooper Institute, to catch a glimpse of Lincoln. That walk still takes a visitor past some of New York's oldest and most charming houses.

PETER BURCHARD
The late Peter Burchard was an author, designer, and illustrator.

Although he had little formal education himself, the industrialist and philanthropist Peter Cooper envisioned a college of the first rank for the working-class and immigrant children of New York City. Strategically and symbolically placed between the Bowery and the more prosperous neighborhoods uptown, the tuition-free college was intended by its founder to break through the class boundary. As pointed out in a characteristic passage by Horatio Alger Jr., the building has entrances uptown and downtown, but the clock and its light face the Bowery.

A national and city historic landmark, the Italianate Foundation Building was designed by Frederick Peterson and, in 1859, was the tallest building in New York City. As the first thoroughly fireproof structure in the city, it set a standard for public safety in construction. It also included the round shaft requested by Peter Cooper in anticipation of the invention of the elevator. When the interior of the building was completely rebuilt in the 1970s, modern technology permitted the old rectangular elevator to be replaced by a cylindrical one.

Abolitionist William Lloyd Garrison and feminists Susan B. Anthony and Victoria Woodhull rallied against the injustices of their time and spearheaded great change in their speeches in the Great Hall of the Foundation Building, and it was there that Albert Einstein presented his transcendent ideas in physics.

GEORGE CAMPBELL JR.
Former president (retired), The Cooper Union for the Advancement of Science and Art

`5.37` Merchant's House Museum

1832
29 East 4th Street between Lafayette Street and Bowery
☎ 212 777 1089; www.merchantshouse.com

In 1835, for eighteen thousand dollars, the merchant Seabury Tredwell bought an elegant three-year-old Greek Revival/Late Federal-style house on the outskirts of New York, at East 4th Street, and moved in with his large family, including five daughters and two sons. Five years later, his last daughter, Gertrude, was born. Seabury, whose ancestors had come over on the *Mayflower*, was a stern and devout man, and when Gertrude wanted to marry an Irish

Catholic doctor, he forbade her. She never married and continued to live in the house her whole life, first with her parents, then with three spinster sisters, and finally, when her money was gone, with paying guests. She died in the house in 1933 at ninety-three years of age. By then the area had changed from a wealthy and respectable suburb to one of the Lower East Side's crowded tenement neighborhoods, known for its bars and brothels. Outside the house, the world was altered completely, but inside, time stood still. Except for a very few modernizations, the house remained as it had been when Gertrude was young. According to one legend, Gertrude's haunting story was the inspiration for Henry James's *Washington Square*.

After her death, the house was given to the city, and it has been a museum ever since—one of the few places where you can see, not a re-creation of Victorian life, but the real thing. The lower floor houses the pantry, the family dining room, and the kitchen, where dishes and cookware still sit. The room is dominated by the black woodstove (which replaced the original fireplace). The sink is worked by a pump connected to a cistern filled with rainwater. Next to it stands the little round tub the family used for bathing. The legs on the pie safe are corroded where they were stood in glasses of water to keep vermin from the baked goods.

Visitors came to the elegant ground floor, containing the dining room and formal parlor decorated with columns, elaborate plasterwork, and magnificent marble fireplaces. To satisfy the Greek Revival desire for symmetry, the parlor was built with two heavy wooden doors—one to use, and a dummy that opens onto a blank brick wall, revealing the structure of the walls. Mrs. Tredwell redecorated in the 1860s to show the family's prosperity—she was trying to marry off six daughters. (Only two ever married.) The piano the girls used to entertain their guests, with an extra pedal meant to imitate an organ, stands by the window.

Upstairs are a small guest room and two separate bed-rooms for Mr. and Mrs. Tredwell, connected by a private passageway. Mrs. Tredwell's mirror is lit by gas jets shaped to look like morning glories twining around the edge. The effect is very pretty, but it's a little frightening to imagine her doing up her hair just inches from two open jets of flame. Although the rooms are large and expensively decorated with gilded pressed-tin ornamentation, there are no closets. Houses were taxed according to the number of rooms, and closets counted as rooms. After Gertrude's death, the magnificent red damask bed curtains were found to be too decayed to salvage, but there was no need to try a modern re-creation; bolts of the original fabric were still stored in the attic.

There is a charming little garden in back, which now looks out on brick walls and barbed wire, but once backed onto the Vauxhall Pleasure Garden. You can see the domed top of the cistern, fed by a drainpipe from the roof, but the outhouse has been removed.

If you want to pretend you're a Victorian, the Old Merchant's House is the place to do it. And if you want to be reminded why you're glad you're not a Victorian, con-sideration of the throne-like mahogany commode in the bedroom, the small hand-filled and hand-emptied bathtub, or Gertrude's terrifyingly narrow corset should do it.

JANET B. PASCAL
Writer and production editor, Viking Children's Books

5.38 Former Asch Building, now the Brown Building

29 Washington Place at Greene Street

On March 25, 1911, a fire in the Asch building, one block east of Washington Square, took the lives of a hundred and forty-six garment workers, most of them young women, some little more than children. The Triangle Shirtwaist

Company occupied the top three floors of the ten-story building. The company's vast workrooms were packed with seamstresses and flammable materials. It was nearly quitting time when fire broke out on the eighth floor and spread swiftly to the upper floors. Flames blocked the only un-locked exits. A *New York Times* reporter wrote: "The girls rushed to the windows and looked down at Greene Street, a hundred feet below them. One poor little creature jumped. Then they all began to drop. A girl, who waved her hand-kerchief at the crowd, leaped from a window. Her dress caught on a wire and the crowd watched her hang there until the dress burned free and she came toppling down."

Social worker and reformer Frances Perkins, who was in the neighborhood when the fire alarms were sounded, rushed to Greene Street, where she saw heaps of broken bodies lying on the slate sidewalk. Outraged by the careless-ness and greed that had made escape impossible, Perkins joined a campaign to eliminate the irresponsible and cruel labor practices that had led to the disaster. Workers like Rosie Yussum, who survived the fire, made it impossible to forget the people who had perished. Rosie said, "They didn't want to jump. They was afraid. They was saying their prayers first, and putting rags over their eyes so they should not see."

PETER BURCHARD
The late Peter Burchard was an author, designer, and illustrator.

CHAPTER 6

LOWER EAST SIDE & EAST VILLAGE

LOWER EAST SIDE

6.1 **Angel Orensanz Foundation**
1850, Alexander Saeltzer
172 Norfolk Street between Stanton and East Houston Streets
☎ 212 780 0175; www.orensanz.org

Designed under the spell of Hegel, Schinkel, Schiller, Heinrich Heine, and the German Romantic movement, this building was erected at the time of the great buildings of central Berlin of the 1840s—the Altes Museum, the Neue Museum, the Berlin Opera, the Berlin Concert Hall, Humboldt University, the Friedrichswerdesche Kirche, and others. The German-Jewish community that arrived in Manhattan in the 1840s asked Berlin architect Alexander Saeltzer to build a synagogue on Norfolk Street that would replicate the glory of the Cologne cathedral and the humanistic splendors of central Berlin. From here, the Jewish Reform movement would transform the cultural horizon of New York and the country.

Angel Orensanz Foundation, formerly the Congregation of Ansche Chesed, has a neo-Gothic main space of about seven thousand square feet with fifty-foot-high blue cathedral ceilings and soaring balconies. There is also an Assembly Room of about four thousand square feet. In 1986, the Angel Orensanz Foundation, established by sculptor Angel Orensanz, rescued the building from demolition. Some of New York's most creative recent projects have been staged here, including *City, Garbage and Death* by Rainer Werner Fassbinder; Alexander McQueen's first American fashion show; Mandy Patinkin's *Mamaloshen*; and George Frideric Handel's *Esther*, in its first full staging since the eighteenth century. This unique, breathtaking space has been used by a diverse group of people in the arts: Philip Glass, John Zorn, Lou Reed, the Kronos Quartet, Whitney Houston, Mariah Carey, Spike Lee, Cecil Taylor, Elie Wiesel, Maya Angelou, and Erica Jong, among others. As a space for culture, spirit, and high learning, the Orensanz Foundation sustains the vision and dream of those ninteenth-century reformers and humanists.

AL ORENSANZ
Director, Angel Orensanz Foundation

6

Loisada

6.2 **Russ & Daughters**
179 East Houston Street between Orchard and Allen Streets
☎ 212 475 4880; www.russanddaughters.com

6.3 **Katz's Delicatessen**
205 East Houston Street at Ludlow Street
☎ 212 254 2246; www.katzdeli.com

6.6 **El Castillo de Jagua**
113 Rivington Street between Essex and Ludlow Streets
☎ 212 982 6412

6.7 **First Roumanian-American Congregation Synagogue**
c. 1860
89-93 Rivington Street between Ludlow and Orchard Streets
☎ 212 673 2835

6.8 **Rosario's Pizza**
173 Orchard Street at Stanton Street
☎ 212 777 9813

6.9 **Sara D. Roosevelt Park**
East Houston Street to Canal Street between Chrystie and Forsyth Streets
www.nycgovparks.org

6.10 **Yonah Schimmel's Knishes Bakery**

137 East Houston Street at Forsyth Street

☎ 212 477 2858; www.knishery.com

For every American of Jewish descent there is a one-in-three chance that they had an ancestor who, upon arrival in this country, lived in the Lower East Side. One in three Puerto Ricans who have settled in the continental U.S. has a relative who has lived in that crowded corner of Lower Manhattan. The same one-in-three odds also apply to parents all over the U.S. who may have had a child run off to New York to be an artist. Unlike many sections of Manhattan where ethnic or cultural groups come and go, usually leaving nothing more than a few plaques or cleverly named coffee shops to commemorate their presence, the Lower East Side (LES), or Loisada if you're Latino or "down," still pulses with the energy of each of these groups.

Begin at Houston Street (pronounced HOW-stun) and Orchard, which used to be the center of the Lower East Side when its boundaries extended north to 14th Street. (The blocks between Houston and 14th Street east of the Bowery are now called the "East Village," a designation begun in the 1950s to compete with the hip West Village.) Now Houston and Orchard is the northernmost part of the LES. Though there is no official signpost, two neon fish glowing over 179 East Houston Street can serve as your markers. They're perpetually swimming over Russ & Daughters, the last and best of the smoked fish and delicacy stores that used to dot the neighborhood. Though the space has remained small and unassuming, Russ & Daughters' selection and quality make stores like Zabar's and Dean & DeLuca look like, as my grandmother would say, "they don't know from fish." The place is a true microcosm of the LES, with Latin countermen who can banter with customers in Spanish-laced Yiddish (Spiddish) and the owner of the store, Mark Russ Federman, who manages it all with his Colombian wife, Maria. More Jews swear by their whitefish salad than they do by the Torah. Order a bagel to go, or get a few pounds of Gaspé salmon packed in ice and a tub of their incomparable whipped cream cheese. With one foot in 1900 and another in the present, you can grab an old-fashioned licorice whip and a cappuccino as you walk out the door.

A block east, on the corner of Ludlow, is Katz's Deli. Since 1888, Katz's has been churning out the best pastrami and corned beef in the city. You'll be given a ticket as you enter—your bill, which you will be expected to produce when you leave. Start at the counter on the far right with a hot dog, so you have something to nosh while countermen with flashing knives prepare your sandwiches. When a chunk of pastrami flies your way, it's not a mistake, you're being offered a taste (be sure to tip). You can even eat your sandwich in the same spot where Meg Ryan faked an orgasm in *When Harry Met Sally* (or the same chair in which my Uncle Irving did not fake it in 1944 over a particularly good brisket on rye).

Take a right upon leaving Katz's and stroll south down Ludlow. Remarkably, the thirty or so new bars that have sprung up over the past few years have not seriously impacted the authentic tenement feel of the street. Many original shop signs remain, though the stores they advertised are long gone. Have a drink at any of these hipster bars. There's a fifty-fifty chance that the grungy-looking kid sitting next to you is either an artist you just read about in *The Times* or an N.Y.U. student cutting class.

A couple of blocks south at 113 Rivington Street on the corner of Essex is one of the best inexpensive Latin restaurants in the city, El Castillo de Jagua. As a paroled friend of mine once said, "Any place where you can frequently find six or seven Latin cops eating has to be good." If matzo ball soup can cure a cold, their chicken (*sopa de pollo*) could raise the dead. It's just how your Jewish grandmother would have made it if she were Dominican, and yucca and cilantro had been available anywhere near Kiev. Castillo is especially known for seafood, so try their paella Valencia (yellow rice with seafood). And be sure to spend at least a dollar on the jukebox to get a crash course on the hottest salsa music. Unlike many other bars and restaurants in the city, you will have no problem hearing your selections playing, even a couple of blocks away. Any Jewish patrons feeling guilty from too much roast pork or *arroz con longosta* can walk a few blocks west to 89 Rivington to the First Roumanian-American Congregation Synagogue. Though not packed the way it would have been ninety years ago, there's rarely trouble getting a minyan for the 5 p.m. daily services.

About a block north on the corner of Stanton and Orchard is Rosario's Pizza, a neighborhood institution for more than thirty-eight years. The place is run by Salvatore Bartolomeo, who will also be heating up your slice, the best in the city. You'll recognize Sal because the walls of Rosario's are covered with photos of him, taken by numerous appreciative neighborhood photographers whom Sal feeds late into the night, even after he's posted the "Closed" sign.

Now take a slice three blocks west and one north to Sara D. Roosevelt Park, which runs from Houston to Canal between Chrystie and Forsyth. On the way, stop into any of the neighborhood bodegas and brown-bag a 40-ounce beer. Make it a malt liquor. Plant yourself on a park bench within this island of towering trees and basketball courts. You can watch a game of pickup or read Henry Roth's *Call It Sleep* and let the Yinglish of the kids in the book who played in the neighborhood eighty years ago mingle in your mind with the Spanglish of today's inhabitants.

For dessert, walk about twenty steps east to 137 Houston, since 1910 home of Yonah Schimmel's Knishes. As you ascend the step into the doorway of the shop, you'll see an interior barely changed since its opening. You could be in Poland or Russia of a hundred years ago, except for the fact that punk rockers were probably having sex in that very doorway only hours before. Substitute Cossacks for punks and cross the threshold. Order a cheese knish. It's as though you've stepped into an Isaac Bashevis Singer novel, but better. In the shtetl you wouldn't hear motorcycles revving outside of the Hells Angels's headquarters a few blocks north or the Puerto Rican man on the corner, scraping a huge block of ice to make mango-flavored snow cones.

DAVID BAR KATZ
Writer and director

6.4 Orchard Corset Center

157 Orchard Street between Rivington and Stanton Streets
☎ 212 674 0786; www.orchardcorset.com

🎁 If you get your thrills wearing daring little pearl thongs, this is not the place for you. If, on the other hand, you prefer more serious support, then pay a visit to Ralph Berk at the Orchard Corset Center. Berk has an uncanny talent for serious bra counsel: from the outline of your shirt he'll guess your size with remarkable accuracy. And the prices! Wacoals—those French gifts to D-cups—are always on sale.

DANY LEVY
Founder, DailyCandy.com

6.5 Economy Candy

108 Rivington Street between Ludlow and Essex Streets
☎ 800 352 4544, www.economycandy.com

🎁 Started in the midst of the post-Depression era when candy still came in barrels, Economy Candy is a rickety little Lower East Side spot owned by Jerry Cohen, a grizzly New York City native with an auctioneer's voice and an attitude to match. This vintage candy warehouse brims floor to ceiling (literally—a stepladder is required) with jawbreakers, licorice whips, chocolate-covered raisins, root beer barrels, Chiclets, Pixy Stix, kosher gourmet jellybeans, and other Willy Wonka-like delicacies. A favorite of Jerry Lewis, Red Buttons, and Tony Curtis, Economy Candy was described by *Gourmet* magazine as "the penny-candy store elevated to an art form."

Other favorites include rock-candy swizzle sticks (red, blue, amber, yellow, pink, and green), Jordan Almonds, Atomic Fireballs, candy necklaces, eighteen kinds of halvah, chocolate-covered pretzels (milk, dark, and white), and Pez in every imaginable size and form. In fact, the only candy you won't find here is Chunky. "It's my favorite," says Cohen. "I don't sell it because I'd eat it all day long." At least the man shows some restraint.

DANY LEVY
Founder, DailyCandy.com

6.11 Lower East Side Tenement Museum

108 Orchard Street between Delancey and Broome Streets
📞 212 431 0233; www.tenement.org
Guided tours only.

This is a breathtaking discovery, perfectly preserved on a busy Lower East Side street. You can touch and smell the world of the original immigrants and see what was overcome to succeed in New York City.

Here is the Lower East Side as gateway to America: the heart of this museum, the tenement at 97 Orchard Street, was home to an estimated seven thousand people from more than twenty nations between 1863 and 1935. It is now a National Historic Landmark. Visit and tour carefully-restored tenement apartments of actual past residents: German Jews (1870s), Eastern European Jews (1900s), and Italian Catholics (1930s). There is also a living-history program focusing on Sephardic Jews from Turkey (1916). There will soon be apartments that interpret an 1893 sweatshop and an Irish family in residence during the Civil War.

JOHN PENOTTI
Founding partner, GreeneStreet Films

This museum is not your conventional installation of precious objects. Instead its apartments are more like a collection of time capsules ranging from the Civil War era to the early part of the twentieth century, each bearing witness to succeeding generations of immigration into the Lower East Side. Furnished with authentic period furniture and artifacts, these humble shelters for the genteel working poor give the visitor an almost eerie sense of association with the families who called these apartments home.

Be sure to take the complete tour with one of the very knowledgeable and enthusiastic guides. Any wait time can be put to good use wandering the narrow old streets nearby and maybe heading for one of the few remaining ethnic delis for some New York specialties. You'll feel like you're on the set of the *The Godfather*.

EVELYN AND PETER KRAUS
Proprietors, Ursus Books and Prints

6.12 Williamsburg Bridge

1903, Leffert L. Buck
From Delancey and Clinton Streets in Manhattan
to Washington Plaza in Brooklyn

South Passage
Manhattan entrance at Delancey and Ridge Streets
Brooklyn entrance at Broadway and Roebling Street

In a rapidly gentrifying city, this temporary metal mesh cage provides a glimpse of the gritty, graffiti-covered dystopia of the 1970s. Built to protect bikers and pedestrians during

the bridge's interminable reconstruction, this poor man's
Pompidou offers the river and skyline to the south and the
wheels and sparks of the adjacent J train to the north.
SEBASTIAN HARDY
Urban planner

6.13 **Doughnut Plant**

379 Grand Street between Essex and Norfolk Streets
☎ 212 505 3700; www.doughnutplant.com
Open Tuesdays to Sundays, from 6:30 a.m. until the
doughnuts sell out.

Sandwiched between a thrift shop and a row of brick
apartments, Doughnut Plant's storefront is easy to miss.
But what lies within puts the franchise doughnut stores
to shame.

One day, while sifting through boxes, Mark Isreal happened on some of his grandfather's recipes, so he whipped
up a batch of doughnuts and tried selling them to his local
coffee shop. The orders poured in literally overnight, and
today Mark's doughnuts grace the counters at, among
others, Dean & Deluca, Zabar's, and Balducci's. But for
the real experience, head down to Grand Street and meet the
man behind the doughnut.

This is not your average cop food. Flavors range from
classic vanilla bean to ginger, lime, pistachio, and rose water,
all hand-cut, hand-rolled, and fried in canola oil. Best of
all, each doughnut measures roughly the size of a human
head. In the words of *The New York Times*' Florence
Fabricant, "a plusher chocolate doughnut than his Valrhona
would be hard to find."
DANY LEVY
Founder, DailyCandy.com

6.14 **Eldridge Street Synagogue**

1887, Peter Herter & Francis Herter
12 Eldridge Street between Canal and Division Streets
The Museum at Eldridge Street
☎ 212 219 0888; www.eldridgestreet.org

Completed in 1887, Eldridge Street was the first synagogue in America built by Eastern European Jews. Which is to say, this synagogue is a link to an older New York that everybody knows about, some have family ties to, and hardly anyone has any contact with. The building itself, with seventy-foot ceilings, Moorish design, and a vast skylight, is beautiful. The fact that it still stands, and, amazingly, is still used for worship, is incredibly moving. The Museum at Eldridge Street hosts readings, concerts, and educational events at the synagogue; volunteer docents lead tours, complete with details that summon the old neighborhood and the synagogue's central place in its life. Imagine: mounted policemen were required for crowd control on the high holidays; people paid rent to reserve their seats in the pews. After exploring the synagogue, which also has a display of signs advertising rabbinical services and a collection of plaques depicting the Ten Commandments under the guard of carved lions—made by the same craftsmen who made the elaborate carousel horses then popular—take a look around the neighborhood. Part of Chinatown now (albeit far off the tourist track), it continues to serve new arrivals and provide an anchor for the next generation of New Yorkers.

MARTHA SCHULMAN
Writer and teacher

6.15   **East River Park Tennis Courts**
FDR Drive north of Delancey Street
☎ 212 533 0656; www.nycgovparks.org

For me, the quintessential New York experience must involve playing tennis. Where Delancey Street meets the river, there are twelve outdoor hard-surface courts at the Brian Watkins Tennis Center, in East River Park under the Williamsburg Bridge.

The most amazing thing about the experience of playing there, aside from seeing the same cronies every time (the guy who never has a racket or tennis shoes, but beats anyone and everyone, the "coach" who gives lessons but looks like he's too large to move around the court, the rooster who feeds on platters of rice and beans) is the incredible urban context in which the courts are situated. To one side is the East River with its stream of maritime traffic; above, the never-ending road-and-rail din of the Williamsburg Bridge; to the south, gatherings of family and friends, with music of the Caribbean islands, Puerto Rico, and the Dominican Republic often blaring from loudspeakers; and to the west, the East River Drive, a frequent route for fire engines and police cars.

With all this around you, it's imperative you work out some type of sign-language system with your partner for communicating (you can forget about even trying to hear the ball bounce!). Yet, despite the dissonance, one whiff of "sea" breeze can relax even the most stressed-out New Yorker.

All it requires is a fifty-dollar permit (good for one season, April 15 to October 15, at any city park court), available online, at Paragon Sporting Goods (867 Broadway between 17th and 18th Streets, ☎ 212 255 8036), and the courts in Central Park. Get there at least forty-five minutes before the hour to secure a court. If the winter is mild,

the nets don't come down and you can play all year long.
Diehards have been known to show up with their own.
STEFANIE SILVERMAN
Architect

EAST VILLAGE

6.16   **East River Park**
East 12th Street to Montgomery Street between the East
River and FDR Drive
www.nycgovparks.org

Grand Street Park, as it was known back then, was enlarged
in 1946 when Marshall Plan Aid was taking food to
bombed-out Europe. They needed ballast on the way back
for the empty boats. When they got back to New York, they
had to get rid of the ballast. The cheapest way was to dump
it in the East River, off Grand Street Park, and enlarge the
park. This kind of thing has been done for three hundred
years, you know. Manhattan had about ten percent less
acreage back in those days, maybe even less. Now when kids
hopscotch in the park, they're doing it on Hitler's bunker.
PETE SEEGER
Songwriter

6.17   **Tompkins Square Park**
1834
East 7th Street to East 10th Street between Avenues A and B

Slocum Memorial Fountain
Mid-park near 9th Street
www.nycgovparks.org

When you walk through Tompkins Square Park, you pass
clusters of old Ukrainians, old Italians, and old Slovaks;
young Latino families, picnickers, skaters, people walking

their dogs (or vice versa), "artsy" kids paying eighteen hundred dollars a month or more for studios in Old Law tenement buildings in the neighborhood, and a multitude of homeless folk.

If you walk east through the park on the path closest to 10th Street, until you are almost all the way to Avenue B, you will come to a small Parks Department building. If you look north through the walkway of this building, you will see a rose-colored eight-foot marble stela with a small lion-head fountain and a shallow relief image of children looking out to sea on its south face. The inscription on this face reads: "They were earth's purest children, young and fair."

The stela was "dedicated by the Sympathy Society of German Ladies" in "the year of Our Lord MCMVI...in memory of those who lost their lives in the disaster to the Steamer *General Slocum*" on June 15, 1904.

In 1904, Tompkins Square was in the very center of a neighborhood called Kleindeutschland or Little Germany. The neighborhood was home to more than a hundred and fifty-thousand Germans and German-Americans; a German free library, hospital, town hall, and schools; numerous German Socialist organizations; and the thriving congregation of St. Mark's Evangelical Lutheran Church on East 6th Street.

On June 15, 1904, St. Mark's Evangelical Lutheran Church leased the *General Slocum* to take the women and children of the congregation to their annual Sunday school picnic in Locust Grove, Long Island. Somewhere around 125th Street, the boat caught on fire. It is still not known what caused the fire, although various sources cite a galley fire, illegally stowed hay placed too near kerosene, a cigar smoked near oil cans, and a fallen match or cigarette. What is known is that the captain did not heed the warnings that the boat was on fire until it was too late to pull into safe harbor at one of the many working piers along the way, the crew had not been trained in emergency procedures, the boat's original hoses had never been replaced and were no longer functioning, its six lifeboats had been painted and wired to the ship and could no longer be pried free, its life vests crumbled and sank when used, and—although scores of people saw the burning boat and battled the East River currents and the intense heat from the flames to try to reach it—by the time the *Slocum* pulled into North Brother Island, at least one thousand and twenty-one women and children had been drowned, killed by the churning wheel of the steamship as they tried to escape the boat, or burnt to death.

Almost every family in Kleindeutschland lost a family member to the disaster and within a very short time Kleindeutschland was no more. The Germans moved uptown to the previously smaller German community of Yorkville, where they could be both closer to the cigar factories where many of them worked and far away from the devastating memories of June 15, 1904—making numerous apartments between the East River and the Bowery, and between Division, Grand, and 14th Streets, available for the next wave of immigrants, some of whose now aged children can be found sitting and chatting in the park today.

There are a few mementos left of the old German neighborhood: the sign for the free German library ("Freie Bibliothek u. Lesehalle") above the doorway of the Ottendorfer Branch of the New York Public Library on Second Avenue between St. Mark's Place and 9th Street, and the sign for the German hospital ("Deutsches Dispensary") above the doorway of Cabrini Medical Center's Stuyvesant Polyclinic next door. But the Germans themselves are long gone, and today fewer and fewer people know about either the *Slocum* disaster or the monument to its victims in Tompkins Square Park.

KATE HARTNICK
President, Hartnick Consulting

6.18 **Tompkins Square Park Dog Run**
9th Street entrance, near Avenue B

One of the best dog runs in the city, complete with a giant wooden statue of a bone.
ERIC STOLTZ
Actor

6.19 **Russian Turkish Baths**
268 East 10th Street between First Avenue and Avenue A
📞 212 674 9250; www.russianturkishbaths.com

You've been tramping around the city and it's finally beginning to get to you: the noise, the traffic, the constant press of human beings. You want to do something that will put you in a completely different frame of mind. Go to the Russian baths. You are surrounded mostly by people in their sixties, seventies, and eighties, many of them speaking Russian. You sit in a hot steam room and every once in a while you leave and jump into a cold pool.

There are small surrounding rooms where you can get different types of massages. The most unusual is the one using branches of oak leaves. You lie on a slab in the main steam room and an attendant rubs and massages your body and beats you with wet oak leaves; as you heat up from the steam, the attendant pours cool water on you and continues to beat and rub. I sent a friend of mine who described it as a religious experience.
MARGOT ADLER
Correspondent, National Public Radio

Go up the red steps. At the register, deposit your money and jewelry into a safe-deposit box. Go behind a curtain, take a cotton robe and a pair of plastic slippers, and put your clothes, along with your modesty, into a locker. Don your robe and slippers and go down a flight of steps to the Russian Turkish baths, where you may enter a traditional sauna, a sauna with a pull-chain shower, a steam room, an ice-cold pool, or—best of all—the radiant heat room. The first time I went into the radiant heat room, I was handed a bucket of icy water. Puzzled, I entered a stone room lined with two tiers of wooden benches. I have never experienced such intense heat. Within seven minutes I had overturned the bucket on my head; it was wonderful. For a modest fee you can spend hours at leisure. Founded in 1892, the baths are a rare New York treat, but the days and hours vary for single-sex and co-ed bathing; call to be sure.

MARGARET A. BRUCIA
Latin teacher and scholar

6.20 Monday Night Magic
Theater 80
80 Saint Marks Place between First and Second Avenues
☎ 212 615 6432; www.mondaynightmagic.com

Fun! Thrills! Comedy! Magic! Imagine a different full-length magic show presented each week in an intimate setting and you've got Monday Night Magic, where the best magicians from all over the world come to perform for an appreciative and enthusiastic audience. In addition to performances on the stage, with no seat more than four or five rows away, intermission features close-up magic where the miracles happen right in front of your disbelieving eyes. In addition to magicians, you'll often find sideshow performers, escape artists, comedy-magicians, jugglers, and Wild West whip-crackers on the bill. This is New York's longest-running magic show.

MATTHEW FIELD
Editor, Magic Circular magazine

6.22 St. Mark's-in-the-Bowery Church

1795–1799; 1828, steeple designed by Martin E. Thompson and Ithiel Towne
131 East 10th Street at Second Avenue
The Poetry Project: ☎ 212 674-091; www.poetryproject.com

When it was completed in 1799, St. Mark's-in-the-Bowery was already more than a hundred years old, having started in 1660 as a Dutch chapel on Peter Stuyvesant's farm. It stands today as the second-oldest site of worship in New York City after St. Paul's Chapel. The Bowery, to the left of St. Mark's, was the road leading to the New Amsterdam governor's farm.

If slightly weary from all the changes around it, St. Mark's is still the most vocal member of the community. The old bronze bell tolled for John F. Kennedy and Martin Luther King, and rang to celebrate the end of the Vietnam War. Cracked in the fire of 1978, it now sits in the courtyard. After years of fundraising, the church was restored and rededicated in 1983.

There is a sublime simplicity to St. Mark's. The inside of the church looks more Quaker than Episcopalian. The sun streams into the large white room over wooden floors—a place where one is as likely to hear the voices of poets as prayers. There is little sign of the arboreal splendor that marked the Stuyvesant farmland, but beautiful trees still grace the courtyard with a skyline of green. With your back to Stuyvesant Street, you can imagine the small colonial town of 1650. Just as easily, you will feel the history of community involvement and countercultural movements. Always a forum for common and radical beliefs alike, St. Mark's is a symbol of peaceful acceptance as well as protest.

St. Mark's has been home to the Poetry Project, scene of the only joint reading by Robert Lowell and Allen Ginsberg, since its founding in 1966. Readers have included Amiri

Baraka, John Ashbery, Yoko Ono, Kenneth Koch, Adrienne Rich, and many adventurous unknowns. A small dogwood in the courtyard honors Allen Ginsberg, who wrote: "The Poetry Project burns like red hot coal in New York's snow." Nearby, flowering trees memorialize W. H. Auden, Paul Blackburn, and Frank O'Hara. A brass plate on the Parish wall quotes Auden: "Thousands live without love, not one without water."

6

I love St. Mark's for the two women eating lunch on the porch and the man practicing tai chi in the courtyard, the gravel barely moving under his light but deliberate steps. Growing up, we used the vault markers as bases. I walked quickly past Peter Stuyvesant's bust as if he were the authoritative parent of a friend. I kissed my first kiss amidst the charred stones. St. Mark's church—eternal home to seven generations of Stuyvesants—reminds us that among the hustle and bustle of Second Avenue, poetry thrives and New York, with its gritty past, is still beautiful.

LAURIE DUCHOVNY
Teacher

6.24 Gem Spa Newsstand

131 Second Avenue at St. Marks Place
☎ 212 995 1866

In my opinion this Manhattan newsstand serves the best version of that world-famous concoction of milk, seltzer, and syrup that is often described as the quintessential New York beverage. Once you've got the proportions and ingredients right, the trick to a great egg cream is using very, very cold milk, and Gem Spa keeps theirs in an ice-cream freezer. The mixologists at Gem Spa have one fault, however. They will ask you what flavor you want. Scoff at them. Any real New Yorker knows that egg creams only come in chocolate.

MICHAEL MISCIONE
Manhattan Borough Historian

Best Old Barrooms

6.25 **McSorley's Old Ale House**
15 East 7th Street between Second and Third Avenues
☎ 212 473 9148; www.mcsorleysnewyork.com

4.16 **Fanelli's Cafe**
94 Prince Street at Mercer Street
☎ 212 226 9412

8.12 **Old Town Bar and Restaurant**
45 East 18th Street between Broadway and Park Avenue South
☎ 212 529 6732; www.oldtownbar.com

🍴 McSorley's Old Ale House, the "wonderful saloon"
chronicled by Joseph Mitchell and painted by John Sloan,
may be the last remnant of a New York we all dreamed
about long ago. "To a devoted McSorley customer, most
other New York City saloons are tense and disquieting,"
Mitchell wrote. "It is possible to relax in McSorley's. For
one thing, it is dark and gloomy, and repose comes easy
in a gloomy place.... Also, there is a thick, musty smell
that acts as a balm to jerky nerves; it is really a rich com-
pound of the smells of pine sawdust, tap drippings, pipe
tobacco, coal smoke, and onions." Despite a few modifi-
cations, including the first female face behind the bar,
McSorley's is much as it was when Mitchell brilliantly captured it for *The New Yorker* almost sixty years ago; much
as it was when the doors first opened in 1854. Dim and
crowded (avoid it at all costs on Saint Paddy's Day), it has
the same bar taps, the same pot-bellied stove, and it serves
just two kinds of beer—McSorley's own light and dark.

If McSorley's is the place to be pleasantly melancholy,
then Fanelli's is the place to be happy. It's practically the
last genuine establishment left in SoHo, once a gritty
factory neighborhood and now full of relentlessly trendy
shops. The beautifully intact speakeasy interior hasn't

changed much since the repeal of Prohibition. And even though the gallery-goers and local loft-dwellers who dart in and out may whip out Palm Pilots at the drop of a hat, Fanelli's remains without pretensions, offering generous drinks and plates of honest grub at fair prices. A friend once compared it to the bar in *Cheers*, but to my mind it's more like the bar in *Northern Exposure*: completely non-judgmental. Prada and Yohji Yamamoto rub elbows with well-worn workshirts and the seersucker jacket and madras tie on the gentleman to your left.

If you've seen the opener of *Late Night with David Letterman*, with that grand sweep of mahogany bar (it seats forty), then you've seen the Old Town. It's pretty great. And when it comes to being conducive to talking (or eaves-dropping), there is nothing like it. Go early, when the serious drinkers are there, and slide into one of the intimate booths opposite the bar. There's a good selection of brew on tap, but there's something about the tone of the place that makes the choice of Bud in a bottle almost automatic. And the food—burgers, real bar sandwiches, terrific fries—is popular with neighborhood loyalists.

JANE DANIELS LEAR
Food and travel writer

7

Pier 83

Lincoln Tunnel

West Side Hwy (Joe DiMaggio Hwy)

Eleventh Avenue

Tenth Avenue

W 42nd St

W 41st St   Dyer Av

W 40th St

W 39th St

W 38th St

W 37th St

W 36th St

W 35th St   Dyer Av

W 34th St

W 33rd St

W 31st St

W 30th St

W 29th St

W 28th St

Chelsea Park

W 27th St

W 26th St

W 25th St

W 24th St

W 23rd St

W 22nd St

W 21st St

W 20th St

W 19th St

W 18th St

W 17th St

W 16th St

W 15th St

W 14th St

Ninth Avenue

Eighth Avenue

Port Authority Bus Terminal

Ⓜ

🚇 **15**

🚇 **10**

Garment District

Madison Square Garden

Penn Station

Ⓜ

🚇 **7**

Chelsea

Ⓜ

🚇 **6**

🚇 **1**

Twelfth Avenue

Pier 64

Eleventh Avenue

🚇 **2**

🚇 **3**

🚇 **4**

🚇 **5**

Tenth Avenue

Ninth Avenue

Eighth Avenue

Ⓜ

Meat Packing District

W 13th St

Little W 12th St

Greenwich Aven

Horatio St

W 4th St

14

13

12   11

9   10

7   8

3   5
    4
2   6

1

Map labels:

W 46th St · E 46th St
W 45th St · E 45th St
W 44th St · E 44th St
W 43rd St · E 43rd St
Grand Central Terminal
Vanderbilt Avenue
W 42nd St · E 42nd St
New York Public Library
Bryant Park
E 41st St
W 40th St · E 40th St
W 39th St · E 39th St
W 38th St · E 38th St
W 37th St · E 37th St
W 36th St · E 36th St
W 35th St · E 35th St
W 34th St · E 34th St
Sixth Avenue (Avenue of the Americas)
Fifth Avenue
Madison Avenue
Park Avenue
E 33rd St
E 32nd St
E 31st St
E 30th St
E 29th St
E 28th St
Park Avenue South
E 27th St
E 26th St
E 25th St
Madison Avenue
Madison Square Park
E 24th St
E 23rd St
Flatiron
E 22nd St
E 21st St
E 20th St
Broadway
E 19th St
E 18th St
E 17th St
E 16th St
E 15th St
Union Square
E 14th St
E 13th St
E 12th St
Greenwich Village
E 11th St

CHELSEA & GARMENT DISTRICT

CHELSEA

7.1 **Starrett-Lehigh Building**
1931, Russell G. Cory & Walter M. Cory, and Yasuo Matsui
601 West 26th Street between Eleventh and Twelfth Avenues

The streamlined Art Moderne Starrett-Lehigh Building
anchors a full city block like a hulking dry-docked tanker.
Russell and Walter Cory and Yasuo Matsui designed the
2.5 million-square-foot shipwreck for the Starrett Brothers
(contractors for the Empire State Building) and the Lehigh
Valley Railroad. An early Modernist landmark work of
the Machine Age, its gently curved corners are wrapped
with nine miles of strip windows and brick. Freight train
cars were ferried across the Hudson River, rode the elevated
High Line rail inside and were hoisted to the upper floors
fully loaded by super-powered Otis elevators. For a brief
moment, the former factory and warehouse housed hundreds
of dot.coms. Remaining tenants include the do-it-yourself
diva Martha Stewart, who delights in driving door-to-door
(via the freight elevator) to her empire designed by architect
Dan Rowan.
FREDERIC SCHWARTZ AND TRACEY HUMMER
Architect and Writer

7.2 **General Theological Seminary Garden**
175 Ninth Avenue between West 20th and West 21st Streets
☏ 212 243 5150

Stroll past the bookstore and onto the grounds of the
oldest seminary of the Episcopal church in the U.S.

(founded in 1817 and a New York City landmark since 1826). You'll find a central garden or "close," with expansive lawns and towering trees, that is an absolute surprise. Wander in for a bit of Boston in New York. It's beautiful, peaceful, and free.

ERIC STOLTZ
Actor

Skybridges
West 15th Street between Ninth and Tenth Avenues
Tenth Avenue between West 15th and West 16th Streets
East 60th Street between Lexington and Third Avenues

The autogyros and skyline freeways of Hugh Ferriss's Metropolis of Tomorrow never appeared, and dirigibles don't moor at the spire of the Empire State Building. However, these simple bridges cantilevered over Manhattan's streets serve both the prosaic purpose of linking showroom and warehouse and providing a sliver of the romantic comic book city of Gotham amid Manhattan's relentless grid.

SEBASTIAN HARDY
Urban planner

7.3 ## Chelsea Market
75 Ninth Avenue between West 15th and West 16th Streets
www.chelseamarket.com

The old Nabisco Factory where the original Oreo Cookie was made in 1912 is once again a center for good food. Since 1995, it has housed the Chelsea Market complex of shops. The factory building fills the entire block between Ninth and Tenth Avenues and 15th and 16th Streets. Developer Irwin Cohen drew on the area's history as New

York's meatpacking and wholesale produce district at the end of the nineteenth century and came up with a design that lightheartedly recalls the building's industrial past. A corridor, originally part of the railroad that carried supplies from the Hudson River, runs through the center, lined with shops like the main street of a village. Halfway through, a factory pipe has been made into an indoor waterfall. All along the walk, gears, bits of old brick, and other machinery now serve as sculptures. (There is also, somewhat oddly, a series of stone carvings of various parts of the human body.) The shops do a large part of their business wholesale, using the original loading bays. Each also sells retail from a storefront, offering the same products used at many of New York's most elegant restaurants at excellent prices. In a particularly nice touch, the wholesale kitchens are all on display behind glass, so you can watch huge batches of cookies, breads, and soups being made. The old factory still contains many bakeries, among them the famous Sarabeth's Bakery and Amy's Bread. Other shops offer meat, wine, fresh milk in glass bottles, soups, freshly squeezed fruit juices, Thai food, imported Italian goods, and produce, including some hard-to-find fruits and vegetables. A kitchen supply store sells both new and used kitchen equipment, including some huge professional ovens and restaurant fixtures. There is a flower shop, a hardware store, and a gift basket creator. Several places offer free samples. Many establishments include small restaurant areas, and there are also benches along the central corridor, so you can assemble a picnic and eat it right there. The market and the shops in it sponsor occasional events such as food and wine tastings, and on Saturday evenings there is free tango dancing (Triangulo, ☎212 633 6445; www.triangulonyc.com).

JANET B. PASCAL
Writer and production editor, Viking Children's Books

The Renaissance Street Singers
www.streetsingers.org

On a Sunday somewhere in the five boroughs, you may come
upon a small semicircle of musicians singing fifteenth- and
sixteenth-century a cappella motets on the sidewalk. These
are the Renaissance Street Singers, a group founded in 1973
by John Hetland. The concerts are always free (and the group
returns any donations people try to leave for them), given
simply for love of the music and as a gift to the City of New
York. For twenty-eight years, the group has sung in any
public space they can find (unless someone kicks them out).
Some favorite spots are the corner of Christopher and
Bleecker Streets in Greenwich Village, Chelsea Market (see
p. 127), the corner of Henry and Montague Streets in
Brooklyn Heights, and Cleopatra's Needle in Central Park.
They perform two or three Sundays a month, usually from
2 p.m. to 4 p.m. If you're interested in tracking them down,
the location of the forthcoming Sunday's concert can be
found on their website.

JANET B. PASCAL
Writer and production editor, Viking Children's Books

7.4 ## Former Port of New York Authority Commerce Building
1932, Abbott, Merkt & Co
111 Eighth Avenue between West 15th and West 16th Streets

In this full-block structure, find an elevator large enough
for semi tractor-trailers, ramps for same, an elevator machine
room straight out of Charlie Chaplin's *Modern Times*, and
a circular elevated helicopter landing pad with a giant red
"x" raised above the roof.

TERENCE RILEY
Architect

If you tilted this muscular 1930s Art Moderne behemoth on its end, it would rise as tall as the Woolworth Building. With more than two million sprawling square feet of space, this is the fourth-largest building in New York City. Its enormous footprint (two hundred by eight hundred feet) encompasses one of the city's biggest blocks and merits its own subway entrance. This was formerly the Port Authority's headquarters, where six giant elevators once hoisted trucks to thirty loading docks in the sky.

TRACEY HUMMER
Writer

7.5   La Taza de Oro

96 Eighth Avenue between West 14th and West 15th Streets
212 243 9946
Closed Sundays.

There is really no reason to pay all that money at Starbucks when you can get such a superior product at this popular Puerto Rican diner. A dollar flat will get you a generous cup of *café con leche*. The brew is foamy and rich, with more than enough caffeine to get you through a morning's worth of Chelsea gallery-hopping or a shopping expedition at Jeffrey. If you need more fuel, sit down to a plate of delectable roast chicken with rice and beans.

MARY CLARKE
Editor

7.6   El Quijote

226 West 23rd Street between Seventh and Eighth Avenues
212 929 1855; www.elquijoterestaurant.com

You wouldn't say there's a scene to make at El Quijote, but the place is generally crowded with actual New Yorkers there to eat the excellent lobster and paella, to drink some sangria or Marques de Riscal, and to spend some time in the very cool atmosphere of this handsome and sturdy seventy-year-old Spanish restaurant. The Quijote is a survivor, and the better part of its patrons—writers, models, hospital workers, legitimately eccentric denizens of the Chelsea Hotel—appear to be among those who have gone too far down their chosen road to contemplate turning back. The Dulcinea Room and the Cervantes Room are attractive, in a slightly Miss Havishamesque way, but the main dining room, with its terra-cotta walls painted with duotone Quixote murals, is the best spot to take in the underlit defunct elegance of the place. Owner Manny Ramirez says he's a direct descendant of Don Quixote, a claim worthy of the Man of La Mancha himself. Dig into the big portions and the red wine.

CHRISTOPHER CAHILL
Author, and director of the American Irish Historical Society

Most people go to El Quijote, the oldest Spanish lobster palace in the city, for its generous portions of paella, and the staggering surf-and-turf platters. Few go for the bar, which is one of the best spots for revisiting the New York of fedoras, furs, and cigarettes cases. It's one of those places where "old" New York isn't re-created—it simply never left. The bartenders wear uniforms with undersized bow ties and engraved nameplates on their vests. Exceedingly polite and formal, it's clear they consider restaurant service an honorable profession—just one of the many subtleties that places the restaurant in another era. The bar is old-fashioned, too, with its large frosted glass etched with lobsters, and backlit a pale blue. Quixote figures form an odd parade along the bar, filling every space not occupied by bottles. The spirits collection includes crème de menthe, Dubonnet, and sloe gin—things you'd think no one has ordered in years until the night you come in here for a perfect Manhattan and you see a woman of tattered beauty—maybe a 1948 Miss Nassau County or a former showgirl—nursing one of those retro drinks in the curve of her arm. Hemmed into her space by the couples from Jersey or the Island, the guy with slicked-back hair and the well-toned date, and the art types from the Chelsea Hotel, she's a character type that's all but forgotten.

From the bar you have the perfect vantage point from which to see the dining room. Red banquettes line the walls, which in turn are lined with the original black-and-white and burnt-sienna murals depicting Quixote's adventures. Windmills turn slowly along the back wall—the only sluggish element in this bustling place, where waiters hustle at breakneck speed, swooping into the dining room with large trays overhead.

There's no pretension here. There's no kitsch, no irony, and no attitude. It's earnest, authentic, delicious—and you'll get a perfect Manhattan at an old-fashioned price.

LANA BORTOLOT
Writer

7.7 Biricchino Northern Italian Restaurant

260 West 29th Street between Seventh and Eighth Avenues

📞 212 695 6690; www.biricchino.com

📞 212 736 7376; www.salumeriabiellese.com

🍴 Go to Biricchino (don't be put off by the decor) and try
🎁 a sample appetizer of five of their sausages. The sausages and salamis are made fresh by Salumeria Biellesse, their deli next door, and are served at New York's finest restaurants including the Four Seasons and Alain Ducasse. When there's a game at Madison Square Garden, people with season tickets also appear to have reservations for tables at the restaurant, until exactly 7:20 p.m. The place stops serving at 9 p.m., so go early.

LIONEL TIGER
Darwin Professor of Anthropology, Rutgers University, and Co-research Director, Guggenheim Foundation

7.8 Capitol Fishing Tackle Co.

132 West 36th Street between Broadway and Seventh Avenue

📞 212 929 6132; www.capitolfishing.com

🎁 I've attempted to fish only a few unsuccessful times in my life. But whenever I happen to walk by Capitol Fishing Tackle, I find myself stopping in to browse the extensive array of fishing paraphernalia and equipment. The beauty, humor, and inventiveness of the vast inventory of lures is astonishing. Their line-up of reels may not rival in diversity the Metropolitan Museum's collection of early weaponry, but it does provide an impressive display of variations on a theme—a kind of simple mechanical beauty either eliminated or hidden in most current product design. For the avid fisher or anyone who likes cool stuff, it's worth a visit. They also carry a decent collection of T-shirts emblazoned with all kinds of piscine imagery.

BILL KOMOSKI
Artist

GARMENT DISTRICT

7.11 Tinsel Trading

1 West 37th Street between Fifth and Sixth Avenues
📞 212 730 1030; www.tinseltrading.com

🎁 The family story of Tinsel Trading is hidden from the casual shopper on this Garment District street. But it's hard to ignore the extraordinary nature of the trims and ribbons sold in this store. Marcia Ceppos inherited this business from her grandfather Arch Bergoffen. In the 1930s, Mr. Bergoffen sold gold trim for military uniforms. He gradually expanded to include many trims using metal thread, handmade raffia flowers from Italy, and straw trims from Switzerland. When things went out of style, he put them away. When Ms. Ceppos found this treasure trove, some of which had not been looked at in fifty years, she decided to keep the business not only going, but in the family.

CHARLES SUISMAN AND CAROL MOLESWORTH
Co-authors of Manhattan User's Guide

7.12 The New York Public Library
1911, Carrère & Hastings
Fifth Avenue and 42nd Street
☎ 212 340 0833; www.nypl.org

Rose Main Reading Room
Restoration 1998, Davis Brody Bond
General Research Division, third floor

Salomon Room
Third Floor

Newly renovated, the Main Reading Room of the New York Public Library is one of the premier public spaces in the city. Take a morning to visit the library, perhaps to order a fine or obscure book from the stacks for perusing at one of the long reading tables. Then, walk across the hall to the Salomon Room (now a wireless reading and study room), where you'll find curious or arresting exhibits drawn from the library's collection of books, manuscripts, and papers. Afterwards, lunch or dine at the Bryant Park Grill behind the library and stroll along the park path, taking in the sculpture and the people.

PAUL KANE
Poet and professor of English, Vassar College

Children's Center
Ground Floor, Room 84

Stop in at the Central Children's Room and you'll discover an old friend in a glass case (they say it's bulletproof). It's the world's most famous teddy bear, Winnie-the-Pooh. Given to the New York Public Library in 1987 and part of a *cause célèbre* when a member of the British Parliament tried unsuccessfully to extradite him in 1998, he waits for fans old and young to pay homage.

JOHANNA HURWITZ
Author of children's books

7.13 **Bryant Park**
1871; 1934, redesigned by Lusby Simpson
Sixth Avenue between West 40th and West 42nd Streets

Bryant Park Grill
25 West 40th Street between Fifth and Sixth Avenues
Upper terrace, behind the library
☎ 212 840 6500; www.bryantpark.org

One of the best ways to spend an hour in Midtown is in Bryant Park, the oasis behind the New York Public Library—by some miracle restored rather than replaced like its counterparts in London and Paris. Ask to see the outdoor roof garden at the Bryant Park Grill. You'll be shown a dark, hidden staircase that takes you to the roof with a wonderful wide view of the elegant park ringed with skyscrapers. Tired from reading, your eyes take in the grassy rectangle below, edged by rows of lush perennials and greenery, partially shaded by rows of tall, graceful trees, and anchored by kiosks selling drinks, tickets, and fresh flowers.
LAURIE LISLE
Journalist and biographer

7.10 **Drama Book Shop**
250 West 40th Street between Seventh and Eighth Avenues
☎ 212 944 0595; www.dramabookshop.com

If you're interested in the theater, don't miss the Drama Book Shop. You'll see stars of tomorrow stretched out in chairs and on the floor, reading scripts for auditions and not buying. The management doesn't mind.
JOHN GUARE
Playwright

7.15   **Former Empire Theater, now AMC Empire 25**
Façade 1912, Thomas W. Lamb
234 West 42nd Street between Seventh and Eighth Avenues
☏ 212 398 7843

How can a vast new twenty-five-screen multiplex on 42nd Street be called a city secret? What makes the AMC worth a careful look is the way the building expresses that it is the largest structure in New York City ever to be physically moved. The remaining signs of that 1998 move are fascinating.

As a boy, I spent happy days on old West 42nd Street, visiting magic shops and Hubert's Flea Circus. The exterior of the new AMC was there then. It was built in 1912 as the Eltinge Theater, named after Julian Eltinge, a famed cross-dressing actor of the era—a work by theater architect Thomas W. Lamb, who in New York also did the lost Strand, Ziegfeld, Rialto, Rivoli, Capitol, and Loew's 72nd Street, and the still extant Cort and Mark Hellinger theaters. Over the decades, the building's function changed from comedy playhouse to burlesque theater to cinema, and its name changed to the Empire in 1954, after it became a second-run movie house. When 42nd Street was rebuilt in the last few years, it was decided to transform the Empire into a multiplex. The single auditorium space became super-fluous, but the building façade and elements within were thought worth preserving as major historic constituents of what eventually became an internally linked, mixed old and new architectural ensemble.

The front of the Eltinge/Empire that in 1998 rolled a hundred and seventy feet west from its original position weighed 7.4 million pounds, including its temporary struc-tural reinforcement. (Though preparations had taken months, the distance was covered in a single day.) What's architec-turally interesting is how the completed design expresses the assemblage of parts, the old façade providing an ad hoc component for the amalgamation. The dome over the lobby, visible behind exterior glazing, covers a surprisingly kinetic space when one walks in. Two transparent-sided escalators merrily penetrate what used to be the old proscenium arch, carrying customers out of the ticketing area into the hinterland of screened auditoriums and eateries. All this can be visited and viewed without buying a ticket.

The lobby interior's largely scenographic decoration includes a restored mural uncovered before the move. It depicts three muses, probably the likenesses of Julian Eltinge in drag. A final transformation for you, sir!

NATHAN SILVER
Architect, critic, and writer

CHAPTER 8

Gramercy, Flatiron District, Midtown South & Murray Hill

GRAMERCY

8.1 **Gramercy Park**
1831, Samuel Ruggles
East 20th to East 21st Street between Park Avenue South
and Third Avenue
Open to the public on Christmas Eve.

It may look like a London square, but Gramercy Park is a
microcosm of old and new New York. Though most of the
houses that surround it were built in a subdued Greek Revival
style in the 1840s and '50s, most were updated, enlarged
or—on the north and east sides, especially—replaced over
the years, so that today the place is a little museum of local
architectural history up to about 1930.

The red brick house (No. 5, dated 1843), at the corner
of 20th and Gramercy Park West, gives the best impression
of the original type. It would have had a wrought-iron
veranda like that which its elegant neighbors at Nos. 3 and
4 (dated 1847) still have. The house at No. 2 later received
an additional story, paired pilasters, and a balustrade.
Two houses purchased by Samuel Tilden at No. 15 were
"Victorianized" inside and out by Vaux & Radford in 1884;
they are now home to the National Arts Club (see p. 141).
After the actor Edwin Booth bought a house with Gothic
trim next door (No. 16) in 1887, Stanford White converted
it to a clubhouse for the Players. The houses at Nos. 13
and 14 were remodeled in the 1930s with large casement
windows, but because one is still red brick with its classical
cornice intact, it passes for being older. Their now

International Style neighbor—painted white with bright yellow trim on the windows— had its cornice removed to emphasize the flat roof. The apartment houses that rose on the other edges of the park include: the polite Federal-style tower of duplexes at 24 Gramercy Park; the Gramercy (No. 34), a Queen Anne fortress dated 1883; the neo-Gothic terra-cotta extravaganza (1910) at No. 36 (complete with metallic-colored knights guarding the door); the collegiate Tudor tower at No. 44; the vaguely Deco building at No. 45; Emery Roth's 1928 New York apartment house with Spanish trim at No. 60; and the massive brick building at 1 Lexington Avenue.

JAYNE MERKEL
Architectural historian and critic

8

8.2 The National Arts Club

1884, Calvert Vaux
15 Gramercy Park South between Park Avenue South and Irving Place
☎ 212 475 3424; www.nationalartsclub.org

This magnificent former residence of Samuel Tilden is now a national landmark and home to the hundred-year-old National Arts Club. Overlooking Gramercy Park, the Victorian mansion is a cynosure from a bygone era in one of the city's loveliest neighborhoods. Although the club is private and its finest rooms are open only to members, the space can be rented for functions, and most of the art galleries are open to walk-in visitors. If possible, sneak a peek at the glorious blue bubble-glass ceiling above the bar. It's a jewel by John La Farge, Louis Comfort Tiffany's great rival.

ALEXANDRA STYRON
Writer

Irving Place Stroll

Pete's Tavern
129 East 18th Street at Irving Place
☎ 212 473 7676

71 Irving Espresso and Tea Bar
71 Irving Place between East 18th and 19th Streets
☎ 212 995 5252; www.irvingfarm.com

80 Irving Place
At East 19th Street

Gramercy Park
1831, Samuel Ruggles
East 20th to East 21st Street between Park Avenue South
and Third Avenue
Open to the public on Christmas Eve.

Yama
122 East 17th Street at Irving Place
☎ 212 475 0969; www.yamarestaurant.com

Choshi
77 Irving Place at East 19th Street
☎ 212 420 1419; www.sushichoshi.com

The Inn at Irving Place
56 Irving Place between East 17th and East 18th Streets
☎ 212 533 4600; www.innatirving.com

If not for Gramercy Park, Lexington Avenue would storm
right down to 14th Street. Luckily, the park deflects
Lexington at 21st Street, leaving a six-block oasis in its
stead: Irving Place. A tree-lined, quiet, two-way street, Irving
radiates a unique feeling. One senses the absence of an
avenue where an avenue should be, and the particular
tranquility created by this vacuum.

Pete's Tavern, at the corner of 18th, is the heart of Irving Place. Founded in 1864, it is the longest continuously operating saloon in New York. Two staples of the American literary canon were created in this corner pub: O'Henry's "The Gift of the Magi" and Ludwig Bemelmans's *Madeline*. Bring a pen and maybe you'll get lucky; clearly something magic is in the beer. Today Pete's draws mostly young corporate types, but don't let that scare you off. In the pantheon of old New York gin mills, it holds a hallowed niche between the dusty Irishness of McSorley's and the Dylan Thomas romanticism of the White Horse Tavern.

8

Across the street percolates a fun little cafe called 71 Irving. They have fresh bread they'll toast and butter for you, and you can have the satisfaction of buying coffee from a small-business person rather than a huge multinational. Across, at 19th, stands a wonderful house (No. 80) —home to Sigourney Weaver's character in the movie *Working Girl*, but truly triumphant because of its two-car garage. Living in Manhattan, one gets inured to trappings of luxury, but a two-car garage still impresses.

At 20th is Gramercy Park (see p. 140), the only private park left in New York. You can wander around the wrought-iron gates, looking inside at the kids with their nannies and the octogenarians on the benches. This is actually the best way to see Gramercy Park; everything shines brighter when you're on the outside looking in.

A brick house on the corner of 17th has a plaque suggesting that Washington Irving once lived there. Irving, creator of "Rip Van Winkle" and "The Legend of Sleepy Hollow," certainly gave his name to the street, but my sources doubt that he ever called that address home. However, in the basement, the sushi restaurant Yama serves up fist-sized pieces of yellowtail and *toro*, so delicious that the horseman would wish he had a head, so sublime they would wake Rip Van Winkle. So yummy, in fact, that the line is often around the corner. If it is, go up the block to Choshi.

Their portions aren't as generous, but they have a pleasant outdoor seating area and I recommend their Kinoko sauté, a delicious blend of Asian mushrooms in soy sauce and butter.

If you're looking for a place to stay and you don't feel like dealing with the madness of Midtown, try the Inn at Irving Place. The luxuriously cozy bed and breakfast occupies a double-wide town house between 17th and 18th Streets, a perfect base from which to enjoy the charms of Irving.

SAM HOFFMAN
Filmmaker

FLATIRON DISTRICT

8.9 **Arts for Transit: *Framing Union Square***
1998, Mary Miss & Lee Pomeroy
www.mta.info/mta/aft

If you visit the grand outdoor greenmarket at Union Square, spend some time exploring the archaeological layers of the subway station, brilliantly elucidated by artist Mary Miss and architect Lee Pomeroy. Three stations, built in 1904, 1914, and 1930 for now-intersecting lines, are joined and have been recently renovated. Pomeroy and Miss have revealed the layers and history of the site through bright red enameled frames in 115 locations. Framed vertical slits, some with faceted mirrored interiors, indicate the workings of the system (electrical panel boxes, message slots, telephone wiring, ceiling light fixtures, holding cells, mesh and wire grates, concrete arches between the columns, cables), or cut through the walls of one level to another so visitors can view the passage of trains. Red horizontal frames border details that were excavated during construction (particularly bands of patterning and lettering in earlier

styles). There are massive hunks of freestanding wall decorated with mosaics and glazed, cast ceramic eagles along
an upper-level corridor, outlined with red girders to draw
our attention. In fact, this signature red is used throughout on signs, pipes, railings, and poles as a marker, even
alternating with white diagonal stripes along the train
walls; in this way, infrastructure is highlighted through a
contemporary graphic process.
JOYCE KOZLOFF
Artist

8

Lower Midtown Squares

8.10 **Union Square**
*1839; redesigned 1872 by Frederick Law Olmsted and Calvert
Vaux; restored in 1985*
East 14th Street to East 17th Street between Union Square
West (Broadway) and Union Square East (Park Avenue South)
☎ 212 460 1200; www.unionsquarenyc.org

8.1 **Gramercy Park**
1831, Samuel Ruggles
East 20th to East 21st Street between Park Avenue
South and Third Avenue
Open to the public on Christmas Eve.

8.18 **Madison Square Park**
1847, Ignatz Pilat
East 23rd to East 26th Street between Fifth and
Madison Avenues
www.madisonsquarepark.org

8.11 **Union Square Greenmarket**
Union Square Park
☎ 212 788 7476; www.grownyc.org

I love the "necklace" formed by Union Square, Gramercy,
and Madison Square parks so much that I have chosen to

conduct my entire personal and professional life around those jewels. It's Manhattan at its most civilized scale, and no neighborhood better combines beautifully preserved historic architecture with a dynamic sense of modern style. One could say that this is where "Ladies' Mile" meets "Silicon Alley." Architects, publishers, and new-media executives commingle with young family residents, green-market farmers, and the city's densest population of excellent restaurants. The trick to any stroll through this zone is to look up. Each building brings an animated story to the streetscape, and many have been lovingly restored and given meaningful, modern uses. The Union Square Greenmarket—open Monday, Wednesday, Friday, and Saturday, but at its abundant and bustling best on Wednesday and Saturday—is New York's closest thing to a vital Italian piazza. It is perhaps the only place in the city where New Yorkers choose to slow down, smell the smells, and talk to each other.

DANNY MEYER
Restaurateur and cookbook author

8.13 Housing Works Thrift Shop

143 West 17th Street between Sixth and Seventh Avenues
☎ 718 838 5050; www.shophousingworks.com

A treasure trove in Chelsea. Like thrift shops everywhere, the merchandise is donated, but here the stuff is fabulous. Antiques, furniture, art, collectibles, jewelry, and tchotchkes, often comparable to those found in Madison Avenue antique shops, are to be had at less-than-flea-market prices. There are also racks of gently worn designer and vintage clothing, and from time to time some top-notch designers donate samples. And as if this weren't rewarding enough, all proceeds go to AIDS assistance. Housing Works also operates the terrific used-book store and cafe at 126 Crosby Street.

BINNIE KIRSHENBAUM
Writer, and chair of the M.F.A. program, Columbia University

8.14 Eisenberg Sandwich Shop

174 Fifth Avenue between West 22nd and West 23rd Streets
☎ 212 675 5096; www.eisenbergsnyc.com

Step in the front door here and leave the new millennium behind; inside, it's 1942. To your left, a long row of swiveling stools. To your right, a few tables if you're dining *à deux*. If you're alone, slide onto a stool and peruse the menu, which hangs from wooden plaques on the wall that look like they've been there since, well, 1942. Choose corned beef or pastrami at a fraction of the price of the snob uptown delis, meatloaf (always a special—alas, now served with instant mashed potatoes), or matzo ball soup bobbing with namesakes bigger than tennis balls. Wash it all down with a Dr. Brown's cream soda. When you're done, there's no check; just tell the cashier what you had. No one running the place seems to be Jewish anymore—the countermen are Hispanic, the cashiers Asian. No matter. In a happy, plastic McDonald's world, Eisenberg's is the real deal.

SUSAN WYLAND
Magazine consultant

8.15 Masonic Hall

1910, Napoleon Le Brun
71 West 23rd Street at Sixth Avenue
☎ 212 337 6602; www.nymasons.org

One of the finest edifices in New York is the Masonic Hall and home of the Grand Lodge of Free and Accepted Masons of the State of New York, as well as Holland Lodge No. 8. Founded in 1787, Holland Lodge's many distinguished members have included Samuel Fraunces (famous tavernkeeper), Baron von Steuben, John Jacob Astor, and F. D.R. The building is of granite and its construction in the early 1900s cost more than a million dollars. Its frontage on 23rd Street is a hundred and forty feet, and its height to the capstone is two hundred and

forty feet. The principal entrance on 23rd Street is through
a Doric portico; at the entrances to the lodge rooms are
plaster columns of the Egyptian order emblematic of
"strength and beauty" and representative of the two great
pillars set up at the appointed entrance of King Solomon's
Temple at Jerusalem. The inside is also beautifully decorated.
GORDON J. WHITING
Managing director, Angelo, Gordon & Co.

8.16 Water Supply Maintenance Cabin

c. 1935, attributed to Aymar Embury II
Worth Square, at the intersection of Fifth Avenue, Broadway,
West 24th and West 25th Streets

Just across Fifth Avenue from Madison Square, this gem of
a self-effacing little black hut is easily mistaken for a disused
comfort station. It was erected in 1935 or soon after for the
City of New York Department of Water Supply, Gas and
Electricity, in order to replace an "eyesore" of a wooden
cabin. Short and chunky, flat-roofed as well as flat-faced,
this little one-story structure turns its back to downtown
and to the adjacent monument of General Worth, with a
single bronze window in either short side, while its curved,
northerly face bows segmentally out from end to end,
inflected only by a central bronze door. The whole, diminutive as it is, is faced with great large rectangles of black
granite, with the corner joints sealed by a kind of Chanel-
style piping along the seams. Fine materials and radically
simple form. This is a stunningly fine, plain little honed
box. Upstaged by the general's ho-hum obelisk (1857), it is
a little unsung hero.
JOSEPH MASHECK
Art historian

8.17 **General Worth Monument**
1857, James G. Batterson
Worth Square, at the intersection of Fifth Avenue, Broadway, West 24th and West 25th Streets

Researching a novel set in a fictional version of my hometown of Hudson, New York, I came across a complicated figure born there, General William Jenkins Worth. He was born in 1794 and made his name in the War of 1812 (the Seminole and Mexican wars), specializing in the massacre of Native Americans. His other claim to fame was as a dancer; the "General Worth Quickstep" was all the rage in the early 1830s. But his arrogance defeated him, and he died of cholera in San Antonio in 1849. Fort Worth and Lake Worth are named after General Worth, as is Worth Street in lower Manhattan. He is buried under this obelisk, which is hard to get close enough to, to really inspect, but if you dare, you can see all his victorious battles carved on the stone—Chapultepec, Vera Cruz, Churubusco, Florida, Lundy's Lane, Puebla, Monterrey, Perote—exotic names, some barely remembered anymore. *Sic transit gloria,* although the inscription on the monolith says *Ducit amor patriae,* "Love of Country."
SAMUEL SHEM
Psychiatrist, author, and professor of psychiatry, Harvard Medical School

8.19 **TADA!**
15 West 28th Street between Fifth and Sixth Avenues
☏ 212 252 1619; www.tadatheater.com

As you walk along West 28th Street, surrounded by the jungle-like greenery of the wholesale plant district, a bright red banner flying above might catch your eye. The banner heralds TADA!, a not-for-profit children's theater company where talented New York kids perform original musicals. The performers range in age from seven to eighteen and come from all different cultural, economic, and social backgrounds. They work for an intensive six-week rehearsal process, and the results are often spectacular. The ensemble sparkles, the songs are catchy, and the performances always seem to have an energy and freshness that simply comes from the actors being kids. TADA! puts on a winter, spring, and summer show; the tickets are cheap and it's easy to make reservations.

CAITLIN PETRE
Journalist

8.20 Flower District

West 28th Street between Sixth and Seventh Avenues
The shops are open Mondays to Saturdays from 4:30 a.m. to early afternoon.

If you are an early riser and want to feel the city hum at daybreak, jump on the subway and head to 28th Street. Follow your nose east to New York's sweetest spot, the wholesale Flower District. (The parking police are unrelentingly vigilant on noncommercial vehicles; do not take your car.) While shops spill a few blocks up and down Sixth Avenue, the premier vendors are squeezed between Sixth and Seventh Avenues on 28th Street. Monday through Saturday, cut-flower vendors open as early as 4:30 a.m., and a bustling business peaks between 5:30 and 7 a.m. French tulips with individual netted caps; Gerber daisies, their heads arranged like bubble-gum-colored checkerboards, and lotus blossoms plucked from island lagoons arrive daily from across America and around the world—California and Canada, South Africa and Holland, New Zealand and Australia, Israel and Italy. Double-parked trucks are unloaded and loaded again at a dizzying speed, while men, shouldering piles of yard-long boxes labeled in multiple languages, maneuver, hips swaying hula-style, through the crowded sidewalks. Other men hose the topiary-lined pavement and sweep up dead flower heads, their fragrance ripened into heady perfume. Inside the shops, rub shoulders—literally, as quarters are notoriously cramped—with the city's foremost party-meisters, floral designers, and flower-shop owners and listen as they vie for five-foot, true-blue delphiniums or tiny nosegays of violets, majestic Stargazer lilies, or rainbows of sweet peas. While the market is strictly wholesale, carry a little cash in your pocket and quietly pick up a bouquet of garden roses, fit for Redouté's brush, for a few dollars.

STARR OCKENGA
Garden photographer and writer

8

MIDTOWN SOUTH

8.21 Church and Friary of St. Francis of Assisi
135 West 31st Street between Sixth and Seventh Avenues
☎ 212 736 8500; www.stfrancisnyc.org

The Great Mosaic
1930, Rudolph Margreiter (design) and Joseph Wild (construction)

The lovely Church of St. Francis of Assisi is a peaceful haven in one of the most bustling areas of New York. The original church, built in 1844, was demolished and rebuilt in its present form in 1892. Embellished with Italian marble, the church also incorporates Vermont marble, Mexican onyx, and white oak into its design. Its most impressive feature, however, is the huge mosaic in the sanctuary. Unveiled in 1925 and known as the Great Mosaic because it was the largest mosaic in America at the time of its execution, it covers more than sixteen hundred square feet. It features Mary and includes scenes from the life of Saint Francis and famous Franciscan saints.

Saint Francis founded an order of friars dedicated to leading a simple life and to helping the poor. Those ideals were put into action in Manhattan shortly after the stock market crash of 1929. The friars of St. Francis organized the distribution of bread and alms to the poor and hungry of New York. The number of alms-seekers grew as the Depression continued until it was not unusual for more than four thousand people to receive assistance each day.

Today, many New Yorkers take a short detour from wherever they are headed and pause in the courtyard of the church to touch the bronze statue of Saint Francis. Kneeling in prayer with head tilted upward, the right heel, hand, and knees of the statue are shiny from rubbing.

JAMES J. BRUCIA AND MARGARET BRUCIA
Justice (retired), New York State Supreme Court. The late Margaret Brucia was a schoolteacher.

8.22 I Trulli

122 East 27th Street at Lexington Avenue

☎ 212 481 7372; www.itrulli.com

I Trulli is one of the few restaurants in New York to special-ize in the food of Puglia, and Nicola Marzovilla and his family make sure it tastes that way. Nicola's mother comes in every morning to make pasta by hand—not because she has to, but because she "has" to. Unless you're lucky enough to have a mother who makes homemade pasta for you, this shouldn't be missed.

I Trulli is also the only restaurant in New York where you will find a *panzerotti*. When you translate the southern Italian slang, you'll find it means "busted gut." I won't even try to describe what *panzerotti* is. You'll have to go find out for yourself.

FRANK PUGLIESE

Playwright, screenwriter, and director

8.23 Paddy Reilly's Music Bar

519 Second Avenue at East 29th Street

☎ 212 686 1210; www.paddyreillysmusicbar.us

In much of Manhattan, you can barely stumble down a block without encountering an Irish pub; in some places, several. But not even in Ireland will you find a drinking establishment that serves nothing on its taps but Guinness, as is the case at Paddy Reilly's Music Bar. In fact, it was only at the urging of the sales reps from Guinness that pub owner Steve Duggan, a former Gaelic footballer, agreed to offer wine, liquor, and even other beer in bottles. But the nine shining taps that stand sentry over his chipped oak landmark bar bleed the bitter only, and thanks to Duggan's care in storing the suds at exactly forty-one degrees, I chal-lenge you to find a better cup of it this side of the Atlantic.

But that's only the beginning of what sets Paddy's apart from New York's other Irish pubs (and from the nondescript strip of Second Avenue on which it's located). This relatively small bar—which gets downright cozy at night with its old copper lanterns looming down from the bar ceiling and candles glowing on the tables—is well-known in music circles as an incubator of the finest Irish music talent on the East Coast. Catch it here seven nights a week, starting around 10:30 p.m., when the place fills with locals, music lovers, the occasional celebrity, and the lively sound of the old country.

JULIAN RUBINSTEIN
Author and journalist

8.24 Kalustyan's

123 Lexington Avenue between East 28th and East
29th Streets

📞 212 685 3451; www.kalustyans.com

The best source for ingredients for the cuisines of Greece, Turkey, Indonesia, Morocco, and India—all of Asia and the Middle East, in fact—is Kalustyan's, a souk of sorts tucked away in the aromatic neighborhood of Little India. Enter this bright and orderly store and prepare yourself for the widest and highest-quality array of exotic products in Manhattan.

Upon entering, a shopper spies large, zippered bags of basmati and jasmine rice and, above them, beautifully designed metal tins of saffron, dec ffed with a nineteenth-century engraving titled "The Gathering of Saffron." Next, take a look at the piles of delectable dried fruits and nuts, including lemon pistachios, masala cashews, and cinnamon-sugar-honey almonds.

The meticulously organized shelves along the right wall are devoted to condiments. The first section holds chutneys (lime-pickle, mango, lime and ginger, mixed-pickle). Next, you'll find a stunning array of oils, curry pastes, marinade-and cooking sauces, including fish sauces. Supposedly

Cambodia's is the best in the world; a splash enriches almost any soup, as does a dash of the *muhamma* hot-pepper dip. Four shelves of hot sauces include my personal favorite, Linghams from Malaysia. *Harissa*, the Moroccan hot sauce, is available in a tube. I consider another item, *zhoug*, a Yemenite chili paste with coriander, a magic ingredient when spread on a fish fillet.

On a low shelf you'll find three dozen varieties of dried beans with irresistible names, including rattlesnake, European soldier bean, Steuben yellow, Jacob's cattle bean, calypso, Jackson wonder, rice bean, and scarlet runner. Then move into the lentils, couscous, and rices. Something called brown *teff* is "the smallest grain in the world," according to the label.

There are beverages, too: Arab sorrel tea, which the Bedouins drink to quench their thirst in the desert, as well as the beautiful pink hibiscus flower tea. Then there's the simply named Mountain Tea, a peasant drink from Greece, as well as many varieties of coffee. Some of the syrups here, including flavors such as quince-lemon and sun-baked pure mulberry, can be added to sparkling water for refreshing drinks; I haven't tried Rooh Afza, "the summer drink of the East."

The freezers hold an abundance of fresh frozen items, such as Kafir lime leaves, lemongrass, banana leaves, and *galangal*, a sort of ginger root, for Thai soups. Preserved lemons, essential for Moroccan cooking, are available here, too. There are delicious samosas and other prepared foods, as well as interesting-sounding ice creams, including fig and saffron-pistachio.

In the bakery department is a sweet bread filled with dates, which can be found alongside naan, tahini bread, and Zaatar bread.

The housewares are beautiful objects in themselves. The copper beakers are lovely, as are the brass spice grinders.

There are small iron woks with loopy metal handles, Indian sifters with four interchangeable screens, a rolling pin for chapati, and a wooden hand mixer that looks like a giant champagne aerator. There are strings of dried okra, cosmetics, and many, many more things.

Upstairs, you'll find more housewares as well as a small snack bar with a couple of tables overlooking the street where you can have a delicious lunch of food made on the premises. Order a portion of olives, or wash down a *basturma* sandwich (air-dried beef in a pita with cumin, pepper, tomatoes, and yogurt hot sauce) with a passion-fruit drink or a ginger beer.

HELEN MARDEN
Artist

8.25   Paul J. Bosco

149 Madison Avenue, entrance on 32nd Street
Closed on Sundays.
☎ 212 758 2646; www.pauljbosco.com

The owner, Paul Bosco, has been collecting coins and medallions for more than forty years. The currency spans ancient coins to modern subway tokens. The medallions (struck to commemorate people and events) range from the Renaissance to the present day. Here you can find a portrait of an Italian noble by the early Renaissance artist Pisanello—the first and finest of the medallists—or perhaps the official medal from the 1925 Exposition des Arts Décoratifs from Pierre Turin, the Art Deco master. Although Mr. Bosco caters to serious collectors, including museums, there is plenty here for the rest of us. It is possible to find a coin or medallion covering almost any subject—actually, the place is "organizationally challenged," so that it is almost impossible to find anything without Mr. Bosco's help. Among the hundreds of themes covered are world fairs and world wars, bridges and bunny rabbits, cemeteries and cathedrals, magic and mythology. I have bought subject-specific gifts for architects and doctors as well as playwrights and actors (although in the last instance, any shiny object with a reflective surface would have done the trick). Mr. Bosco also has an assortment of objets d'art, mostly acquired because he just couldn't say No. The last time I was there, he handed me an old letter opener with a decorative handle and asked if I knew what it was. After a few minutes, I answered that it looked as if the entire object was made from a single piece of carefully twisted metal. He then handed me its leather case, which read, "Compliments of John A. Roebling's Sons Company"; it was a nineteenth-century "giveaway" from the inventors of the steel cable and designers of the Brooklyn Bridge.

ROBERT KAHN
Architect

8.26 Former Della Robbia Bar
1913, Warren & Wetmore
4 Park Avenue at East 33rd Street

A remarkable space has survived in the former Vanderbilt Hotel. The hotel has a beautiful ceramic rathskeller, which was originally known as The Crypt, and later the Della Robbia Bar, and now Wolfgang's Steakhouse. The ceilings are embellished with polychrome terra-cotta ornaments made by the renowned Rookwood Pottery (Cincinnati, Ohio) and surrounded by Guastavino tiled arches. The room was declared a New York City Landmark on April 15, 1994, and is one of the rare restaurant interiors with such a distinction.

SUSAN TUNICK
Artist and writer

8.27 **Empire State Building**

1931, Shreve, Lamb & Harmon
350 Fifth Avenue at West 34th Street
www.esbnyc.com

Yep. It's worth it. Especially right before closing time, at around 10:30 at night. Take a date, it's stunning.
ERIC STOLTZ
Actor

Viewed from the south at sunset, the parallel lines of stainless steel trim catch the light, gleaming with a red-orange glow that shimmers along the thousand-foot shaft to the wings of the crown and television mast above. Surprisingly, lightning travels *up* the building as well as down, and often before it hits, a spiral of fire jumps up from the top of the tower to guide the electric current to the clouds above. The mysterious Saint Elmo's fire, the hovering light seen on ships at sea, is also a phenomenon of the upper realms of the tower, and when it appears, it is accompanied by a hissing sound. On the 102nd floor, a solid gold rivet tops off the steel structure, driven in by then governor Al Smith.
ALEX GORLIN
Architect

Although the Empire State Building is no secret, there are secret times to visit. My favorite is in the morning after a snowstorm, when the air is crisp and clean and all of New York City's rooftops are covered with snow. The building creates peculiar wind currents and there are times when it snows up rather than down. Rain, on the other hand, travels around the building sideways and sometimes when it is raining at the top, the street below is completely dry. When the clouds conceal the city beneath, you feel like you're floating, weightless, above land.

Back down to earth, try to find out when the fluorescent lobby lights are scheduled for their yearly cleaning. When the cleaners remove the translucent panels that cover them, the lobby's original decoratively painted ceiling is exposed and you can see where the original chandeliers once hung. It's like being transported to the great Art Deco days of the 1930s.

RONNETTE RILEY
Architect

City Lights

As New Yorkers, we instinctively chafe at playing second fiddle, gathering our "bests" and "firsts" and "largests" honors as a matter of birthright and taking umbrage when other cities have the temerity to make a claim to fame that we think really ought to be ours. Some distinctions are of little interest: the St. Louis Arch? Don't want it.

Staffordshire thinks of itself as the ceramics capital of the world? Let them have it. Paris's boast, though, that it's the City of Lights, was bound to be seen as a gauntlet thrown, and one advertising executive decided to take it up.

Douglas Leigh was known for masterminding kinetic billboard ads that included the Times Square smoking Camel sign and one for Pepsi with a block-long waterfall. Having spent enough time in Times Square to see the light, he decided to brighten up some of the city beyond the theater district.

Mr. Leigh knew that the Empire State Building, opened in 1931, had remained short of tenants as a result of the Depression. He had the idea of getting Coca-Cola to take the top floors and proposed that the tower have changing lights that would serve as a weather forecast. Coke would package bottles with a small guide to decipher the colors. By late 1941, Coke had agreed, but following Pearl Harbor, the lights of the city were darkened. The government suddenly needed a lot of office space, filling up much of the Empire State Building, and the Coke deal fell by the wayside. After the war, they decided to use a different, simpler lighting scheme.

More immediate success in creating a night skyline is in evidence with his designs for the Crown Building, Citicorp, John Jay College, New York Life, 90 West Street, and 2 Park Avenue. Among his most successful is one for the Helmsley Building at 230 Park Avenue. When the decision was made to illuminate the building, the owners agreed to add plenty of gilding (including the sculptures and the clock) to enhance the effect, and a gold band around the lower part of the pyramid roof. The yellow (high-pressure sodium) light is focused on the tower from beneath and glows through the balustrades and onto the cupola. It gives a spectacular focus to the vista down Park Avenue.

More than three decades passed before Mr. Leigh had another crack at the Empire. In 1976, he was made chairman of City Decor to welcome the Democratic Convention and visitors for the Bicentennial. This time, he suggested to the ESB's owners that the lights be colored red, white, and blue. It was an instant success, and they were left that way until the end of that year. Mr. Leigh then offered the idea of tying the lights to different holidays, rather than the weather, which is the fundamental scheme still in effect today.

The great Broadway lighting designer Abe Feder also made an enormous contribution to the city at night when he was asked to light Rockefeller Center from four sides. He decided to project light up the building (about eight hundred and fifty feet), but the bulbs he used in the theater only projected eighty or so feet. Bulbs used in sports arenas projected greater distances, but they were meant to be on for a shorter period of time and were already big in size. In the end, he took these as a prototype and developed a bulb that had the power wattage increased from four hundred watts to fifteen hundred watts without increasing its size. In all, three hundred and forty two lights now illuminate Rockefeller Center from many locations, and Mr. Feder focused each one individually. The lighting was unveiled on December 3, 1984, at 5:15 p.m. before the lighting of the Christmas tree.

Bright lights in the big city are also on display at the Chrysler Building, the Four Seasons Hotel, Park Avenue Tower, Met Life, Con Ed, the Woolworth Building, and American International. For an exhilarating rush of warm light, though, it's hard to beat crossing the street at Fifth Avenue and 55th Street. Two hotels, the St. Regis and the Peninsula, straddle the thoroughfare, so pause as long as you can in the middle of it and look up. The luminosity from both buildings merges mid-avenue in such a great wash that even if New York isn't the City of Lights, its burnished glow stays with you.

CHARLES SUISMAN AND CAROL MOLESWORTH
Co-authors of Manhattan User's Guide

8.28 Louis Tannen Inc.
45 West 34th Street between Broadway and Sixth Avenue
Sixth floor

📞 212 929 4500; www.tannens.com

🎁 You might never guess that this smallish shop is the largest magic store in the country, but then, nothing here is what it appears to be. You may see a silvery orb float inexplicably through space, a borrowed object vanish...only to re-appear in your pocket, or a card you have visualized rise, slowly and unaided, from its deck. But, of all the tricks—and there are hundreds of them displayed behind glass cases—the most amazing is the transformation of suspicious adults into bewildered children and vociferous children into speechless beings of pure joy.

The salesmen perform their legerdemain with enthusiasm and aplomb and, of course, as a means of selling the illusions. The customers—celebrities and CEOs, teachers and cops—watch in total amazement. The more magically advanced discuss and compare techniques against a learned history of prestidigitation and, maybe, show off their own variations.

Beware: this is a lifelong addiction. You may walk in to pick up some magician's wax or to discuss the "perfect Faro shuffle," when, before you know it, you have purchased all eight volumes of the *Tarbell Course in Magic*, first published in 1927, and presto...your money has vanished.

ROBERT KAHN
Architect

MURRAY HILL

8.29 **Mid-Manhattan Library**
455 Fifth Avenue at 40th Street
☎ 212 340 0833; www.nypl.org; www.digitalgallery.nypl.org

Picture Collection
Third floor

The Picture Collection at the Mid-Manhattan Library started out in 1915 as a modest collection of pictorial images. Today it is a huge circulating and reference archive containing more than five million images—illustrations clipped from books, magazines, newspapers, catalogs, and pamphlets, as well as postcards, linecuts, prints, and photographs—organized into nearly twelve thousand subject categories. In this unique collection, history is served up visually, in images that reflect the constant evolution of popular taste and trends. This archive is an unparalleled resource for research and brainstorming, and it is turned to regularly not only by designers, illustrators, and picture researchers, but also by visual artists, historians, students, writers, and professionals from advertising, interior design, book publishing, theater, fashion, and film. You can borrow any useful image, and people do, at the rate of half a million pictures loaned out each year.

MUNTADAS
Artist

8.30 Bronze Architectural Plaques

1996, Gregg LeFevre
Block encompassing 41st Street (south side, towards Lexington), Park Avenue (east side) and 40th Street (north side, towards Lexington)

8

Few people would think of shifting their gaze downward to view Midtown's famous towers, but doing so in the block of Park Avenue bounded by 40th and 41st Streets allows you to see the rich details of Midtown's skyscrapers without straining your eyes or craning your neck. Go to the east side of the Pershing Square overpass and start looking down. Seventeen bronze plaques are imbedded along the sidewalk, each depicting a famous building in the immediate vicinity. Artist Gregg LeFevre, well known for his public art, was commissioned to create the plaques, which celebrate the Grand Central area's rich architectural heritage.

The Modernist buildings—the Seagram, Pan Am, and Lever House—don't translate well to the medium; their geometry is better appreciated when you're standing in front of them. But the Art Deco jewels—particularly the Chanin, French, G.E., and the Daily News buildings—are beautifully rendered in bronze, with details that you can't see from the street. In particular, note the Egyptian styling of the French Building, showing mythical animals and lounging figures in high relief; the decorative detail in the fiery crown of the G.E. Building; the Aztec geometry of the Chrysler Building doorway; and the original decorative elements of the Bowery Savings Bank portal (some of which have been removed from the building). Some of these buildings are within a two-minute walk, so after you see them in bronze, you can see them for real.

Or, opt for a free guided tour with an urban historian, sponsored by the Grand Central Partnership (☎ 212 883 2468; www.grandcentralpartnership.org).

LANA BORTOLOT
Writer

Historic Savings Banks

In Manhattan:

4.22 **Bowery Savings Bank**
1895, Stanford White of McKim, Mead & White
130 Bowery between Grand and Broome Streets
www.nyc-architecture.com

8.31 **Former Bowery Savings Bank, now Cipriani's 42nd Street**
1923, York & Sawyer
110 East 42nd Street between Park and Lexington Avenues
www.nyc-architecture.com

12.29 **Former Central Savings Bank, now Apple Bank for Savings**
1928, York & Sawyer
2100 Broadway at West 73rd Street

7.9 **Former Greenwich Savings Bank, now Republic National Bank**
1924, York & Sawyer
1352–1362 Broadway at West 36th Street

In Brooklyn:

The Dime Savings Bank of New York
1908, Mowbray & Uffinger; 1932, expanded by Halsey, McCormack & Helmer
9 DeKalb Avenue, off Fulton Street (not on map)

Former Williamsburgh Savings Bank Tower, now Republic National Bank

1929, Halsey, McCormack & Helmer
1 Hanson Place at Ashland Place (not on map)

The ATM has made them an endangered species, but from the 1890s to the 1930s the explosion of savings banks eager to house the pennies of New Yorkers created spaces that surpass many of the city's civic buildings and churches in awe-inspiring splendor. Hurry to see them before 3 p.m. closing and before yet another one becomes a Duane Reade drugstore (it happened at the corner of West 96th Street and Amsterdam Avenue) or a Gap (East 85th Street). In most cases the grand but solemn exterior hardly prepares one for the luxury of both space and materials that greets you within. We instinctively become quiet, as if in a church—the only place, it seems, where Americans are hesitant to talk up about money. Moralism and patriotism are also good incentives for squirreling away your cash—be sure and read the inscriptions on the benches provided at my personal favorite, downtown Brooklyn's Dime Savings Bank, before you sit down to wait for your turn at the teller's booth.

BARRY BERGDOLL
Philip Johnson Chief Curator of Architecture and Design, MoMA

CHAPTER 9

Times Square & Midtown West

TIMES SQUARE

Restaurant Row

9.1 **Barbetta**
321 West 46th Street between Eighth and Ninth Avenues
☎ 212 246 9171; www.barbettarestaurant.com

9.2 **Joe Allen's**
326 West 46th Street between Eighth and Ninth Avenues
☎ 212 581 6464; www.joeallenrestaurant.com

9.3 **Becco**
335 West 46th Street between Eighth and Ninth Avenues
☎ 212 397 7597; www.becco-nyc.com

9.4 **Lattanzi**
361 West 46th Street between Eighth and Ninth Avenues
☎ 212 315 0980; www.lattanzinyc.com

9.5 **FireBird Russian Restaurant**
365 West 46th Street between Eighth and Ninth Avenues
☎ 212 586 0244; www.firebirdrestaurant.com

🍴 Before or after the theater, "Restaurant Row," West 46th
Street between Eighth and Ninth Avenues, with almost
every building occupied by a restaurant, offers a wide
choice of cuisines—American, French, Italian, Spanish,
Russian, kosher—at a wide range of prices. My favorites:
Becco for pasta; Joe Allen's for atmosphere; FireBird
for decor; Barbetta for old-fashioned elegant service; and
Lattanzi for the delicacies of the Roman ghetto.
KENNETH SEEMAN GINIGER
Publisher, editor, and author

9.6 **Frankie & Johnnie's Steakhouse**
269 West 45th Street between Seventh and Eighth Avenues
☎ 212 997 9494; www.frankieandjohnnies.com

For a living glimpse of Damon Runyon's Manhattan, that gin-drinking, hat-wearing, Lucky-smoking town, get yourself seated at the table next to the first full window on the left as you enter Frankie & Johnnie's, which since 1926 has been feeding Broadway types and theatergoers. The steak house is on the second floor, and you will be looking past the ironwork of an artfully placed fire escape down to a slice of Eighth Avenue that encompasses the half-century-old neon signage proclaiming the presence of Smith's Bar, while above the saloon's roof rises the superb 1931 Art Moderne tower of Raymond Hood's original McGraw-Hill Building, over on 42nd Street. The view is good at twilight, wonderful in rainy twilight, and the steak you must have while taking it in won't disappoint you either.
RICHARD SNOW
Historian and author

9.7 **Edison Hotel**
228 West 47th Street between Broadway and Eighth Avenue

Cafe Edison
In the Edison Hotel
☎ 212 354 0368; www.edisonhotelnyc.com

This Midtown restaurant is nicknamed "the Polish Tea Room" (to distinguish it from its infinitely snootier Russian cousin) by the Broadway producers, directors, and actors who often lunch there. While you eat the classic deli food, served by that New York rarity, a waitstaff that isn't comprised of actors, you may well overhear what's in the works for next year's Broadway season.
GREGORY MOSHER
Theater director and producer

9.8   I. Miller Building

1929, Louis H. Friedland
167 West 46th Street at Seventh Avenue

As you stroll down Broadway after your matinee, stop and glance at the inscription on the façade of 167 West 46th Street (close to the northeast corner of Seventh Avenue and 46th Street), the site of the I. Miller shoe shop that served New Yorkers from 1929 into the 1970s. The words "The Show Folks Shoe Shop Dedicated to Beauty in Footwear" describe I. Miller's two passions—shoes and stars. As an added attraction, four statues by Alexander Stirling Calder (father of Alexander Calder of mobile fame) appear in niches below the inscription. Miller invited the public to vote for their favorite actresses as models. The winners were Ethel Barrymore as Ophelia, Mary Pickford as Little Lord Fauntleroy, Marilyn Miller as Sunny, and Rosa Ponselle as Norma.

THERESA CRAIG
Writer

9.9   Church of St. Mary the Virgin

1895, Napoleon Le Brun & Sons
145 West 46th Street between Sixth and Seventh Avenues
☏ 212 869 5830; www.stmvirgin.org

Established in 1868 as the first Episcopalian church in America to combine the Roman Catholic liturgical tradition with the Protestant tenets of the Anglican church, St. Mary's is a bastion of the "high church" ceremonial tradition in America. The church is famous for its use of incense, which hangs particularly heavy on humid days, and enjoys the nickname "Smoky Mary's." The second and current building has the distinction of being the first church façade in New York City to be adorned with religious statues, counter to the prevailing Puritan tradition eschewing religious iconography. Fewer than forty years later the climate had changed dramatically. The "new" building completed in 1895 is one of the surprises of New York's grid of streets, which hides some of the city's best assets. Located mid-block on 46th Street between Sixth and Seventh Avenues, just steps from Times Square, the building, with its eighty-foot nave, was once the tallest and most prominent structure in the neighborhood. Now the church lies virtually buried in the skyscrapers of the last century. Ironically, it was the skyscraper technology that allowed this impressive complex of church, mission house, and rectory to be constructed in fewer than two years. New visitors and the many pilgrims who find their way here each day are agape at the splendid interior, decorated in the French Gothic taste with a sky-blue ceiling and gold stars. This combination is steep competition to the nexus of neon and bright lights less than a block away. No single work of art dominates the space; instead it is the sum of its parts: the four marble altars, probably a hundred statues, and the exceptional late-Victorian metal, glass, and woodwork. The Aeolian-Skinner organ is one of the most famous church organs in the world and is partic- ularly well suited to the building. These elements combine to enhance the most ceremonious celebration of the Mass. The services, especially High Mass at 11 a.m. on Sunday, have particular style and dignity. While the social tradition of the church has progressed (there are women priests, and gays and lesbians are welcomed), the service has a decidedly old-fashioned air. After the 11 a.m. service there is coffee hour where a great cross section of the city is present. Over homemade cakes and cookies, you are just as likely to meet a visiting bishop, a homeless person, or a Park Avenue matron.

THOMAS JAYNE
Interior designer

Cherished Churches

`9.16` St. Thomas Church
1914, Cram, Goodhue & Ferguson
1 West 53rd Street at Fifth Avenue
☎ 212 757 7013, www.saintthomaschurch.org

`12.27` Christ and St. Stephen's Church
1880, William H. Day
120 West 69th Street between Broadway and Columbus Avenue
☎ 212 787 2755; www.csschurch.org

`9.10` St. Malachy's Roman Catholic Church
1903, Joseph H. McGuire
239 West 49th Street between Broadway and Eighth Avenue
☎ 212 489 1340; www.actorschapel.org

`5.3` Church of the Ascension
1841, Richard Upjohn; 1889, interior renovated by McKim, Mead & White
36–38 Fifth Avenue at West 10th Street
☎ 212 254 8620; www.ascensionnyc.org

New York, unlike European capitals, is not too faithful to her treasures. Paris wouldn't have let the wrecking ball get anywhere near the Empire Theatre (see p. 136), that elegant little jewel box, or the marvelous, stately Metropolitan Opera House (the old one, not the Lincoln Center World's Fair-ish one).

But God and the Chamber of Commerce willing, some of my favorite icons are still around. To start with, I'm a church junkie—not so much for the grandiose cathedrals like St. John the Divine and St. Pat's. But I love St. Thomas; its stained-glass rose window is hard to beat.

Christ and St. Stephen's Church has wonderful windows, too. They were designed by Sir Edward Burne-Jones, a nineteenth-century painter.

The actors' chapel in St. Malachy's Roman Catholic Church is beloved, of course, by all us showbiz types who appreciate their staying open late so that those who work in Broadway shows can worship after the curtains come down.

I have a sentimental spot in my heart for Church of the Ascension. It's not at all grand, but in the halcyon days of the 1930s when I first attempted to storm Manhattan's bastions, it was open all night. I shed many a tear on its altar as I asked God please to let me find work so I could stay in this glittering, improbable city and not have to retreat in defeat to Alabama.

HUGH MARTIN

The late Hugh Martin was a songwriter. He wrote the score for Meet Me in St. Louis, *in which Judy Garland sings "The Trolley Song" and "Have Yourself a Merry Little Christmas."*

MIDTOWN WEST

9.11 The Russian Samovar

256 West 52nd Street between Broadway and Eighth Avenue
212 757 0168; www.russiansamovar.com

When Joseph Brodsky was alive, he and I would often go to the Russian Samovar to drink and talk about poetry. It was always vodka—many flavors of it. Joseph would usually have cilantro. I would have cranberry. We talked and talked, stopping now and then to take large bites of smoked salmon, smoked sturgeon, and pickled herring, usually with black bread. And the caviar we consumed! The food, like the vodka, was excellent. But what made the Russian Samovar special was its owner, Roman Kaplan, who knew Joseph before he came to this country. He is one of the warmest and most generous men that I have ever known. Whenever I go to New York, I go to the Russian Samovar, sit down, have some vodka, and talk with

Roman. A gifted pianist plays sad Russian songs. Almost everyone in the restaurant is speaking Russian. Mikhail Baryshnikov, who is a part owner, is a frequent patron. Joseph hovers nearby.

MARK STRAND
Poet

9.12 Gallagher's Steak House

228 West 52nd Street between Broadway and Eighth Avenue
📞 212 245 5336; www.gallaghersnysteakhouse.com

🍴 This sprawling speakeasy-turned-restaurant has been here since 1927 when Helen Gallagher (a former Ziegfeld girl) and Jack Solomon opened the place. Take a peek at the meat from the street—the front window offers a prime view of the walk-in locker loaded with aging marbleized beef at this classic steak house just off the Great White Way. The wood-paneled walls are covered with portraits of celebrities, sports heroes, and legendary racehorses—from Jackie O to Joe DiMaggio to Man o' War. Sit "under the bull" (one of the best seats in the house) or perhaps at Marilyn Monroe's table (Number 83), where one night she was thrilled when the mutually starstruck Myrna Loy, and then Henry Fonda, paid calls to her corner banquette. Joe DiMaggio (Number 84) was a regular, too. When a young boy requested his autograph, "Broadway" Joe Namath responded by grabbing a roll from the bread basket and telling the kid he'd sign only if he ran deep for a pass. Liza Minelli and her mom, Judy Garland, considered Gallagher's a real New York joint. The red-and-white checkered tablecloths attest to its zero-pretension, comfortable comfort-food attitude.

Gallagher's legendary late owner, Jerome Brody, was the founder of Restaurant Associates and at one time also owned the Four Seasons, the Oyster Bar, and the Rainbow Room. The friendly waiters and bartenders have been here for years and treat everyone like a celebrity. The oval racetrack of a bar is its centerpiece. Down a couple of rounds pre-theater and come back for a great steak after the show.

TRACEY HUMMER AND FREDERIC SCHWARTZ
Writer and Architect

9.13   ## Museum of Arts & Design

1964, original building designed by Edward Durell Stone;
2008, redesigned by Brad Cloepfil, Allied Works Architecture
2 Columbus Circle
212 299 7777; www.madmuseum.org
Closed Mondays.

9

I've never been to an exhibition at the Museum of Arts and Design that I didn't find completely fascinating, whether it be of cut paper, three hundred miniature chairs, or modern radiators. The museum's curators manage to explore the fine lines between art, design, and craft in ways that are exhilarating and awe inspiring.

The restaurant, Robert, is a lovely place to have lunch or tea. Situated on the ninth floor, it has the most spectacular of Central Park that I have ever seen.

The building itself is noteworthy. It was designed in 1964 by Edward Durell Stone for Huntington Hartford, heir to the A&P Supermarket fortune, to display his art collection. (Stone was the designer, with Philip S. Goodwin, of the original Museum of Modern Art.) The building was listed as one of America's 11 Most Endangered Historical Places by the National Trust for Historic Preservation in 2004, and the World Monument Fund included it on its Watch List of 100 Most Endangered Sites in 2006—yet the Museum of Arts and Design had the building radically redesigned. Once dubbed "the building New Yorkers love to hate," now it's "the building New Yorkers hate to miss."

FIONA KAHN
Managing editor of City Secrets and co-founder of Fang Duff Kahn Publishers

9.14 Henri Bendel (former Coty Building)
1909, façade by Woodruff Leeming
714 Fifth Avenue between 55th and 56th Streets

Lalique windows
1912, René Lalique

While you're window-shopping at Henri Bendel, look up to the top three floors to see René Lalique's lead-crystal Art Nouveau windows, the only example of his architectural glass in New York, and one of few examples in the United States.

Go to the back of the store and up the winding staircase to each mezzanine, where you can see the etchings up close. Merchandise sometimes obscures the view, but you can still get a good look at the tulips and vines crisscrossing gracefully through the panes. Lalique also designed the original interior, commissioned by the French perfumer Coty, for whom the building was built. Messieurs Coty and Lalique had neighboring businesses on Place Vendôme in Paris and, as a designer for the perfume labels and bottles, Lalique was the natural choice for Coty's flagship store in the United States. Though the Lalique interior no longer exists—the entire store was renovated in the 1990s—the windows (also recently restored) are a sparkling piece of Belle Epoque Paris in Midtown Manhattan.

LANA BORTOLOT
Writer

9.16 St. Thomas Church
1 West 53rd Street at Fifth Avenue
☎ 212 757 7013; www.saintthomaschurch.org
Check the website for a schedule of choral services.

The St. Thomas Choir of Men and Boys is recognized as the premiere choral ensemble of the Anglican musical tradition in the United States today, and as one of the world's finest choral groups. Patterned after the Continental and English cathedral and collegiate chapel choir models, and comprised of men and boys, it consists of twelve professionals from the New York City metropolitan region singing countertenor, tenor, and bass parts, while eighteen boys from the St. Thomas Choir School provide the soprano section. The school is the only church-related residential choir school in the country, and one of only four schools of this type remaining worldwide.

Go for Handel's *Messiah* just before Christmas, one of three major concerts yearly with accompanying orchestra. On a wintry evening, New Yorkers can pretend they are climbing the steps of the Imperial Chapel in Vienna. Or go for one of the numerous occasions between mid-September and May, on which you can hear this choir's large and beautiful repertory of mass settings, canticles, anthems, cantatas, and oratorios at services. The combination of voice, music, and magical Gothic setting is uplifting.

JANE FISHER
Marketing consultant

`9.18` ## The Paley Center for Media
1991, John Burgee and Philip Johnson
25 West 52nd Street between Fifth and Sixth Avenues
☎ 212 621 6600; www.paleycenter.org

John Burgee and Philip Johnson's building attempts to discipline the twentieth century's unruly mass media inside a tight little tower of respectability and historic allusion, exemplified by a grand country house window above a Romanesque doorway. Fat chance.

Everyone has a favorite treasure in this seductive archive of history and entertainment (formerly the Museum of Television and Media)—Roosevelt, HUAC, Bankhead, Benny, *I Love Lucy*, *The War of the Worlds*—but respectability has little to do with it. More like a need to connect with the lost anarchies of showbiz and the compulsiveness of the filmed past.

My first choice is always Imogene Coca, sublime clown and stooge to Sid Caesar in *Your Show of Shows* (1950–1954), the benchmark series from America's heroic age of television comedy, when programs went out live and scary. Pop-eyed, toothy, and built like a collapsible bird, Coca is the token girl in a Manhattan boys' town—the gagsters joining Caesar in the famous room above City Center included Carl Reiner, Mel Brooks, Neil Simon, and Woody Allen—and when she is on screen you don't even look at the star. Caesar is brilliant but very aggressive; Coca distills an air of eagerness, gentility, and incompetence that would be funny with no script at all. I never tire of "The Clock," in which C and C run amok as malign, desynchronized figures on a Mittel-European timepiece; or "The Lorelei," in which our heroine acquires a tutu and falls over the scenery while trying to stay out of sight. *Swan Lake* was never the same after that.

Reserve your viewings from the catalog in the lobby as you arrive; you will then be allotted a booth in a viewing room. There are also public showings from the collection of more than fifty thousand items every day. One drawback: no café, but here in Midtown you'll hardly go short, and MoMA is on the next block.

MICHAEL RATCLIFFE
Former literary editor and chief book critic, The Times (London)

9.20   Rockefeller Center

1932–1940, The Associated Architects: Reinhard & Hofmeister, Corbett, Harrison & MacMurray; Raymond Hood, Godley & Fouilhoux
West 48th Street to West 51st Street between Fifth and Sixth Avenues
☎ 212 632 3975; www.rockefellercenter.com

New York State has many architecturally notable venues. Given the variety of scale, use, and context, it is extremely difficult to single out just a few projects. Some of the indigenous styles, like the rhythmical Manhattan brownstones, the rich expressions of the cast-iron district, the glorious skyscrapers, the parks, and many cultural centers, are wonderments in themselves. But on the basis of enrichment to the human experience, I would have to rank Rockefeller Center at the top. This complex of buildings, larger than some cities, is a marvel of urban design, enduring architecture, and integrated art.

The composition of massing and open space has made Rockefeller Center the most powerful and dramatic man-made environment in the world. Upon entering the complex from Fifth Avenue between 49th and 50th Streets, one is immediately struck by the intimacy of the axial allée with its refined low-scaled flanking buildings, central gardens, and restrained storefronts. As the gardens gently slope toward the delightful, oasis-like central plaza with its sunken courtyard, they form a perfectly proportioned forecourt for the soaring sixty-story RCA Building (now the G.E. Building). Beyond the face of this multiple-slab tower, form immediately draws the eye up and marks the focal point of the center.

Each building in the ensemble is beautifully scaled and balanced to support the overall composition. While the components forming the central axis are symmetrical, the remainder of the buildings vary in height and bulk, thereby blending naturally into the surrounding urban fabric. Remarkably, there is no clear demarcation of Rockefeller Center. Except for the sunken plaza area and an unusual sense of visual order with a consistently high quality of architectural expression in a similar vocabulary, the streetscape does not dramatically change from adjoining neighborhoods.

The architectural vocabulary, a unique blend of Art Deco and vertical modern, consists primarily of naturally cleft limestone, refined bronze storefronts, and metal spandrel panels. The lower elevations are solid stone with elegantly balanced combinations of ribbon glass and punched retail windows. As the buildings rise, the façades turn to exquisitely composed vertical bands of limestone, alternating with windows and recessed limestone or rippled cast-aluminum spandrels that create a dramatic soaring effect. These vertical elements continue to the top of each wall plane, building energy as they rise and meet the sky.

Each building has a unique entry that creates visual interest and identity at the pedestrian level. The Fifth Avenue buildings have nicely scaled, recessed courtyards that appropriately relieve the congestion on the crowded sidewalk and create dramatic settings for the huge bronze sculptures. Most entries are marked by polychrome reliefs above the openings, each with its own theme relating to the original tenancy of the respective buildings. The lobbies—all different—have their own ambience, with large wall murals, black granite Deco motifs, terrazzo floors, and wainscot. Some are more successful than others, but all are executed with an artistic flair and sense of permanence. The underground network of shopping concourses, subway access, and service corridors, linking the buildings to the sunken plaza as well as to each other, is a marvel in itself.

No aspect was overlooked in the design of this remarkable complex, and it works just as well today as it did when it opened seventy years ago! This is urban design at its finest—holistic, timeless, futuristic, culturally enriching, uplifting, pedestrian-oriented, and economically viable. It may never be matched.

BRUCE S. FOWLE
Architect

Rock's Paper, Scissors

7.14 **Books Kinokuniya**
1073 Sixth Avenue between 40th and 41st Streets
☎ 212 869 1700; www.kinokuniya.com

9.21 **Minamoto Kitchoan**
608 Fifth Avenue between West 48th and West 49th Streets
☎ 212 489-3747; www.kitchoan.com

A visit to the Japanese bookstore Kinokuniya makes an exhilarating field trip for those interested in books, graphics, and the visual refreshment of the Eastern aesthetic. The store specializes in Japanese books, magazines, and English books on Japan (check out the collection of Japanese cookbooks in English). Although those not fluent in Japanese can only appreciate the graphics, anyone should be able to follow the diagrams in the sophisticated and specialized assortment of origami manuals. For a lovely inventory of origami paper, walk upstairs to the mezzanine level—and if you are someone who has been known to lust after a beautifully engineered and designed notebook, buckle your seat belt. You will find a sublime assortment here, along with an irresistible array of stationery, paper goods, and all manner of related items. Several of the binders here can be customized by choosing from a wide array of inserts: dividers, clear envelopes, paper with different colors, lines, and grids, and more. Even the staple removers are a delight, as are many of the pens, clips, drawing pads, notebooks, and blank books. The discriminating calligrapher will appreciate the wide selection of paints, inks, and brushes. There are clipboards, erasers, and pencil cases for the design-forward student. Stickers for kids. Chic aluminum containers as well as cardboard drawers and nesting boxes.

This is the place to find the gift you won't find elsewhere: sachets wrapped in printed silk and tucked in a beautiful wooden box; or metal, ceramic, and lacquer paperweights and desk accessories, which will be appreciated by an executive or an aesthete. Wrap it up in one of the decorative papers, available by the sheet, printed with traditional Japanese designs.

There is a small snack counter on the main floor of Kinokuniya that serves teas, coffees, soft drinks, sandwiches, and cakes. For more elaborate fare, walk down the block to Minamoto Kitchoan, a Japanese confectionery filled with exotic sweet delicacies artfully displayed.

ANGELA HEDERMAN
Publisher

9.23   ### Hudson River Powerhouse

1900–1904, McKim, Mead & White
12th Avenue between West 58th and West 59th Streets
646 918 7917; www.hudsonriverpowerhouse.com

The IRT powerhouse is one of the most unusual architectural monuments in America. Designed by McKim, Mead & White in 1900 to power the very first section of the New York City subway system, it was the largest powerhouse in the world, and used the most sophisticated technology in the production of electrical power at that time. The delicately adorned exterior of the powerhouse was designed in the Beaux-Arts style, reflecting the civic-minded ideals of the City Beautiful movement. In 1904, *The New York Times* described it as " . . . an ornament to the west side that enhances rather than diminishes the value of the surrounding property. But for its stacks, it might suggest an art museum or public library rather than a powerhouse."

In 1959, the building was sold to Con Edison for use as a power station for the New York City steam system. The utility promptly built a flat brick addition to the building, covering its western façade. As the demand for steam waned over the last twenty years, Con Edison has decommissioned most of the building and recently demolished the last of the original five smokestacks. The once majestic turbine hall stands largely empty. Decades of neglect have left other scars: steel loading doors have damaged the finely carved terra-cotta friezes and the original building cornice is entirely gone.

Efforts to designate the building a historic landmark, in 1979 and 1990, failed in the face of the powerful public utility. In 2007, The Hudson River Powerhouse Group was formed to lobby the city to designate the powerhouse a landmark, raise funds to restore the building, and re-purpose this once grand powerhouse as a public space. It remains to be seen if this gem will be preserved or demolished.

BASIL WALTER
Architect

CHAPTER 10

MIDTOWN

Midtown

10.1   **The New York Yacht Club**
1900, Warren & Wetmore
37 West 44th Street between Fifth and Sixth Avenues
☎ 212 382 1000; www.nyyc.org
Not open to the public.

The architects of Grand Central Terminal, Warren &
Wetmore, humored their seafaring Gilded Age clients with
this outrageous 1900 Beaux Arts façade. Among the
building's stately columns and arches are fantastic nautical
motifs pirated from the designs of High Renaissance
galleons and grottoes. Into each tall clubhouse window, an
old ship appears to have just sailed, trailing sea foam in its
wake which pretends to pour over the stone ledges and
into the street.

COLTA IVES
Curator of drawings and prints, The Metropolitan Museum of Art

10.2   **Grand Central Terminal**
1913, Reed & Stem and Warren & Wetmore
East 42nd Street at Park Avenue

As Sun Tzu, author of *The Art of War*, might have put it,
"Never stand between a commuter and his train." The vast
marble floor of Grand Central Terminal is the prime
vantage point for observing the remarkable sight of New
Yorkers walking. Unlike out-of-towners, who walk four
abreast, arms swinging widely, or who stand stolidly
unmoving when you try to get past, New Yorkers walk
sleekly, rapidly as surgeons on rounds. They dodge and
shift, adjusting shoulders and briefcases to allow one
another to pass with minute precision. You can see them
on any New York street, their shoulders drawn in, arms

barely swinging, advancing with long strides. You can see them inching into traffic, jockeying on corners, waiting for their moment of opportunity. They juggle coffee cups, cigarettes, briefcases, groceries, and gym bags, and still manage to have a hand free to hail a cab or gesticulate to their companion. But the newly scrubbed Grand Central is the best place to watch New Yorkers walk. Stand on the steps leading to Vanderbilt Avenue and look down at the wonderful ballet. Each person is on an urgent mission, each must take the shortest path to their train or office or shrink; they cannot yield, but none collide. It is the essence of New York's grace.

DAVID HELLERSTEIN
Psychiatrist, author, journalist, and professor

10

The Whispering Gallery

In Grand Central Terminal, East 42nd Street and Vanderbilt Avenue entrance

When I was a boy, it seemed to me that this acoustical oddity was pretty well known, but in recent years nobody I've mentioned it to has heard of it. The Whispering Gallery offers another reason (not that one is needed) to visit the magnificently restored Grand Central Terminal. Once in the station, go to the Oyster Bar and at the main entrance, which is on the ramp to the lower level, turn your back to the restaurant, look up, and you'll see a tawny, supple Guastavino tile dome riding on four piers. Go to one of these piers and stand with your face close into the corner; send a companion to the one diagonally across the way. Then speak softly; your voices will sound in each other's ears, as close, intimate, and audible as if you were sitting together in a small car rather than murmuring across a broad concourse full of urgent clatter.

RICHARD SNOW
Historian and author

In the bowels of the bustling terminal, not far from the Oyster Bar, is a remarkable corner best visited in the dead of night. A crossing pair of vaulted arches creates an acoustically perfect spot. Two lovers may stand at opposite ends of the cavern, whisper sweet nothings, and be heard only by each other.

JOHN JILER
Playwright and author

Oyster Bar
In Grand Central Terminal
East 42nd Street and Vanderbilt Avenue
☎ 212 490 6650; www.oysterbarny.com

⑪ A pearl, a treasure, this vast, bustling eighty-eight-year old classic is tucked under Guastavino's vaulted tiled ceilings at the foot of Grand Central Terminal's great ramps. Not exactly a secret, this New York institution serves the freshest and widest range of seafood in the city. Choose from more than two dozen different types of oysters and more than two dozen types of fish. A real New Yorker will skip the dining room, sit at the lunch counter and ask Charlotte for a half-dozen briny, luscious cherrystones, followed by the creamy, plump oyster pan roast. You'll be back tomorrow for more.

TRACEY HUMMER AND FREDERIC SCHWARTZ
Writer and Architect

10.3 Sakagura
211 East 43rd Street, B1F, between Second and Third Avenues
☎ 212 953 7253; www.sakagura.com

⑪ You'll find the best sushi in New York at Sakagura, an elegant sake bar improbably located in the basement of a Midtown office building.

ALEXANDER DUFF
Restaurateur

10.4   Edward J. Kaufmann Conference Rooms

1965, Alvar Aalto
In the Institute of International Education
809 United Nations Plaza (First Avenue) between East 45th
and East 46th Streets
For tours: ☎ 212 963 8687; www.un.org/tours

Alvar Aalto (1898–1976) was one of the most important
and influential Modernist masters of the twentieth century.
Frank Lloyd Wright briefly put his ego in the backseat to
praise him as a genius and, with this endorsement, architectural historian Edgar J. Kaufmann Jr. (of Fallingwater
family fame) commissioned Aalto to design the twelfth-
floor conference room in 1965. Located in the Institute of
International Education, the space overlooks the United
Nations and the East River. The only place in New York
where one can experience the Finnish architect's work, his
convertible, blond-on-blond interior seamlessly combines
fluidity and sensuousness with practical and functional
details. The undulating walls include Aalto's signature
hockey-stick-like birchwood slat sculpture and sedate ash
panels. For a splash of color, Aalto framed openings in the
entry hall with cobalt blue tiles. Jump at the chance to see
this somewhat secret spot, recently "saved" by the Municipal
Art Society.
TRACEY HUMMER AND FREDERIC SCHWARTZ
Writer and Architect

10.5   United Nations Headquarters

1953, International Committee of Architects
United Nations Plaza (First Avenue) between East 42nd and
East 48th Streets
Guided tours only: ☎ 212 963 8687; www.un.org/tours

A world unto itself stretching six blocks, from 42nd to
48th Streets along First Avenue and the East River, the

U.N. Headquarters complex is the architectural apotheosis of modern functionalism and the embodiment of post-World War II optimism. On land given to the U.N. by John D. Rockefeller, the buildings we see today include the Secretariat, a thirty-nine-story glass-and-aluminum curtain-wall skyscraper, the low-slung profile of the General Assembly with its awkward dome, the Conference Building overlooking the river, and a library. Given the geopolitical structure of the U.N., perhaps it is not surprising that the buildings are the result of design by committee. In 1947, New York architect Wallace Harrison chaired an international board of design comprised of ten architects from various member countries, including Le Corbusier from France and Oscar Niemeyer from Brazil, whose ideas were seminal to the final outcome. Harrison hoped that the "workshop for peace," an economical, functional, and efficient modern design, would symbolize the rational ideals of the member nations. The unfortunate addition of the dome over the Assembly chamber had been requested by the American Representative to the U.N., Senator Warren Austin, because he believed this traditional architectural element was a necessary symbol for a new world capitol.

The interior is well worth a tour, as much to observe the ambitious, complex work of the organization as to enjoy the art (such as the Fernand Léger murals in the Assembly chamber), interior design, and views from the dining room overlooking the river, from which one sees the southern tip of Roosevelt Island (which still awaits its presidential memorial), and the giant, decades-old Pepsi sign in Queens. Near the visitors' entrance, one can also mail cards and letters with unique U.N. stamps from the post office on the lower level. Take note of the three council chambers, each designed by a Scandinavian at the time when the concept of "Scandinavian design" was born. Finn Juhl (Denmark) designed the Trusteeship Council, Sven Markelius (Sweden) designed the Economic and Social Council, and Arnstein Arneberg (Norway) the Security Council. As any student of modern architecture must realize, the renowned Alvar Aalto of Finland, who was at the peak of his career, is absent from this architectural constellation—this, for the simple and unfortunate reason that Finland was not yet a member country of the U.N. Interestingly, some years later, in 1965, this omission was corrected when Aalto was given an opportunity to design his surrogate council chamber across from the U.N. atop the former Institute of International Education. Believing that New York deserved a work by the Finnish master, Edgar Kaufmann Jr. commissioned Aalto to design the Edgar J. Kaufmann Conference Rooms, to be named after his father. The elder Kaufmann was a Pittsburgh merchant who also had a strong design sensibility: he commissioned Frank Lloyd Wright for his home, Fallingwater. The Kaufmann Conference Rooms are one of only three works by Aalto in the United States.

PETER REED
Senior deputy director for cultural affairs, MoMA

Peace Bell

1952, Chiyoji Nakagawa
In the Garden of Peace, northwest of the Secretariat
☎ 212 963 8687; www.un.org/tours

A grand Shinto bell gong of two hundred and fifty six pounds is sheltered in a shrine on the grounds of the United Nations. Cast in Japan of tinkling coins from more than sixty countries, its history is magical.

In 1952, sixty United Nations officials at a Paris conference table dreamed aloud, searching for a symbol whose language people of the world would understand. Discussion led to each tossing coins from his pocket onto the table. An observer delegate from Japan offered to have an esteemed bell foundry cast them into a giant bell, adding pennies from the children of Japan. Famous throughout history, Asian bells have been forged of molten metal, often including donated coins to add to the sentiment and tone of the bells. This one is inscribed "Long Live Absolute World Peace" in Japanese.

Each September, there is a celebrated ringing of the bell to open the General Assembly of the U.N. It also rings for Earth Day in the spring and other special occasions.

TERRY MAYER
Jewelery designer and bellologist

53rd Street Stroll

10.6 **United Nations Plaza Apartments**
First Avenue at 44th Street

10.7 **Mitchell Place**
East 49th Street between First Avenue and Beekman Place

10.8 **Beekman Tower**
1928, John Mead Howells
3 Mitchell Place, 49th Street east of First Avenue

10.8 **Top of the Tower Restaurant**
3 Mitchell Place, 26th floor
📞 212 980 4796; www.thetopofthetower.com

10.9 **Luxembourg Mission to the United Nations**
17 Beekman Place at East 50th Street
📞 212 935 3589; www.un.int/luxembourg

10.10 **Former Home of Paul Rudolph**
1987, Paul Rudolph
23 Beekman Place at East 50th Street

10.11   **Wood Frame Houses**
312 and 314 East 53rd Street between First and Second Avenues

10.13   **Seagram Building**
1958, Ludwig Mies van der Rohe (with Philip Johnson;
also Kahn & Jacobs)
375 Park Avenue between East 52nd and East 53rd Streets
www.nyc-architecture.com

10.13   **Brasserie**
2002, Diller and Scofidio
100 East 53rd Street between Park and Lexington Avenues
☎ 212 751 4840; www.patinagroup.com

10.13   **The Four Seasons**
1959, Philip Johnson & Associates
In the Seagram Building
99 East 52nd Street
☎ 212 754 9494; www.fourseasonsrestaurant.com

10.15   **Lever House**
1952, Gordon Bunshaft of Skidmore, Owings & Merrill
390 Park Avenue between East 53rd and East 54th Streets

10.16   **Racquet and Tennis Club**
1918, McKim, Mead & White
370 Park Avenue between East 52nd and East 53rd Streets
☎ 212 753 9700
Not open to the public.

10.18   **Segment of Berlin Wall**
On East 53rd Street between Fifth and Madison Avenues,
east of Samuel Paley Plaza

10.19   **Samuel Paley Plaza**
1967, Robert Zion and Harold Breen in association
with Albert Preston Moore
3 East 53rd Street between Fifth and Madison Avenues

9.16 St. Thomas Church and Parish House
1914, Cram, Goodhue & Ferguson
1 West 53rd Street at Fifth Avenue
📞 212 757 7013; www.saintthomaschurch.org

9.19 Former Tishman Building
666 Fifth Avenue between 52nd and 53rd Streets

9.15 The Museum of Modern Art
11 West 53rd Street between Fifth and Sixth Avenues
📞 212 7089400; www.moma.org

9.17 CBS Building
1965, Eero Saarinen & Associates
51 West 52nd Street at Sixth Avenue
www.nyc-architecture.com

A walk west across 53rd Street from Beekman Place
to Sixth Avenue offers an unrivaled concentration of
architectural gems.

Start at the monolithic United Nations Plaza Apart-
ments at 44th Street and First Avenue, home to Truman
Capote in the last years of his life, and the residence
Robert Kennedy established when he ran for the U.S.
Senate in 1964.

Walk north to 49th Street and cross the avenue to a little
one-block street, Mitchell Place, named for a distinguished
nineteenth-century jurist. The major structure on this small,
inclined street (corner of First and Mitchell) is Beekman
Tower. Originally the Panhellenic Hotel, built as a proper
residence for college alumnae who were sorority members,
some of the bricks in this 1930s modern building bear the
Greek letters of prominent college sororities. Occupying the
crown of the twenty-six-story suite hotel is the aggressively
Art Moderne Top of the Tower Restaurant and cocktail
lounge. Its architectural furniture, wrought-iron and
obsidian-glass tabletops, and grand piano allow me to close

my eyes and see William Powell and Myrna Loy bobbing for olives, or Ginger Rogers dancing backward with Fred Astaire.

Continue up the street to the understated luxury of Beekman Place. The toponymic street was part of the Beekman family farm during the Colonial and Revolutionary War eras. Young Nathan Hale, Yale graduate, schoolteacher, and America's first spy, was allegedly hanged on the "north forty" of Beekman's farm.

On the east side of this cul-de-sac (corner of 50th Street, No. 17), is an elegant townhouse that now bears the coat of arms of the Grand Duchy of Luxembourg, a relatively new tenant in the large limestone structure with its splendid East River view. This newly minted consulate was the home of American composer and lyricist Irving Berlin for the last forty-two years of his life.

Born in Russia as Izzy Ballin, Berlin died at age one-hundred-and-one (1888–1989), outliving the copyrights on a number of his songs. He wrote "White Christmas" and "God Bless America," as well as the music and lyrics to such Broadway classics as *Annie Get Your Gun*. After his death, his daughters sold the house to the Grand Duchy. It was fitting, since Berlin's last major Broadway hit, *Call Me Madam*, was set in that tiny nation.

After this medley of memories and an envious look at the late architect Paul Rudolph's house on the northeast corner of 50th Street and Beekman Place and the wrought-iron balconies on the adjoining town houses, briskly make your way to 53rd Street. Find there an anachronistic pair—the last two wood frame houses in Midtown Manhattan. These well-maintained Federal-era dwellings are on the south side of 53rd Street between First and Second Avenues (Nos. 314 and 312).

On the left side of 53rd Street as we approach Park Avenue is New York's only Mies van der Rohe—the Seagram Building. This bronze and bronze-glass tower brought the plaza back to New York. Its two reflecting pools are coolly inviting in the warm weather, and when the illuminated Christmas trees are set afloat on them during the holiday season, who the hell needs tickets to *The Nutcracker*? If this monument to the International School and the geniuses of the Bauhaus wasn't enough as an edifice, it also houses two unique restaurants, the Brasserie on the 53rd Street side of the building, and on the 52nd Street side the remarkably consistent and glorious forty-three-year-old Four Seasons (see p. 200). The latter has a liberal sprinkling of Van der Rohe's Barcelona chairs, a well-placed Picasso or two, and interiors so striking that the restaurant has its own designation as an official landmark.

Catercorner to the Seagram Building is another icon of the International Style, Lever House. Designed by Gordon Bunshaft of Skidmore, Owings & Merrill, it has been designated a landmark by the New York City Landmarks Preservation Commission. Lever House was the first glass-and-steel curtain-wall building erected on Park Avenue (1952). The Anglo-Dutch firm sacrificed certain economies of scale by letting Mr. Bunshaft open up the site as much as possible. The office tower itself is offset to the right on top of a windowed and landscaped one-story pavilion. Between the columns of the pavilion sits a plaza area and interior spaces fit for art exhibitions and, at Christmastime, the joyful Lever House carousel.

In 1952, Lever House was a jolt of emerald glass and stainless steel on neo-Renaissance Park Avenue. This L-shaped new resident was particularly striking as it reflected the heavy stonework of that bastion of the Brahmins, the Racquet and Tennis Club, designed by McKim, Mead & White. The Racquet and Tennis Club sold its air rights and, in 1981, a dense application of the floor-area ratio was used with brutal effectiveness by Skidmore, Owings & Merrill in its design of that forty-four-story giant that runs from 52nd to 53rd Streets.

At 520 Madison Avenue, a segment of the Berlin Wall is mounted by a fountain in a well-hidden plaza at the southwest end of the building between Madison and Fifth. The side of the wall that faced West Berlin is filled with graffiti in an Abstract Expressionist mode, while the side that faced east is pristine concrete, with the exception of some pockmarks approximately nine millimeters in diameter.

It is time for an island of elegant tranquility—Samuel Paley Plaza, also known as Paley Park, just west of 520 Madison. The gentle cascades of the waterfall running down the back wall of New York's first vest-pocket park are not only visually relaxing, but also provide a baffle against the cacophony of a busy crosstown street. Conveniently placed Bertoia chairs and a discreet snack bar make Paley Park a perfect urban oasis.

Refreshed in a literal sense at Paley Park, cross Fifth Avenue and gratify your spiritual sense at Cram, Goodhue & Ferguson's superb French Gothic St. Thomas Church and Parish House. Although its exterior and interior designs are of the French style, St. Thomas keeps its Anglican connection with windows by Whitefriars of London. St. Thomas is noted for its superb male choir (see p. 176), and it is fitting that a magnificent choir should have a majestic reredos (choir screen). Bertram Goodhue designed the reredos with sculptures by Lee Lawrie.

The one-million-square-foot embossed aluminum-clad siding on the southwest corner of 53rd and Fifth, 666 Fifth Avenue, formerly known as the Tishman Building, has its own hidden treasure—a lobby waterfall by the late Isamu Noguchi (enter from 53rd Street).

Press onward to view the Museum of Modern Art. Its original structure, plus its expansions and additions, were

done by an all-star team of architects: Edward Durell
Stone, Philip Johnson, Philip Goodwin, and Cesar Pelli.

Your walk ends on the southeast corner of 53rd Street
and Sixth Avenue, at the only high-rise building designed
by Eero Saarinen. Its honed and beveled columns of gray
granite have earned it the sobriquet "Black Rock." The CBS
Building (see p. 194), commissioned by company founder,
the late William Paley, has been designated an official New
York City landmark.

Saarinen designed the building inside and out, with a
lot of input from art connoisseur Paley and the vice president for corporate design, Louis Dorfsman (Dorfsman's
signature typeface, CBS News, abounds throughout the
building). The Finnish-American master even specified the
ashtrays in the reception areas on each floor. True to his
Northern European roots, Saarinen chose the late lament-
ed Scandinavian retailer Bonniers to supply the ashtrays.
This masterpiece of creativity and entrepreneurship stands
in its recessed plaza like an elegant maître d'hotel in a
classic temple of haute cuisine.

LEE GELBER
Urban historian and tour guide

10.12 **St. Peter's Lutheran Church**
1977, Hugh Stubbins & Associates
619 Lexington Avenue at East 54th Street, in the
Citicorp Center
☎ 212 935 2200; www.saintpeters.org/art

Environmental Sculpture
1977, Louise Nevelson
Erol Beker Chapel of the Good Shepherd

Enter the still space of St. Peter's Church. Concerts are
given here; art exhibits change. But I come to seek out
a permanent installation—the painted-wood sculpted

environmental mystery by Louise Nevelson. It is designed to be entered, wandered into, stayed with. The structure waits like a building with an address, yet you must come upon its door by accident. Passageways are walled by constructions of boxes, dowels, some recognizable as drawer handles or newel posts, perhaps, but no part is any longer an object apart, with any name or function separate from the whole. Inner spaces contain opposites, as though shadow and light were equal and the same; surfaces simultaneously invite touch and warn against probe. I go back to this space as to a recurrent dream of a place familiar and fascinating.

CHARLOTTE MANDEL
Poet

10

Black and White

10.13 **Seagram Building**
1958, Ludwig Mies van der Rohe, with Philip Johnson;
Kahn & Jacobs
375 Park Avenue between East 52nd and East 53rd Streets

9.17 **CBS Building**
1965, Eero Saarinen & Associates
51 West 52nd Street at Sixth Avenue

1.12 **Marine Midland Bank**
1967, Skidmore, Owings & Merrill
140 Broadway between Liberty and Cedar Streets

I used to think that, with the exception of Frank Lloyd Wright's Guggenheim Museum, the best works of architecture built in New York City during the last half of the twentieth century were the black buildings: the Seagram Building designed by Mies van der Rohe, the CBS ("Black Rock") building designed by Eero Saarinen, and the Marine

Midland Bank designed by Skidmore, Owings & Merrill.

But as the world we live in has grown more ominous, I think it will be the white buildings that will stand out, adding their much-needed light to the third millennium.

RICHARD MEIER
Architect

10.13 Seagram Building

1958, Ludwig Mies van der Rohe, with Philip Johnson;
Kahn & Jacobs
375 Park Avenue between East 52nd and East 53rd Streets

It happens that this great building contributed to my becoming an art historian. While it was under construction, the Museum of Modern Art installed in one of their regular galleries a full-size mockup of a stretch of the bronze facing, with I-beam moldings between the bays. How vividly I remember the amazing way this was mirrored on floor and ceiling. I was still in school, but looking back, this and Mondrian really did it for me.

Pay attention to certain, perhaps underappreciated, features: the unfussy disposition and lofty but unintimidating proportions of the lobby as a space of transition from the terrace, and the relation of the tower to the shorter block behind. My single favorite view is looking up from the south side entrance on 52nd Street at the asymmetrical, rectilinear composition framing the sky.

JOSEPH MASHECK
Art historian

10.13 The Four Seasons

1959, Philip Johnson & Associates
In the Seagram Building
99 East 52nd Street
☎ 212 754 9494; www.fourseasonsrestaurant.com

🍴 I still love the Four Seasons restaurant in the Seagram Building. At first, Mies and I weren't sure what would go in those spaces. At one point we considered a car show-room. Fortunately, the final decision was for a restaurant. I got to do the interiors since Mies was eager to get back to Chicago.

The Grill Room and the Pool Room are different in feel, but they are two of the prettiest rooms in New York. More than forty years later, these designs still please me greatly. One of the more amusing elements is the chain window coverings. Have you seen how they move with the air currents? I can't take credit for that effect; it's just the way it turned out. Those types of things often just happen in architecture. The entire project was an architect's dream—I was working with not only Mies van der Rohe, but Phyllis Bronfman Lambert.

10

PHILIP JOHNSON
Architect

For only a fraction of the cost of a trip to one of the two main dining rooms, I recommend a drink at the bar of the Four Seasons restaurant, the quintessential New York power scene for more than forty years. From Marie Nichols's fluttering, gold-anodized aluminum curtains (a happy accident of the ventilation system) to Richard Lippold's perilously perched sculpture over the bar, this Philip Johnson-designed space is an appropriate counterpart to the building in which it sits, Ludwig Mies van der Rohe's bronze master-piece, the Seagram Building.

DAVID FISHMAN
Architectural historian

You are walking down the street in Midtown Manhattan when you realize you need a bathroom. This is not a prob-lem. Head directly to the Seagram Building and the Four Seasons restaurant. Go to the bar on the second floor of this wondrous example of Modernist architecture, order a drink and the crab cakes, sit back for thirty seconds and take in the real magic of Mies van der Rohe and Philip Johnson's brilliance, then walk briskly down the stairs to the men's room. There you will encounter the most lush, extravagant, and completely perfect combination of marble and wood man has ever envisioned.

After this Zen-like experience, return to the bar, sip your drink, and marvel at the golden beaded window treatment, pulsing at something roughly equivalent to your new, reduced heart rate. (That Mies and Johnson did not know warm air currents would facilitate this visual effect when they designed the space only proves there is an architectural god out there somewhere.) Finish your crab cakes, have another drink—or not—and now, more slowly than you entered, walk out the middle door leading to the Grill Room and toward Park Avenue.

As you exit, directly in front of and around and above you is Roy Lichtenstein's thirty-two-foot-high black-and-white *Brush Stroke*. Humorous, huge, wonderful, it's a big sculpture—as good as sculpture gets—by a painter. For me, it's the sweetest dessert.

And so there you have it. A Midtown imperative turned into an aesthetic, spiritual, and culinary vacation—all in about thirty minutes.

DENNIS ASHBAUGH
Artist

10.14 Villard Houses

1884, Joseph Wells, façades; Stanford White, interiors;
1981, restored by James Rhodes
451–455 Madison Avenue between East 50th and 51st Streets

The architectural historian Henry-Russell Hitchcock applauded the Renaissance detailing of the houses. For me, however, they are much more, both urbanistically and architecturally. The entry court is New York's first, and perhaps finest, vest-pocket park. The use of brownstone is at once majestic and recalls common row houses. Careful scaling can be seen in the entrance porches, in the conglomeration of six houses—two of which are not entered off the courtyard—in the deflection of the main house to the sunny south, and in the bisection of the main axis into two houses (now lost). All this brings to mind precedents much more varied than the detailing of a simple Renaissance palazzo. Pay no attention to the Palace Hotel except to note that it pretty much leaves the original façades intact.

ROBERT LIVESEY
Architect

10.17 St. Regis-Sheraton Hotel
2 East 55th Street at Fifth Avenue

King Cole Bar and Lounge
1906, Maxfield Parrish
📞 212 753 4500; www.stregisnewyork.com

🍴 Stop for a drink at the King Cole Bar and Lounge and admire the magnificent twenty-eight-foot mural by Maxfield Parrish (1870–1966), whose studio was not far away at 49 East 63rd Street. This spectacular painting illustrates the eponymous nursery rhyme. Commissioned in 1905 by Nicholas Biddle for Colonel Astor, it was originally installed in the Hotel Knickerbocker on Times Square. Astor also owned the St. Regis, and the mural was moved to its present site in the 1930s.

MARGARET A. BRUCIA
Latin teacher and scholar

10.19 Samuel Paley Plaza
1967, Robert Zion and Harold Breen in association with Albert Preston Moore
3 East 53rd Street between Fifth and Madison Avenues

This little vest-pocket park is a lovely spot that easily takes one away from the surrounding bustle of Midtown Manhattan. Replete with waterfall, this park offers a

🍴 bonus during summer months by serving from its tiny food
stand the best hot dog in New York. Grilled and served on
a buttered bun, it is made even better by the surroundings.
JIM CODDINGTON
Chief conservator, MoMA

A civilized oasis in one of the most congested parts of the
city, landscape architects Robert Zion and Harold Breen's
Samuel Paley Plaza was the first and by far the best of the
city's vest-pocket parks. Located on a tight, forty-two-by-
one-hundred-foot site, Zion & Breen expertly manipulated
just a few key ingredients—twelve honey locust trees,
roughly hewn granite pavers, ivy-covered gray brick side
walls, chairs by Harry Bertoia, tables by Eero Saarinen,
and a rear wall of cascading water tumbling over stone that
fortuitously whites out just enough of Midtown's din—to
create a remarkably restrained and sophisticated outdoor
room suitable for contemplation, conversation, a quick snack
(there's a discreet kiosk just to the side of the entrance), or
simply a refreshing rest. Built and maintained with private
🍴 funds, Paley Park is the prototype that has unfortunately
either been ignored or poorly imitated. The good news is
that the original one-tenth-of-an-acre parklet looks—and
works—just like new.
DAVID FISHMAN
Architectural historian

Paley Park has been a favorite spot of mine since I was
a child. It is an utterly urban landscape that cannot help
but suit New York. The space is serene, elegant, and
modern. The water wall is a particularly welcome element
in Midtown. The architect, Robert Zion, worked on land-
scapes with Philip Johnson, which may explain why I feel
such an affinity for the design. How wonderful that a private source, in this case William Paley, could create such a
gem of public space.
HILARY LEWIS
Urban planner and architectural historian

Horological Stroll

10.20 **Cartier**
653 Fifth Avenue at 52nd Street

10.21 **Fifth Avenue Presbyterian Church**
7 West 55th Street at Fifth Avenue

10.22 **Tiffany & Co.**
727 Fifth Avenue at 57th Street

10.23 **Sherry Netherland Clock**
Fifth Avenue at 59th Street
www.nyc-architecture.com

10

12.3 **Delacorte Clock**
1965, Andrea Spadini
Above the arcade between the Wildlife Center and the
Children's Zoo
www.nycgovparks.org

Watch the clock as you take a leisurely stroll up Fifth Avenue
to the southern end of Central Park. Begin at 653 Fifth
Avenue (the southeast corner of 52nd Street) and note the
time on the ornate clock between the windows of Cartier's
second and third floors. As you proceed uptown, notice the
golden hands and numerals of the clock on the Fifth Avenue
Presbyterian Church at 55th Street. Continue north for two
blocks and admire the Tiffany clock, supported by a nine-
foot-tall Atlas. At 59th Street, take a moment to look at the
elegant Sherry Netherland street clock, one of seven clocks
designated as landmarks by the city's Landmarks Preservation
Commission. Cross the street and enter Central Park at the
corner of 60th Street and head north on the walkway to the
zoo. Located above the walkway at 64th Street near the
Arsenal is one of my favorite clocks—the musical Delacorte
Clock. Its clocktower houses two clockfaces on its north
and south sides. Sitting on top of the tower are two bronze

monkeys with hammers who appear to strike a large bell to sound the hours of the day, while six musical animals revolve around the tower to nursery rhyme tunes. The animals give a shorter performance on the half-hour. The best show, of course, is at noon.

BETTY KEIM
Editor, writer, and musicologist

10.24 **Former Pepsi-Cola Building, now ABN AMRO Bank Building**
1960, Gordon Bunshaft and Natalie DuBois of Skidmore, Owings & Merrill
500 Park Avenue at East 59th Street

Anybody who doubts that a simple Modernist grid of aluminum and glass can amount to a composition that is somehow more than just a grid of aluminum and glass, should get a load of this. Superbly proportioned, the building is at once earthbound and light. Each single window unit consists of a broad, horizontal rectangle of plate glass above a narrower aluminum parapet-like panel, with two elements together comprising, to the eye, an approximate square. And these "horizontals-and-a-half" in turn stack up vertically in regular bays. Between are vertical mullions of an astute slenderness, on the scale not of a skyscraper but of an urbane mansion. Here is perhaps a hint of Russian avant-garde suprematism, as well as of the Italian Renaissance.

JOSEPH MASHECK
Art historian

Art Underground

To obtain a free copy of *Art en Route*, send an email to artsfortransit@mtahq.org, or write to MTA Arts for Transit, 347 Madison Avenue, New York, NY 10017. www.mta.info/mta/aft

Take the MTA self-guided tour by using *Art en Route: Your Guide to Art in the MTA Network*. The guide will lead you to over a hundred works of art in the transit system, including works in the subway, Grand Central Terminal, and Penn Station. The tour includes mosaics, sculptures, and faceted glass installations by such internationally known artists as Elizabeth Murray, Maya Lin, and Donald Lipski, as well as works by other well-known and emerging artists. *Art en Route* is organized according to rail and subway lines.
SANDRA BLOODWORTH
Artist, and director of Metropolitan Transportation Authority Arts for Transit program

CHAPTER 11

UPPER EAST SIDE

Upper East Side

11.1 **Serendipity 3**

225 East 60th Street between Second and Third Avenues

☎ 212 838 3531; www.serendipity3.com

🍴 While Holly Golightly was eating breakfast at Tiffany's, all the cool kids in New York City were having frozen hot chocolates at Serendipity. The sandwiches and sodas, which are quite good, are mere obstacles to amazing desserts. The ambience is cozy and fun. Children's treasures, miniature tea sets, stuffed animals, and marbles are sold at the front of the shop. While hectic city life persists on just the other side of the door, this little haven promises nourishment and fun. My particular favorite—grilled cheese and a Coke and a caramel sundae for dessert.

DEBORAH SKELLY
Attorney and author

If you have kids, bring them here and let them gorge on the giant sundaes. Then take them to Central Park so they can run around for eight hours 'til they come down.

ERIC STOLTZ
Actor

11.2 **Arts for Transit: *Blooming***

1996, Elizabeth Murray

In the subway station at 59th Street and Lexington Avenue

www.mta.info/mta/aft

The best way to experience artist Elizabeth Murray's surreal metropolitan masterpiece is to stumble upon it (or rather, into it) by accident—preferably when half asleep. Change subway trains at 59th Street, and you will pass through a work of contemporary art that is also a playful visual pun. In *Blooming*, Murray has conjured a subterranean world of dreamy, evocative images. Gigantic trees with serpentine branches form a blooming dale—a witty allusion to the department store above. Along one wall towers a fantastic high-heeled slipper trailing long golden laces—a lost Manolo Blahnik, possibly? In ribbons of steam, fat yellow coffee cups spill poetic aphorisms: "In dreams begin responsibility," by Delmore Schwartz, and "Conduct your blooming in the noise and whip of the whirlwind," by Gwendolyn Brooks.

A longtime subway rider herself, Elizabeth Murray has said that she created her monumental mosaic for workers on their daily commute from Queens into Manhattan. For the price of a subway token and the willingness to climb a few stairs, you can see it, too. Take the trip. It will wake you up. It will make you smile.

ANN BANKS
Journalist

11.3 Subway Inn

143 East 60th Street between Lexington and Third Avenues
☎ 212 223 8929

This is the end of the line and the last great dive in Midtown. Up and running since 1933, its great neon "Subway Inn" sign has survived outside, as has its original Art Moderne glass-block storefront. Between takes of *The Seven Year Itch*, Marilyn Monroe stepped off the grate and dropped in to throw a few back with fellow straphangers. Photos and paintings of the blonde bombshell line the smoky walls. Once through the doors, you realize that this grimy broken-down joint is for the serious rider and regulars board at noon. When you're down and out, pop some quarters into the great jukebox and down a double Johnnie Walker on the rocks.

TRACEY HUMMER AND FREDERIC SCHWARTZ
Writer and Architect

Go to the Subway Inn on 60th Street and Lexington Avenue, and order a whiskey and a draft beer to back it up, then sit there and soak up one of the last authentic bars in New York. If you have two rounds the tab won't surpass ten bucks.

When you're done, walk outside and look diagonally across Lexington Avenue at the tiny brownstone that seems to be stuck into the enormous skyscraper that surrounds it. The story goes that an old Italian woman lived in the top-floor apartment for decades. When developers wanted to build the skyscraper, they offered her a buyout of her lease—and she refused. They doubled their offer, she still refused. After she turned down a million dollars, they decided to build it around her, which they figured would drive her out. It didn't. When I think about the beautiful stubbornness of New Yorkers, I think about this woman. For years she lived there, keeping her window boxes filled with fresh flowers through the spring, summer, and fall.

DAN ALGRANT
Filmmaker

11.4 Tender Buttons

143 East 62nd Street between Lexington and Third Avenues
☎ 212 758 7004; www.tenderbuttons-nyc.com

Whether you're trying to replace a missing button, looking for the perfect buttons for a homemade sweater, or just in a browsing mood, come to this little button boutique. You may not have thought of buttons as interesting or note-worthy, but step inside this quaint shop (here since 1967) and you'll marvel at the selection. Organized in small self-serve boxes, you can find buttons in every style made from horn, vegetable ivory, silver, leather, crystal, wood, Bakelite, and ranging in price from fifty cents to a few hundred dollars. Framed on the wall and just for show are rare, antique buttons that give the store more of a museum feel. The friendly staff can help you find a particular button or make inspired suggestions.

SARAH CAPLAN
Designer, graphic artist, and writer

11.5 The Metropolitan Club

1894, McKim, Mead & White
1 East 60th Street at Fifth Avenue
☎ 212 838 7400; www.metropolitanclubnyc.org
Not open to the public.

My vote for the prettiest room in the city just might be the
main room of the Metropolitan Club; you might have
trouble getting in, but just go up the stairs and gaze in at a
McKim, Mead & White marble, soaring-ceilinged treasure.
JOHN GUARE
Playwright

11.6 Viand

673 Madison Avenue between East 61st and 62nd Streets
☎ 212 751 6622

11

🍴 If you are looking for a quick bite in Midtown, pop into
Viand for a classic New York coffee shop experience.
Established in 1976, this miracle of Manhattan real estate
caters to a wide cross section of New Yorkers—from the
Upper East Side matron dripping in furs to the neighbor-
hood cop on the beat.

Waiters call out orders like "jack with tommy" (grilled
cheese with tomato), "full house" (grilled cheese with
tomato and bacon), "short stack bac" (two pancakes with
bacon), and "42 whiskey down" (four eggs, two plates,
rye toast). Viand is famous for its fresh turkey sandwiches,
delicious cheeseburgers, and a great tuna salad. The hospitable owner oversees his galleyesque eatery like a captain
on his ship in a storm.
ROBERT KAHN
Architect

11.7 Ursus Books and Prints

699 Madison Avenue, third floor, between East 62nd and
East 63rd Streets
☎ 212 772 8787; www.ursusbooks.com

Ursus offers a vast selection of rare books, fine bindings, and first editions covering a broad range of subjects. Here, you will find manifestos from Marx to Marx, literature from Shakespeare to Joyce, and illustrated books by artists Dürer to Picasso. In the Bs alone, Ursus has had the elusive first edition of *En attendant Godot*, the Complutensian Polyglot Bible, and a twelve-volume first-edition Babar collection. To experience perfect symmetry, locate a first edition of Bemelmans's *Madeline*, then head down to the lobby for a drink in Bemelmans Bar to celebrate your good fortune. Book-loving tourists and book-reading former presidents can be found browsing through the shelves. Ursus also offers a superior selection of art books and a room of decorative prints from the seventeenth through the nineteenth centuries.

ROBERT KAHN
Architect

Nathan Hale Was Here

While Nathan Hale may have said he had "but one life to lose" for his country, there are four places in Manhattan that claim to be where he lost it.

The most visible site is his statue in City Hall Park, placed there on the probably mistaken presumption that that's where the British hanged him as a spy in 1776.

The most invisible site was marked by a plaque in a slaughterhouse on First Avenue in the East 40s, since razed to make way for the United Nations. The plaque was saved and reproduced at the Yale Club at the corner of Vanderbilt Avenue and East 44th Street, across from Grand Central Terminal. It must have seemed logical since Hale was a Yale man (class of 1773). No matter that the plaque says he was hanged "near this site" and the Yale Club is nowhere near any of the alleged sites.

The slaughterhouse claim was nearer, because most

historians now seem to agree that the heroic twenty-one-year-old was hanged from a tree in the British encampment at what is now the intersection of Third Avenue and East 66th Street. A new plaque at the entrance to the Banana Republic at Third and 65th indicates that the dastardly deed was probably done near the 66th Street corner. The Dove Tavern stood there in 1776. It's a Starbucks now.

RICHARD MOONEY
Journalist

11.8 Seventh Regiment Armory

1879, Charles W. Clinton
643 Park Avenue between East 66th and East 67th Streets
☎ 212 616 3930; www.armoryonpark.org

11

The Park Avenue Armory (Seventh Regiment Armory), host to numerous art fairs throughout the year, is a fascinating building to explore. At one end of the ground floor is the Tiffany Room, covered top to bottom with decoration—stained glass, mosaic, and metalwork.

NADINE ORENSTEIN
Curator, Prints and Drawings Department, The Metropolitan Museum of Art

11.9 Urasenke Chanoyu Center

153 East 69th Street between Third and Lexington Avenues
☎ 212 988 6161; www.urasenkeny.org

🍴 Housed in Mark Rothko's old studio is the Urasenke Chanoyu Center, a nonprofit society that cultivates an appreciation of the Japanese tea ceremony. Membership is not required to attend one of the monthly classes, presided over by a kindly older gentleman. The transformation of the space is quite incredible, and the devotion of the staff is touching as they set about educating you about the ceremony, emphasizing the role of the guest as well as that of the host.

Certainly the experience depends on the group you attend with, but the force with which it demands you stop your day and experience the beauty of the ceremony itself, both deliberate and simple, is great. Before and after the actual ceremony there are short lessons about the aesthetics as well as general philosophy of tea and life. While it sometimes stays on a less-than-profound level, it is always pleasant. *Wabi-sabi*, the Japanese aesthetic of imperfect and impermanent beauty, is among the discussions, and guests are encouraged to participate.

LAURIE MCLENDON
The late Laurie McLendon was the owner of Shi and Papivor on Elizabeth Street in Nolita.

11.10   The Frick Collection

1914, Carrère & Hastings; 1935, renovated as a museum by John Russell Pope
1 East 70th Street at Fifth Avenue
☎ 212 288 0700; www.frick.org
Closed Mondays.

It's easy to love the Frick, not only because of its great works of art and sumptuous rooms, gardens, and fountains, but because it is relatively small and intimate for a museum. One can go there for half an hour or forty-five minutes and see the entire collection briefly. The Frick very seldom loans art and rarely moves pictures; and it is this consistency that allows one to retain its artworks so indelibly in one's mind.

AGNES GUND
President Emerita, MoMA; Chairman, Mayor's Cultural Affairs Advisory Commission of New York City

The price of bliss in New York City is eighteen dollars. This is the admission fee to the Frick Collection, a once-private house just steps off Fifth Avenue, where you may enter the enchanted interior garden court. Beneath the vaulted glass ceiling, supported by paired columns, is a grand Roman atrium with year-round plantings of exotic palms, orchids, and ferns. You may want to sit awhile among the carved stone benches and listen to the water-music of the enormous fountain with its squatting frogs. You would certainly want to experience the incredible sense of serenity by gazing at Jean Barbet's *Angel* (1475), whose beautiful face and gently closed wings seem to whisper, "Rest, rest." And when you have recovered your ability to see with fresh eyes, you are ready to stroll along the outer corridors and into the great room to view some of the best-known paintings by the greatest European artists.

JEAN RATHER
Artist

For an exceptional afternoon in New York City, visit the Frick. With its few rooms, this is an incredibly manageable experience. The collection mirrors the weight, substance, and gravitas of Frick himself and contains remarkable paintings by Hans Holbein the Younger (*Sir Thomas More*), Bellini (*Saint Francis in the Desert*), Ingres (*The Comtesse d'Hausonville*), as well as beauties by Vermeer, Rembrandt, and Georges de la Tour. As I tell my students, the only reason Frick is remembered (despite his power, wealth, and "robber baron" status) is because of this magnificent art collection.

SIMON DINNERSTEIN
Artist

The Frick is exquisite, especially the Whistlers.

HUGH MARTIN
Songwriter

Saint Francis in the Desert
c. 1480, Giovanni Bellini
In the Living Hall

One of the more unusual masterpieces of Venetian art from the late fifteenth century, Giovanni Bellini's *Saint Francis in the Desert* is a celebration of God through landscape. Standing on an outcropping of rock outside his cave, Saint Francis curves his spine backwards toward the makeshift study behind him, greeting warm sunlight as it falls over his body. Barefoot, lips parted, and with his palms exposed (perhaps a reference to his receiving the stigmata, although his wounds are already visible), Francis' thin body is dwarfed and humbled by the beauty of his natural surroundings. An olive tree bends toward him, grapevines fall over his study, water spills from a spout in the rock, and a shepherd tends his flock (all details that carry Christian symbolism). With painstaking attention to detail, Bellini has infused his composition with brilliant color, enticing us to feel the same spiritual ecstasy that Francis found in his own backyard.

KATEY BROWN
Art historian

11.11 **Candle Cafe**

1307 Third Avenue between East 74th and East 75th Streets
📞 212 472 0970; www.candlecafe.com

🍴🍷 The best vegan restaurant in the city, in a neighborhood where you'd never expect to find such a thing. The staff is wonderful and the dishes are tasty as well as inventive.

KATHARINE RISTICH
Editor, Theheart.org and Femina.com

Three Paintings

9.15 **Broadway Boogie Woogie**
1943, Piet Mondrian
The Museum of Modern Art
11 West 53rd Street
📞 212 708 9400, www.moma.org

11.10 **Saint Francis in the Desert**
c. 1480, Giovanni Bellini
The Frick Collection
1 East 70th Street at Fifth Avenue
📞 212 288 0700; www.frick.org

11.14 **Juan de Pareja**
1650, Diego Velázquez
The Metropolitan Museum of Art
1000 Fifth Avenue at 82nd Street
Second floor, Gallery 16, The Old Masters Gallery
📞 212 535 7710; www.metmuseum.org

May I present a walk comprised of paintings, which,
at points in my life, were destinations of sustenance and
in which I identified various New York City aspects.
Go straight to the mentioned paintings, and try not to be
distracted by the other beauties calling for attention. Keep
the enterprise clean.

At the Museum of Modern Art, go to Piet Mondrian's
great *Broadway Boogie Woogie*, painted in homage to his
adopted city in reverence for its ongoing energies, movements, sounds, rhythms, and intensities. Give the painting
at least five minutes of concentration. Leave.

Go to the Frick Collection and straight to its Bellini, *Saint
Francis in the Desert*. New York City is a teeming place
(remember *Boogie Woogie*), but it is made up of millions
of pure individuals. Here is Saint Francis, surrounded by
beings, a golden light, his town, but he is alone in com-
munion with an energy directed only to him (see the wind
in the olive tree) in an otherwise still environment. He is
alone, inspired, and fully conscious of his greater self.

It's on up to the Met for a visit with Diego Velázquez's
Juan de Pareja. Stand in awe of Velázquez's total mastery
of the illusion achieved through the workings of the eye, the
hand, and the paint. Be reminded by Pareja, an obviously

11

proud man of color, of our own city's ethnic diversity and
how much that adds to our power and beauty.
BRICE MARDEN
Painter

11.12 Whitney Museum of American Art

*1966, Marcel Breuer & Associates; 1998, addition by Gluckman
Mayner*

945 Madison Avenue at East 75th Street

☎ 212 570 3600; www.whitney.org

Dwellings

1981, Charles Simonds
In the stairwell between the second and third floors

The mysterious ruins of a lost nomadic civilization can
be seen on a second-floor window ledge of a palatial
neo-Classical building at 940 Madison Avenue, across the
street from the Whitney Museum. Seldom noticed by
passersby, the diminutive clay dwellings and ritual towers
are the abandoned habitations of the Little People, a vanished urban tribe that has been fully imagined, chronicled,
mythologized, and architecturally contextualized by the
artist Charles Simonds. *Dwellings*, a three-part site-specific
piece, was commissioned by the Whitney Museum and
installed in 1981. A second part of *Dwellings* is perched on
a chimney at the right back corner of the building and is
also visible to pedestrians from across the avenue (field
glasses helpful here). The principal component of the work
is permanently installed inside the Whitney, above a window
in the airshaft of the main stairwell, between the second and
third floors. From that window, all three parts of *Dwellings*
are visible, although the label describing the piece in the
museum fails to mention that there are two more parts of
the work. If you don't know about the outdoor pieces and
don't, by chance, spot the one on the far right window ledge,
you will miss seeing these extraordinary and beguiling
works of art.

Starting in the early 1970s, Simonds constructed nearly three hundred outdoor pieces representing the abandoned settlements that marked the passage of the Little People. They were deliberately impermanent works, made of unfired clay, sand, twigs, bits of cloth, and other materials that would eventually decay outdoors. Simonds sited the pieces chiefly in the slums of the Lower East Side, half-hidden in the earth and litter of vacant lots, or tucked into crevices of crumbling brick walls. He expected these street pieces would be stolen, destroyed by neglect and weather, or otherwise lost to sight. And they were. The physical traces of these tiny primitivistic villages are gone now, though recorded on film and in photographs. Simonds made similar works on wooden platforms, for indoor viewing, and for keeping. The only outdoor ruins that remain are on pricey Madison Avenue on a building used as a bank until mid-1999, an irony most likely intended by Simonds.

Simonds's constructions strongly evoke the archaeological ruins of the cliff-dwelling Anasazi, who lived in the Four Corners region of the American Southwest from roughly 600 C.E. to 1300 C.E. The Anasazi, precursors of the Pueblo culture, vanished as enigmatically as Simonds's mythical Little People. His invented civilization and its vestigial settlements hint at a nostalgia for a simpler child-like past, but there is nothing sentimental about Simonds's art. His work challenges conventional perceptions of scale, of artwork as precious collectible, of historical record as reliable. What's more, it has powerful narrative appeal. Looking at *Dwellings*, we can't help wondering about the daily lives and dreams and social realities of the Little People, can't help thinking about how and if they differ from us, ordinary folks wandering the canyons of vast and difficult cities. These provocative ruins are small in size only, and certainly worth seeing.

LUCIENNE S. BLOCH
Writer

The Stair at the Whitney

Of all the museums in the city, the Whitney captures the vibe of the local and national art scene the best. The collection is sophisticated yet accessible, raw but accomplished. And Breuer's 1966 building, an idiosyncratic landmark, well reflects the strength, fluidity, and independence of the art inside, even as it complements the staid brownstone fabric of the surrounding neighborhood.

As a visitor moves between floors, the stair becomes a showcase for the structure's finessed tectonics. The massive elements of the museum's construction are delicately assembled and organized in a way that communicates eloquently the various scales at work within the building. In a very confined area, the stair combines poured-in-place concrete walls (with the aggregate carefully exposed), stone slab stair treads suspended from those walls, oversized, elegant bronze balustrades, and wooden handrails and benches, and sets them off with a stepped pane of glass that recalls the inverted ziggurat form of the structure and brings in the light of the city.

Take a break between floors, sit on a bench at one of the landings and talk about the art, feel the building, and watch the crazy cross section of people walking up and down the stairs.

SCOTT GLASS
Architect

11.13 **Bemelmans Bar**

1947, murals by Ludwig Bemelmans
Madison Avenue between East 75th and East 76th Streets
In the Carlyle Hotel
☎ 212 744 1600; www.thecarlyle.com

🍴 Legend has it Bemelmans Bar in the Carlyle Hotel was one of the late Jackie O's favorite haunts, and that her protests, along with cries from others, helped save this landmark from being remodeled into just another Madison Avenue piano lounge ordinaire. Classy, but not fussy, Bemelmans is so elegantly dim that the most shimmering celebrity can be rendered inconspicuous in the shadows of the deep leather booths. Fine, since sighting the rich and famous isn't the appeal here—people come to see the walls. Four walls of murals, once vibrant and now perfectly subdued by half a century of nicotine fumes, teem with characters you will immediately recognize unless you spent your child-hood in a culvert. Ludwig Bemelmans, author, artist, and restaurateur, was best remembered as the creator of the *Madeline* books. In 1947 Bemelmans brought his characters in out of the rain and painted them to life among seasonal views of Central Park. Ever since, twelve little girls in two straight lines, and tweed-clad, shotgun-packing rabbits wel-come regulars famous and not.

For a half-century a self-portrait of Bemelmans near the bar has overseen the preparation of countless thousands of perfect martinis by the white-tuxed, black-tied batenders. The bartenders are no-nonsense veterans, and while only a few could possibly remember Bemelmans himself, they speak of him as if this good friend has just stepped from the room.

I try to visit whenever I'm in New York. One afternoon when I was either dressed well enough or the lights were low enough that I might be mistaken for an Upper East-sider, the barman headed to my booth with a phone in his hand, just like the movies, bowing from the waist—I swear he clicked his heels—and offered me the receiver, inquiring, "Miss Colgate?"

I was tempted by the mischievous Madeline perched just over my shoulder: Take the call, take the call!

"Miss Colgate?"

But gumption failed and I could only reply, "I wish."

The barkeep and I had a good laugh, and a few moments later I was delivered a potent something on the house, which is exactly the type of hospitality Bemelmans himself was loved for.

SARAH STONICH
Writer

For me, an evening at Bemelmans Bar has always been both fanciful and familiar. When I was a young editor just getting started in New York, a visit to Bemelmans meant slowly savored martinis and a meal of homemade chips, rosemary-marinated olives, and divine mixed nuts. I would float through the front door, past the tastefully dressed giraffe with the yellow handbag that graces the wall near the entry, and casually settle in for a cocktail and conversation. Tommy, the friendly Irishman who has been tending the bar for more than forty years, made me feel right at home. I would slip into a tufted leather banquette and slip back in time. By the end of the evening, I felt as though I had stepped out of a Noël Coward play. Today, the experience of turning back the elegant clock at Bemelmans is every bit as transporting. The refined service and urbane pianist, along with the warm glow of the room and Ludwig Bemelmans' amazing wall murals, have endured and I expect always will.

KATE SPADE
Co-founder, Kate Spade New York

11.14 The Metropolitan Museum of Art
1000 Fifth Avenue at 82nd Street
☎ 212 535 7710; www.metmuseum.org

For me, the best expenditure of two hours' recreation in New York City is a visit to the Metropolitan Museum of Art. In fact, I enjoy my trips to the museum so much that

I go about every two weeks. There is always a new exhibition to be seen or an old collection to be revisited in order to learn even more about it. The permanent collections that draw me to visit again and again are the Egyptian Art collection and Arms and Armor.

I have been a frequent visitor to the museum for many years. When I became a Member of Congress in 1969, I compared life in New York City to Washington, D.C. New York came out way ahead for a host of reasons, of which the museum is only one.

EDWARD I. KOCH
Former Mayor of New York City

Greek and Roman Art
First floor

11

Cubiculum from Boscoreale
40–30 B.C.E.

Walking along the sidewalks of New York we sometimes want to know what lies behind the anonymous walls of urban structures. Where are the brilliant salons of Cole Porter where beautiful people chat wittily over cocktails? The period rooms at the Metropolitan Museum of Art allow us to enter elite environments from different periods in history. My favorite is the richly painted *cubiculum* (small bedroom) excavated from the villa of P. Fannius Synister at Boscoreale (just north of Pompeii), now installed in the Greek and Roman Galleries.

It is decorated in what art historians term the Second Style of Roman painting, a system of complex perspectives that may derive from architectural stage backdrops (*frontes scaenarum*). These views appear to open behind the actual wall plane, which is reinforced by painted columns and piers. The ancient viewer would move about the room and imaginatively escape into three different worlds: the courts of urban sanctuaries, cityscapes of jostling buildings, and a rocky landscape. Modern visitors can also suspend belief and project themselves back into the middle of the first century B.C.E. Elsewhere in the galleries are other paintings from the same villa. These feature near-life-size figured scenes (megalography) that derive from the decorations found in Hellenistic royal courts. The paintings, together with some of the statuary and luxury items displayed in the galleries, provide an *Architectural Digest*-like glimpse into the opulent private lives of wealthy Romans.

PETER J. HOLLIDAY
Professor, History of Art and Classical Archaeology, California State University, Long Beach

Metropolitan Museum Figure Tour

The most omnipresent image in the history of art is the figure. At the Metropolitan Museum, you can follow the figure through thousands of years. Unique in this part of the world in offering such a sweeping reach in a single location, the museum provides visitors a view of this entire arc in one of the finest collections anywhere. The striking similarity between the "beginning" and the "present"— between the Cycladic and Brancusi—is a marvelous paradox, which we have the good fortune to witness here.

Third millennium B.C.E.:

Cycladic art
Greek and Roman Art Galleries
First floor

With only crude tools at hand, our forebears created splendid frontal images of themselves in kind. They would have a lasting effect on the making of sculpture into the twentieth century.

Fourteenth century B.C.E.:

Fragment of the Face of a Queen
1353–1336 B.C.E.
Egyptian Art Galleries
First floor

In a glass case near the entrance to the Temple of Dendur, find this piece composed from yellow jasper, the second hardest stone known to man after the diamond. Note the little stand with the metal pin, required when this piece came to the Met in 1926 because there was no drill strong enough to pierce the jasper. Ponder, then, how the contour line of the lip was carved in 1350 B.C.E.

Fourteenth century B.C.E.:

Haremhab as a Scribe of the King
1336–1323 B.C.E.
Egyptian Art Galleries
First floor

11

Find it, also, near the entrance to the Temple of Dendur. This king worked his way up to sovereign without the usual bloodline requirement. This portrayal of him seems to keep that crucial fact in mind, juxtaposing refined elegance and mass, and seeming to say that power can be achieved only through intelligence. It is one of the museum's finest works.

Sixth century B.C.E.:

Kouros (Statue of a Youth)
590–580 B.C.E.
Greek and Roman Art Galleries
First floor

We've returned to the Greeks and Romans. The only tool in Attica at this time was the bull-nose chisel, which limited the ability to achieve a rounded naturalism. Still, look at the way the artist handled the hair, and pushed the chisel to create lifelike anatomy. This is a work of amazing intelligence and liveliness.

Fifth century B.C.E.:

Statue of Diadoumenos
69–96 C.E., Roman copy of a statue by Polykleitos c. 430 B.C.E.
Greek and Roman Art Galleries
First floor

This youth tying a fillet around his head is attributed to Polykleitos, the man who put the class in classical. Polykleitos invented the Classical canon: seven and one-half heads. This canon measures anatomical length in the following fashion: Squint with one eye closed and extend your arm. Using the thumb and index finger of the extended hand, measure the height of the head of the youth. This measurement equals one head. It is then one head again to the nipples. One head to the belly button. Half a head to the pelvic bone. Two heads to the knee. Two heads to the plinth. Total? Seven and one-half. Try it. This method of rendering the figure has lasted until the present day.

Third-Second century B.C.E.:

Veiled and Masked Dancer
Greek and Roman Art Galleries
First floor

Look at this little miracle—so miraculous in fact, so modern, the detailing so perfect, that some believe it is a phony. It's impossible to stay in one place when viewing it; one is forced to walk around it.

First century:

Old Market Woman
Greek and Roman Art Galleries
First floor

Here, genre and type supersede ideal beauty. The result is a startling, lifelike presence. Now leave the ancients and head for the roots of modern Europe.

Twelfth century:

Dancing Celestial
Irving Galleries for the Arts of South and Southeast Asia
Second floor

The apotheosis of figure as decoration. Near the Jain Temple, find this jewel wearing jewels in a pose of unabashed sexuality.

Thirteenth century:

Golden Boy
Charlotte C. Weber Galleries for the Arts of Ancient China
Second floor

This wooden masterpiece hovers between stasis and movement and stands in charmed vibration between the two.

Fifteenth century:

Virgin and Child
c.1420, attributed to Claus de Werve
Medieval Art Galleries
First floor

Take note of the rear view. Compare and contrast it with *Haremhab as a Scribe of the King.*

Fifteenth century:

Adam
1490–1495, Tullio Lombardo
Vélez Blanco Patio
First floor

A masterpiece of sexual sublimation. Here is a startling union: Modern Man's fig leaf on an ancient monumental sculpture, for the first time. Compare with Polykleitos's *Diadoumenos*.

Seventeenth century:

Bacchanal: A Faun Teased by Children
1616–1617, Gian Lorenzo Bernini
European Sculpture and Decorative Arts Galleries, first floor

The prodigy at work, at age nineteen. This piece shows you the master who will soon emerge.

Eighteenth century:

Jack and Belle Linsky Galleries
European Sculpture and Decorative Arts Galleries
First floor

Now you are at the Rococo. Despite the leap of two thousand years, you can find the *Old Market Woman* in these porcelains, on a different scale.

Nineteenth century:

New Hebrides Slit-Gongs
Arts of Africa, Oceania, and the Americas Galleries
First floor

These amazing structures are part functional—serving as drums—and part fertility figures; both male and female gender in one giddy form. Spiritual, too.

Nineteenth century:

Perseus with the Head of Medusa
1804–1806, Antonio Canova
Balcony above the Great Hall
Second floor

We're neo-Classical now and you have two precedents to consider: Polykleitos's *Diadoumenos* and Tullio Lombardo's *Adam*.

Nineteenth century:

Ugolino and His Sons
1865–1867, Jean-Baptiste Carpeaux

Burghers of Calais
1884–1895, Auguste Rodin (cast in 1985)
European Sculpture and Decorative Arts Galleries
Sculpture Court
First floor

Back downstairs to the Carroll & Milton Petrie Sculpture Court. Carpeaux gives us Dante's most harrowing canto brought to life. Rodin's sculpture of the doomed burghers as they make their way to the gallows, hints at Modernism's dialectic between collective suffering and personal growth.

11

Twentieth century:

Sleeping Muse
1920, Constantin Brancusi
Modern Art Galleries
First floor

Brancusi's polished simplicity completes the arc. You've not only journeyed some five-thousand years, you have, in significant ways, traveled full circle back to the Cycladic. One can quibble with this mix of work, but you'll see that the startling parallels overwhelm the inherent differences. It's the most convincing case under one roof for the notion of progress as inconsequential to art-making. Brancusi may have been a happy man when the electric sander was invented, but it didn't make him a better artist.
PIER CONSAGRA
Artist

Arts of Africa, Oceania, and the Americas
Michael C. Rockefeller Wing
First floor

The most internationally renowned collection of
non-Western art on display is a series of treasures
that includes a sixteenth-century ivory pendant mask
depicting a queen mother from the kingdom of Benin,
a primordial couple by a Dogon master, and a majestic
series of monumental Bamana allegorical figures from
present-day Mali.

ALISA LAGAMMA
*Curator, Department of the Arts of Africa, Oceania, and the
Americas, The Metropolitan Museum of Art*

European Sculpture and Decorative Arts
First floor

The Studiolo from the Palace of Duke Federico da Montefeltro at Gubbio
c.1478–1483, Francesco di Giorgio Martini

Among the many treasures in the Metropolitan Museum,
one worth spending some time with is the Gubbio *studiolo*.
Created in Gubbio, central Italy, for the fifteenth-century
humanist scholar and soldier Federico da Montefeltro, Duke
of Urbino, this small private study embodies the diverse
interests of a true Renaissance man. Federico was renowned
for his love of books, art, and learning—he employed forty
scribes in his library and five men to read him the classics
during meals. His *studiolo* is an irregularly shaped room
decorated entirely in perspective intarsia—wood inlay. The
benches jutting into the room, the shelves and cabinets
overflowing with artifacts symbolizing learning, art, and
power, the half-opened cabinets, the organ, the birdcage—
all are created with astonishing realism from thousands of

minute slivers of different colored woods. The room repays careful study, as it is full of delightful tiny details. You can discover distinct strings on the musical instruments, legible text from Virgil's *Aeneid* on an open book, convincingly rendered shadows, a pair of eyeglasses neatly folded in their case, an hourglass full of sand. All the views are calculated for a person about five feet tall. If you crouch, you can see how the perspective works, particularly by watching as the circular headdress casually laid on the bench becomes, from the wrong point of view, a distorted ring with shadows in the wrong places, and then falls back into place as you stand up again. The Met completed its meticulous renovation of this friendly little room in 1996. The museum trustingly put up no barriers in front of the walls, and the light streaming in through the small window convincingly simulates sunlight. Although the *studiolo* was opened with great fanfare, it is now often empty for long stretches. You can easily spend a quarter of an hour there without seeing anyone except the guard, who checks periodically to make sure you don't touch anything.

JANET B. PASCAL
Writer and production editor, Viking Children's Books

One of the gems of the Medieval Department is the *studiolo* (or private study) of Federico da Montefeltro, Duke of Urbino, formerly located in his palace at Gubbio (a hilltown in the Umbria region of Italy). A masterwork of fifteenth-century craftsmanship, this intimate room—approximately sixteen feet by twelve feet—exhibits the illusionistic qualities of intarsia, or wood-inlay technique. Thousands of tiny pieces of wood act like a painter's palette: the multiple varieties, cuts, and grains of wood create the trompe l'oeil appearance of cabinet doors slightly ajar, revealing inside objects dear to a humanist's intellect and curiosity. Books are casually stacked or left open, as if someone has just thumbed through their pages. A parrot sits patiently on a perch in a cage. Lutes, candles, scientific instruments, a portable pipe organ, lectern, sand hourglass, convex mirror, hunting horn, and helmet are all displayed as cherished belongings of perhaps the most renowned *condottiere* (soldier of fortune) of his time. Among the visual rewards for feasting one's eyes in this room are the latticework designs that incorporate the effects of natural light from the window, as well as the use of perspective that invites our eyes to question the two-dimensionality of the flat wall.

KATEY BROWN
Art historian

Sienese Paintings

The Creation of the World and the Expulsion from Paradise
1445, Giovanni di Paolo
The Robert Lehman Collection
First floor

St. Anthony the Abbot in the Wilderness
c.1435, The Osservanza Master
The Robert Lehman Collection
First floor

The Journey of the Magi
c.1420, Sassetta
European Paintings Galleries
Second floor

Sienese painting has always been overshadowed by its more famous cousin, Florentine painting, which broke through to the full-on science of rational representation. By contrast, Sienese paintings are illogical and medieval—but that's exactly what modern viewers love about them. These paintings have spaces more absurd than Cézanne, colors right out of the comics, and images that tamp down academic space and accentuate the expressive. Candy-colored castles! Giant people walking through miniature worlds! Mystical experiences in improbable architectures! If you want to make a little pilgrimage to this uncanny world, there are some great Sienese paintings that you can visit at the Met. They are not presented with much fanfare and can be missed easily.

Go directly to the back of the ground floor of the museum to the Robert Lehman Collection, walk through the glass doors and along the wall on the left with paintings by Degas, Renoir, Cézanne, and Vuillard (some of the Vuillards alone make this worth the trip). Go back around the wall to the left to find the Sienese room, the first of a suite of semi-hidden rooms containing Lehman's collection of older paintings, all fitted out in red velvet and gilded wood to imply a fifteenth-century Italian environment. Hanging here are two outstanding examples of Sienese painting: *Saint Anthony the Abbot in the Wilderness* by the Osservanza Master, and *The Creation of the World and the Expulsion from Paradise* by Giovanni di Paolo. Both artists were active in the second quarter of the fifteenth century in Siena. You will probably find the di Paolo first because it is marked for the Museum's headphone audio tour. This heavily cracked painting shows Adam and Eve's expulsion from the garden set against a chart-like mini-universe that includes the prime mover himself presiding over everything from the circles of hell to the four great drainage ditches of the world.

Across the room is the extraordinary *Saint Anthony the Abbot in the Wilderness* by the Osservanza Master, a small tempera-and-gold painting hanging modestly amidst a wall of more conventional Madonna paintings. In it, a startled-looking Saint Anthony gestures toward a little gray bunny crouching at the base of a bare tree. There is an almost minimalist space and silence between the man and the animal, as though some phantom thing between them has been painted out. What's going on in the background is even weirder. The Osservanza Master seems to have had a background man who was either new at the job or a brilliant pre-Van Gogh hallucinator, four hundred years before his time. Saint Anthony and the mute bunny live in a wild and crazy pink-and-green world inhabited only by listing and hunkering animals. The action twists back along a pebbled path to a variety of green Mister Softee hills, some stuck with what look like cloves. The earth is orange, the castles are hot pink, the sea is bright green with a thrift-store-looking boat in it and, above it all, crows fly in a flaming sky lit up with crimson clouds.

For a comparison, visit the more polished Sassetta in the Met's regular Italian painting collection. Take the main staircase to the second floor, through the doorway straight ahead of you on the right side, into the first room of the corridor of fourteenth- to sixteenth-century Italian paintings. On the right side and behind glass, you will find the truly amazing *Journey of the Magi* by Sassetta, painted in tempera and gold on wood, c.1420. Here's the ubiquitous speckled path, but in this tiny painting all the townspeople march down a hill in a frieze-like procession, which disappears out of the painting as though it were stage left, leaving a lone horse's leg in view as it exits. As the people walk off, swallows pose, storks graze on mottled hills, stars bleed gold, trees lose their branches, and leaves and buildings glow in the distance, all in a painting the size of a piece of typing paper.

AMY SILLMAN
Artist

Islamic Art
Second floor

Deep inside the labyrinthine corridors of the Metropolitan Museum of Art are a series of galleries devoted to the museum's superb collection of Islamic art. These galleries are among the most serene and pleasant spaces within the museum—oases of repose and contemplation where you can see and enjoy works of art of incomparable beauty and power. Located in the southeast corner of the second floor, the galleries were designed in 1975 and they remain among the most intelligent and compelling displays of Islamic art anywhere in the world. They're home to more than twelve thousand works of art from almost every corner of the Islamic world—from Spain to India—that date from the eighth to the eighteenth century. Among my favorite objects, which have fascinated me since I was a graduate student and first encountered them, are the reconstruction of Núr ad-Dín's room from a wealthy Syrian home of the early eighteenth century; the great twelfth-century Seljuk incense burner in the shape of a lion; the dazzling tile mihrab (or prayer niche) from the mid-fourteenth century madrassa (school) of Imami in Isfahan; the majestic early sixteenth-century "Simonetti" carpet from Mamluk, Egypt; and the illustrated pages from the *Shahnama* or *Book of Kings* commissioned by the Safavid ruler Shah Tahmasp (1514–1576), one of the Islamic world's most ardent bibliophiles.

What distinguishes all these works is a precision of line, complexity of design, and a level of craftsmanship and detail that is not only breathtaking, but awe-inspiring. The weave of the "Simonetti" carpet, for instance, is a staggering hundred asymmetrical knots per square inch. Many of the colors used in the painting of the *Shahnama* are made from semi-precious ground minerals such as lapis lazuli and malachite. The lustrous gold backgrounds are, in fact, a thinly applied layer of gold leaf.

GLENN LOWRY
Director, The Museum of Modern Art

European Paintings
Second floor

The View of Toledo
c.1597, El Greco

After you have viewed the city, climb the steps at the
Metropolitan Museum, head to the second floor (European
Paintings), and be transported by El Greco's *The View
of Toledo.*

This is not a painting of the state of grace already fully
realized, like Bellini's wondrous *Saint Francis in the Desert*
at the Frick Museum. Instead, we are in the middle of a
hallucination, in the anxious peripheries of revelation. The
sky is doubt, the landscape ambiguity, and the source of
light a riddle.

As you travel through the painting, sweeping past the
architecture, you are at once pulled by the weight of weather,
human events, botany, history, a familiar world—time-
bound, color-bound, language-bound—up to the prospect
of the skyline that is Toledo. Here the painting abruptly
stops. The skyline is a horizon. There is no beyond. There
is only the above, leading the eye by way of the church spire
to the light that creates the scene. Is it nighttime or day,
twilight or dawn? All you really know is that a supernatural
illumination is eclipsing the scene.

In this spot of time, the world of weather and human
events stops. You have reached the terminus of earthly
experience. There is no beyond, even though there is a
potential for beyond. El Greco takes the scene, arrests it,
holds it. Then, through a series of silvery gleams of light,
he abstracts you from real time to the realm of timeless-
ness. The entire painting unfolds within a shadow—which
confesses to the mystery of spiritual illumination—toward
the opening in the sky, an oculus in the celestial dome.
You are in the exact spot where the ordinary is about to
reach beyond itself to immanence.

This hallucination in light and dark releases the gradations of secular time and distance into a supernatural hilltop and sublimity, heaving upward and pointing, sky beyond sky, to receive God in an instant. As Thoreau would say, it is a light to behold but to dwell not in.

JACK BARTH
Artist

Madonna and Child
c.1480, Carlo Crivelli

Hidden among the many blockbusters in the Metropolitan Museum of Art are some wonderful little jewels that are, unfortunately, often overlooked by the average visitor. Carlo Crivelli's *Madonna and Child* is one of these.

Crivelli originally lived in Venice but left the city after serving a short prison term in 1457 for seducing a married woman. From that time forward he painted in the Provincia di Ancona. While Giovanni Bellini painted with oils in the new Renaissance manner, Crivelli, using egg tempera, created masterpieces more visually aligned with the Gothic painting tradition. The word best used to describe his paintings is sumptuous. His pensive Madonnas are cloaked in fabrics that are gilded and tooled so as to reflect, almost kinetically, a warm golden glow back to the viewer. During the early Renaissance this sheen was believed to be heavenly light.

This particular painting has the Virgin surrounded by a beautiful garland similar to those Andrea Mantegna used to adorn his Madonnas. However, unlike Mantegna, who used exotic assortments of fruits and flowers to construct his garlands, Crivelli preferred everyday fruits and mundane vegetables.

The Madonna has long, elegant, and slightly spidery fingers, a characteristic often found in Crivelli's paintings. She stands before a hanging drapery in Bellini-esque fashion while slivers of the local landscape appear on either side of the cloth. The baby Jesus sits on a bumpy lavender cushion that looks as if it could have been tailored from a hunk of dyed ostrich skin and ponders a housefly (a symbol of evil) the size of his foot. He simultaneously clutches a goldfinch, which, like the giant cuke, symbolizes redemption.

The juxtaposition of these wonderfully strange objects, the impact of the tooled gold, the peaceful, meditative Virgin, and the magnificent use of color, make this a jewel of a painting not to be missed.

FRED WESSEL

Artist and Professor Emeritus, Hartford Art School, University of Hartford

The Triumph of Marius
1729, Giovanni Battista Tiepolo

Elizabeth Farren, Later Countess of Derby
1790, Sir Thomas Lawrence

A brimstone-yellow banner flutters against a hot Italian sky and compels the eye and mind up the great staircase of the Metropolitan and into the collection of European paintings. The dazzling half-smile of an actress out for a walk on a breezy spring day makes further exploration of the English rooms hard to resist. Both these superb paintings display the particular genius of the Metropolitan for leading us effortlessly from one room of the enormous building into the next. Their appeal is immediate and obvious, but they are also about aspirations, both extinct and alive. Tiepolo's rich, shadowed procession of a Roman victory over the Moors reminded Venetians of their claimed—if phony—descent from ancient Rome, and of the political power they had just relinquished. There's a vintage, sulky-lipped Tiepolo matron in the bottom right-hand corner, but basically this is a great painting of a brimstone-yellow banner.

Known as "The Queen of Comedy" at London's Haymarket and Drury Lane theaters, Elizabeth Farren was so furious when Lawrence first catalogued her portrait as

An Actress that she demanded (and received) an apology. He claimed his original title had been *Portrait of a Lady*. Farren also wanted him to make her look fatter—Regency times were just around the corner and gentlemen's tastes were running to the zaftig. Happily, he declined, and gave us the best of everything: Portrait of an Actress Classy Enough to be a Lady. Dressed in oyster satin and furs, her face turning just long enough for the painter to capture its candour, she's gorgeous. The Earl of Derby had been potty about her for years and, Reader, she married him.

MICHAEL RATCLIFFE
Former literary editor and chief book critic, The Times (London)

Asian Art
Second floor

11

The Astor Court
1981

You don't know serenity until you visit the Chinese Scholar's Garden in the Metropolitan Museum. Ask for the Astor Court, named for the philanthropic Mrs. Brooke Astor, whose foundation paid for it. Tucked among the Asian Galleries on the second floor, this island of tranquility is modeled on a Ming dynasty courtyard—in the "Garden of the Master of the Fishing Nets"—in Suzhou, China, a city near Shanghai once renowned for its culture and elegance.

In those ancient times, a learned man had a scrupulously sculptured garden to which he might repair for composing poetic thoughts, maybe for tea and conversation, or just for quiet contemplation. In the Met, you might go to the garden to wonder at the delicacy of its design, to take a break from the hubbub, or even to compose your own verse. Others may be resting there when you enter, never many and always hushed.

The principal entrance is a moon gate—a big round hole in the wall, flanked by lions, under a motto that reveals the

garden's secret in archaic script: "In search of quietude."
The space inside measures about sixty by forty feet. A
sheltered walkway lines two sides, with low walls to sit on.
A graceful pavilion stands opposite, beside a spring trickling
through rocks into a goldfish pond. Windows, cut out in
lattice patterns, frame living bamboo and Asian grasses, while
a large skylight bathes the scene in sunshine (on a good day).
Everything about this lovely space came from China: the tile
from an old imperial kiln reactivated for just this purpose;
eroded rock formations from the bottom of Lake Tai, near
Suzhou; timber from gingko, camphor and fir trees, and the
rare *nan* evergreen. The garden and the fine paneled room
that opens onto it were installed by twenty-seven Chinese
craftsmen in 1980. They created a secret gem.

RICHARD MOONEY
Journalist

Iris and B. Gerald Cantor Roof Garden

1987, Kevin Roche, John Dinkeloo & Associates
Rooftop of Lila Acheson Wallace Wing
Open May to October.

After living in New York and visiting for many years,
I face the challenge—how to see all those old friends and
professional contacts when I'm only in town for a few
days? Answer: arrange a collective rendezvous at 6 p.m.
on Friday on the rooftop terrace of the Metropolitan
Museum (open until 9 p.m. on Fridays and Saturdays).
Cocktails, superb sculpture, views over Central Park of
the capital of capitalism—the apotheosis of civilization.

FENTON JOHNSON
Writer

🍴 Lunch on the roof of the Metropolitan Museum—the
fourth-floor Sculpture Garden—great view of Central Park
and Midtown and Central Park West skylines.

JEAN PARKER PHIFER
Architect

11.15 Neue Galerie New York

1914, Carrère & Hastings
1048 Fifth Avenue at East 86th Street
☎ 212 628 6200; www.neuegalerie.org
Closed Tuesdays and Wednesdays.

If you ever wished for an art museum with an excellent collection that you could survey in its entirety in one visit, the Neue Galerie is for you. This small museum is housed in an elegant former mansion, dating from 1914. Originally designed as a private residence by Carrère & Hastings (who also designed the New York Public Library), it was occupied at one time by Mrs. Cornelius Vanderbilt III. More recently, it was home to the YIVO Institute for Jewish Research.

The collection focuses on German and Austrian fine art and decorative art of the early twentieth century. It is derived from the holdings of Serge Sabarsky and Ronald Lauder, an art dealer and businessman respectively, who share an abiding interest in this field. They purchased the building in 1994. You may or may not be familiar with the several German schools represented, namely, Die Brücke, Der Blaue Reiter, Neue Sachlichkeit, Bauhaus, and Werkbund. You will, however, recognize many of the artists they included, such as Klee, Schiele, Kandinsky, Klimt, Hoffmann, Van der Rohe, and many others who are shown at their very best.

LAWRENCE KAHN
Professor Emeritus of Pediatrics, Washington University

11.16 Solomon R. Guggenheim Museum

1959, Frank Lloyd Wright; 1992, addition by Gwathmey Siegel & Associates
1071 Fifth Avenue between East 88th and East 89th Streets
☎ 212 423 3500; www.guggenheim.org
Closed Thursdays.

Frank Lloyd Wright chose the location for the Guggenheim Museum for its proximity to Central Park, and his design encourages the visitor to communicate with nature, particularly from the vantage point of the small rotunda, or "Monitor Building," as he called it. Here, two glass-enclosed mini-rotundas are inscribed in wide terraces, one rectangular and one round. Although visitors are not allowed access onto these terraces, the new Gwathmey Siegel tower building, completed in 1992, includes a marvelous jewel of a sculpture terrace, which is open to the public. Access is through the fifth-level tower gallery. From this perch, the visitor has a superb view of Central Park and the Reservoir. An added bonus is a sculpture or group of sculptures from the Guggenheim's collection. Go at sunset and enjoy the silhouetted skyline of Central Park West. This is the view of only the privileged few who live on Fifth Avenue overlooking the park. An added attraction is reduced museum admission on Saturdays after 6 p.m.

After the Guggenheim, explore the charming residential neighborhood of Carnegie Hill and the Guggenheim's neighboring museums, including the Smithsonian's Cooper-Hewitt National Design Museum and the Jewish Museum (see p. 246). Pick up a picnic lunch from the museum café or any of the take-out shops on Madison and dine in the park. The most beautiful spot is the Conservatory Garden on Fifth Avenue and 104th Street (see p. 270).

LISA DENNISON
Executive, Sotheby's

11.17 Carnegie Mansion, now Smithsonian's Cooper-Hewitt, National Design Museum

1903, Babb, Cook & Willard
2 East 91st Street at Fifth Avenue
☏ 212 849 8400; www.cooperhewitt.org

Arthur Ross Terrace and Garden

Andrew Carnegie left us a legacy of public libraries across the country, but one of the best places to read is the garden in what was his own backyard. Now the Arthur Ross Terrace and Garden behind the Cooper-Hewitt, this plot of land is a well-kept oasis at the highest elevation on Fifth Avenue, located between 90th and 91st Streets. Descending the steps from Carnegie's former home, one enters a central lawn set among lovely plantings, with the original wisteria still flowering. Along a picturesque path winding around the circumference are welcoming benches, ideal for spending a bucolic afternoon outside while in the city. Looking through the enclosing wrought-iron fence (the only flaw in the view), west to Central Park and south to apartment buildings and the Church of the Heavenly Rest, it is hard to imagine that for the first fifteen years the Carnegies were in residence, the plot across the street held a decrepit wooden shack that sold lemonade, peanuts, ginger cakes, and other snacks. Now, the perfect afternoon in the garden includes a treat from one of Carnegie Hill's nearby gourmet food shops and an absorbing book—Mr. Carnegie no doubt would approve.

11

While neighbors used to be privileged with private keys, now all visitors access the garden through the Carnegie mansion, which Andrew and his wife, Louise, built for his retirement, intended as "the most modest, plainest and most roomy house in New York." (Along the way, take time to look for the charming period details adorning the interior of the house or view the exhibitions featuring objects from the extraordinary collections amassed by the Hewitt sisters.) Daydreaming in the garden, while looking at the southwest corner of the back limestone-and-brick façade, one can imagine Carnegie in his office within his private suite of rooms. Visitors would come seeking donations from Carnegie, who devoted the end of his life to dispensing his wealth for the benefit of society. To get to the philanthropist, suppliants had to pass through a small vestibule with a dropped ceiling then duck through a low doorway (Carnegie was only 5'2") to enter a library dominated by a painted frieze of inspirational quotations, where they would await the small but powerful man.

LISA PODOS
Arts educator

11.18 The Jewish Museum

1908, C. P. H. Gilbert; 1993, addition by Kevin Roche
1109 Fifth Avenue at 92nd Street
☎ 212 423 3200; www.thejewishmuseum.org
Closed Wednesdays.

In the heart of New York City there is a piece of ancient Jerusalem—a foundation stone from a wall that protected the city in the first century that tells a story of desperation, disaster, and transformation. In 66 C.E., the Jews of ancient Israel rebelled against their Roman overlords and hastily completed the city wall as a part of their defense system. The wall did not hold, however; the Roman army breached it, going on to destroy Jerusalem and the Temple, the focus of ancient sacrificial worship. The Jews were exiled from the city and were forced to devise an alternative form of worship, based on prayer in the synagogue and the study of the sacred texts. This new form of worship became the mainstay of Judaism thereafter. All this can be read from a single stone!

The foundation stone is one of more than eight hundred works of art and artifacts on view in the Jewish Museum's permanent exhibition, "Culture and Continuity: The Jewish Journey." Each tells a part of the dramatic story of the Jewish people's artistic and cultural creativity in response to the challenges of preserving and defining their identity over four millennia. I have many favorite objects in the show in addition to the foundation stone. One is a nineteenth-century Hanukkah lamp from Australia, decorated with kangaroos and emus. It started out as a souvenir from Down Under, with an emu egg hanging in the center. When the egg eventually broke, someone decided to convert it into a

Hanukkah lamp. Another favorite, also from the nineteenth century, is a painting by the German artist Moritz Oppenheim titled *The Return of the Jewish Volunteer*. It reflects both the opportunities and conflicts Jews experienced after the Emancipation, when they were allowed for the first time to participate as citizens in the activities of their adopted homeland. In the painting, the soldier has just arrived home from his unit, interrupting his family's Sabbath observance. While he is now free to serve his country, he has broken with his religious tradition by traveling on the Sabbath.

After viewing the permanent exhibition, the visitor might take a rest by examining the museum building itself, which is a gem. It was designed by Charles Prendergast H. Gilbert in the style of a François er French Gothic château. The second floor of the museum retains many of the original details of the rooms from the first half of the twentieth century, when the mansion was occupied by Felix and Frieda Schiff Warburg. In 1993, an addition was made to the building and the interior of the original mansion renovated. Architect Kevin Roche chose to extend the French Gothic façade and interior decoration, and the visitor will be hard-pressed to distinguish the original parts of the mansion from the more recent addition.

SUSAN L. BRAUNSTEIN
Curator of Archaeology and Judaica, The Jewish Museum

11.19 Clapboard House

1852, attributed to Albro Howell
160 East 92nd Street between Lexington and Third Avenues
Not open to the public.

This 1852 two-and-a-half-story residence is one of only a handful of wood frame houses remaining on the Upper East Side. In 1915, it was purchased by Willard Straight and his wife to serve as servants's quarters for their Fifth Avenue mansion on the corner of 94th Street.

The charming house has classical fluted columns on the

first-floor porch and the upper stories have wooden shutters at their windows. Although it's a designated New York City Landmark, this romantic and evocative orphan has received too little loving care in recent years.

MARGOT GAYLE
The late Margot Gayle was a preservationist, and co-founder of the Victorian Society of America.

11.20 Kitchen Arts & Letters

1435 Lexington Avenue between East 93rd and East 94th Streets
☎ 212 876 5550; www.kitchenartsandletters.com
Closed Sundays. (Closed Saturdays and Sundays in July and August.)

Proprietor Nach Waxman carries a marvelous assortment of books on food and wine, culinary history, and food ephemera. It's absolutely top drawer. He sells one food product, which happens to be my favorite olive oil—Alziari, in the beautiful blue can with stars on it. It's from Nice and is suave and full-flavored.

JANE DANIELS LEAR
Food and travel writer

11.21 St. Nicholas Russian Orthodox Cathedral

1902, John Bergesen
15 East 97th Street between Fifth and Madison Avenues
☎ 212 996 6638; www.russianchurchusa.org

St. Nicholas Russian Orthodox Cathedral of New York is the only example of Moscow Baroque in the United States, and a particularly splendid one. It is reminiscent of the world-famous Church of Protection in the historic Russian village of Fili (constructed in 1693), St. Nicholas-the-Great-Cross in Moscow, and several others. The cathedral is decorated with frescoes by the renowned Russian artist Sokolov, and in 1973 was declared a landmark by the City of New York. Few are aware, however, that this building is something of a monument to entirely different Russian-American relations that are today difficult to imagine. These could be characterized as the relations, if not between friends, then between close acquaintances, and span from the cultural to the military. The initial contributions toward the construction of the cathedral were made by the sailors of the Russian warship *Retvizan*, on which could be seen the mark "Made in Philadelphia." The *Retvizan* was sunk in the Russo-Japanese war and a cross from the ship's chapel was saved. Today this cross hangs in the cathedral.

The construction of the cathedral is connected with the then head of the mission of the Russian Church in the United States, Bishop Tikhon (Belavin). Bishop Tikhon was fluent in English and was able to establish strong and useful contacts in New York when he moved his headquarters here from San Francisco. He was to be the famous Moscow Patriarch, elected after Russia's February Revolution, who died in 1925, most likely with the participation of the Bolshevik administration. From 1924 to 1960, St. Nicholas Russian Orthodox Cathedral, in the heart of Manhattan, was the subject of a protracted legal battle over ownership of this remarkable example of Moscow Baroque.

YURI MILOSLAVSKY
Writer

11

11.22 Museum of the City of New York

1930, Joseph H. Freedlander
1220 Fifth Avenue at East 103rd Street
☏ 212 534 1672; www.mcny.org
Closed Mondays.

On Fifth Avenue, a stone's throw away from the magnificent Conservatory Garden in Central Park, is the Museum of the City of New York, home to a wonderful toy collection that tells the story of growing up in New York over the last three centuries. Particularly thrilling is a quiet room filled with antique doll houses dating back to 1769. As you contemplate these miniature universes filled with dolls dressed by long-forgotten children, a lost world begins to shimmer in your mind's eye. The crown jewel of the collection is the Stettheimer Doll House, created in the 1920s by Carrie Walter Stettheimer, hostess to New York City's avant-garde artists and writers. This extraordinarily detailed evocation of the Stettheimer's home and life has its own art gallery, which houses such works as Marcel Duchamp's miniature version of his *Nude Descending a Staircase*, an alabaster *Venus* by Gaston Lachaise, and other works of art by Albert Gleizes, and Marguerite and William Zorach.

Before you leave, take a look at Elizabeth Yandell's treasure box, circa 1885. Elizabeth, orphaned when she was six years old, kept this special box throughout her life, bringing it out on occasion to amuse her own children when they were ill. It's filled with mementos—a piece of rope from a trip to Europe, an autograph album, a favorite wax doll resplendent in a red-tasseled hat and gold-buttoned jacket, an assortment of shells and stones, a stuffed cat and dog, their fur rubbed smooth. Elizabeth's sadnesses and joys come vividly to life, although the child has

> *. . . grown up and gone away,*
> *And it is but a child of air*
> *That lingers in the garden there.*
> —R. L. Stevenson, "To Any Reader."

ANNE LANDSMAN
Novelist

11.23 El Museo del Barrio

1230 Fifth Avenue at East 104th Street
☎ 212 831 7272; www.elmuseo.org
Closed Mondays.

At El Museo del Barrio you will find a permanent exhibit of works by the Taino, a pre-Colombian Caribbean culture, as well as temporary exhibitions that might include such renowned Hispano-American artists as Frida Kahlo and

Diego Rivera (Mexico), Francisco Oller (Puerto Rico), Fernando Botero (Colombia), Amelia Paez (Cuba), and other Latin-American masters of the arts. Through their paintings one gets to know the passions, the imagination, the originality, the devotion, and the fascinating sense of style that has propelled these artists to become international figures in the art world.

ANITA VELEZ-MITCHELL
Writer

11.24 Gracie Mansion

1804, attributed to Ezra Weeks
In Carl Schurz Park, enter at East 88th Street and East End Avenue

📞 212 570 4751; www.nyc.gov/html/artcom
Check website for information about tours.

11

Most Gracie Mansion visitors are drawn by the prospect of seeing the Federal-period house and its collection of fine and decorative art, or by the possibility of catching a glimpse of New York's mayor. However, three lesser-known features reveal traces of previous residents.

Elegant floor-to-ceiling windows in the Mayor's Library overlook the East River. On one windowpane is etched in script, "Millie, 1875," and beneath in a bold scrawl "Margie, 1965." Amalia Hermione Wheaton (Millie) was born at the mansion, and as a young girl scratched her name and birth-date on the window. Almost a century later, the young daughter of newly elected Mayor John Lindsay spotted the window. Her mother, pleased to have Margie bond with her new home, permitted her to write her own name on the glass.

The mansion's front door is framed by a finely carved Adam-style surround. Sharp-eyed guests note an odd, angled notch cut into the right side of the doorjamb. During the mayoralty of Edward I. Koch, the notch held a traditional Jewish mezuzah, a small case containing a piece of parchment. Written on the parchment is the Shema prayer, which

reminds Jews of their obligations toward God. It is customary to kiss the mezuzah in passing. The mezuzah was
removed at the end of Mr. Koch's term.

During early-twentieth-century construction projects,
workers unearthed remains of narrow stone-lined tunnels
leading from the mansion's basement to the riverbank.
Historians identified the tunnels either as an escape route
built during the American Revolution or as a stop on the
Underground Railroad during the Civil War period. Visitors
ask about the rumor that Mayor William O'Dwyer stashed
money missing from city coffers in the tunnels before
abruptly departing for Mexico in 1950. These stories are
not true; modern archaeology has revealed instead that the
tunnels, of the same vintage as the 1799 house, provided
drainage for the basement, which tended to flood. The real
secret is that the basement still floods.

DAVID L. REESE
Director, Gunster Hall, Virginia

11.25 **Sotheby's**
1334 York Avenue at East 72nd Street

Sotheby's Terrace Cafe
Tenth floor
☏ 212 606 7070; www.sothebys.com
Closes at 4 p.m.

Bid
In the lobby
☏ 212 988 7730; www.sothebys.com

🍴 Enter the new Sotheby's building, proceed directly to the
tenth floor, grab a hot *panino* or a salad in the café, and
head outside to the terrace. Linger and enjoy the great city
feel. When you've had enough, walk back inside to the
best new gallery space in New York City...some say in
America. Or wander among French furniture, antiques,

fab jewels, or very affordable prints, all on view on the approximately seventy-five-thousand square feet of exhibition space.

As a more serious alternative to the café, try Bid on the ground floor of Sotheby's: a wonderful "multi-starred" new American restaurant.

GERALDINE NAGER-GRIFFIN
Senior vice president, Sotheby's

11.26 Rockefeller University

1910, York & Sawyer
1230 York Avenue between East 63rd and East 68th Streets

Caspary Auditorium

1957, Harrison & Abramovitz
☎ 212 327 8000; www.rockefeller.edu
Open to the public for events only.

11

Harrison & Abramovitz's dreamy, hemispherical dome could have floated over from a World's Fair. This colossal sunken sphere, a forty-foot-high, ninety-foot-diameter bubble, was once covered with beautiful blue tiles. Slide into an aisle seat to gaze at the convex circles bulging everywhere. Imagine being inside a giant golf ball.

TRACEY HUMMER AND FREDERIC SCHWARTZ
Writer and Architect

11.27 Mount Vernon Hotel Museum & Garden, formerly the Abigail Adams Smith Museum

421 East 61st Street between First and York Avenues
☎ 212 838 6878; www.mvhm.org
Closed Mondays.

This is great fun—an eighteenth-century carriage house hidden in the middle of the city.

In 1796, William Stephens Smith and his wife Abigail Adams Smith, daughter of President John Adams, began construction of an estate on twenty-three acres of Manhattan's Upper East Side, at the time a rural area and a refuge from the congested city to the south. They named it Mount Vernon in honor of George Washington's Virginia home. Unfortunately, beset by financial troubles, the couple had to sell their unfinished property just a year later. By the turn of the century, under a different owner, the main house and stone carriage house (now housing the museum) were completed. In 1826, the main house was destroyed by fire and the carriage house was converted into a posh day resort called the Mount Vernon Hotel. The hotel operated there until 1833 and today is New York City's only surviving day hotel—one of only a handful of sites in the United States affording a window on hotel life in the early nineteenth century. It also contains a beautiful decorative arts collection, along with furniture, costumes, quilts and textiles, and historical documents.

LAURA LINNEY
Actor

Museum Evenings

www.iheartnymuseums.com

A city's best-kept secrets are often in plain sight. As any tour book will tell you in its listing of hours, most of the major museums in New York are open late on Friday and Saturday evenings. As many longtime aficionados of art in the city know, this is the time when tourists head downtown for dinner and the theater, and you can view the art undisturbed.

ELIZABETH WINTHROP
Writer

Museum Evening Hours

Admission is often waived, or discounted, during evening hours. Check websites for times, as they may vary.

Museum of Jewish Heritage (see p. 28)
Wednesdays until 8 p.m.; www.mjhnyc.org

El Museo del Barrio (see p. 250)
Wednesdays until 9 p.m.; www.elmuseo.org

National Museum of the American Indian (see p. 17)
Thursdays until 8 p.m.; www.nmai.si.edu

Paley Centre for Media (see p. 177)
Thursdays until 8 p.m.; www.paleycenter.org

The Jewish Museum (see p. 246)
Thursdays until 8 p.m.; www.thejewishmuseum.org

Museum of Arts & Design (see p. 175)
Thursdays from 6 p.m. to 9 p.m.; www.madmuseum.org

The Museum of Modern Art (see p. 194)
Fridays until 8 p.m.; www.moma.org

Whitney Museum of American Art (see p. 220)
Fridays until 9 p.m.; www.whitney.org

The Studio Museum in Harlem (see p. 307)
Thursdays and Fridays until 9 p.m.; www.studiomuseum.org

Solomon R. Guggenheim Museum (see p. 243)
Saturdays until 7:45 p.m.; www.guggenheim.org

The Metropolitan Museum of Art (see p. 224)
Fridays and Saturdays until 9 p.m.; www.metmuseum.org

12

Cathedral Pkwy
B'way
W 109th St
W 108th St
W 107th St
W 106th St
W 105th St
W 104th St
W 103rd St
W 102nd St
W 101st St
W 100th St
W 99th St
W 98th St

Riverside Dr.
Amsterdam Avenue
Columbus Avenue
Manhattan Avenue
Central Park West

Central Park North

Harlem Meer

Cons
G

The Pool

North Meadow

97th St Transverse

W 97th St
W 96th St
W 95th St
W 94th St
W 93rd St
W 92nd St
W 91st St
W 90th St
W 89th St
W 88th St
W 87th St
W 86th St
W 85th St
W 84th St
W 83rd St
W 82nd St
W 81st St

Central Park

Jacqueline Onassis Reservoir

86th St Transverse

The Great Lawn

Me
M

Riverside Park

West Side Hwy (Henry Hudson Pkwy)

Riverside Drive

West End Avenue

Broadway

Amsterdam Avenue

Columbus Avenue

Central Park West

Upper West Side

Hudson River

W 80th St
W 79th St
W 78th St
W 77th St
W 76th St

American Museum of Natural History

Delacorte Theater
Turtle Pond
Belvedere Castle
79th St Transverse

W 75th St
W 74th St
W 73rd St
W 72nd St
W 71st St
W 70th St
W 69th St
W 68th St
W 67th St
W 66th St
W 65th St

The Ramble

The Lake

West Drive

Strawberry Fields

Terrace Dr.

Cons
V

The Mall

Sheep Meadow

Lincoln Center

Freedom Pl

Joe DiMaggio Hwy

West End Avenue

Amsterdam Avenue

Columbus Avenue

Central Park West

W 64th St
W 63rd St
W 62nd St
W 61st St
W 60th St
W 59th St

65th St Transverse

Carousel
Wollman Rink

Central Drive

East Dr.

The Pon

Columbus Circle
Central Park South

CHAPTER 12

CENTRAL PARK & UPPER WEST SIDE

CENTRAL PARK
1876, Frederick Law Olmsted & Calvert Vaux
Central Park South (59th Street) to Central Park North
(110th Street) between Fifth Avenue and Central Park West

`12.1` Wollman Memorial Rink
1950, rebuilt early 1980s
Southeast corner of park, enter at Fifth Avenue and
East 60th Street
☏ 212 439 6900; www.wollmanskatingrink.com
Open from late October to early April.

New York City has several outdoor ice skating rinks, but
skating at the Wollman Rink in Central Park, especially at
night, is a transcendent experience. I always think of the
opening sequence of Woody Allen's *Manhattan*—you can
almost hear Gershwin playing as you stare at the illuminated skyline of Central Park South. In the early evening
when the kids go home, you can skate to Sinatra, Ella
Fitzgerald, Fred Astaire, and Duke Ellington. There's a sense
of continuity as you imagine the New Yorkers who skated
on this spot a hundred years ago, when this part of New
York was so far uptown it was considered "the country."
They were dressed more formally—long skirts, bonnets,
and fur muffs for the women, suits and overcoats for the
gentlemen. But the delightful feeling of gliding, the shared
silliness, the thrill of being outdoors on a cold night—these
things don't change with the times. Go on "Cheap Skate"
nights, when the admission fee is discounted and there's
usually enough room to fall without taking anyone down
with you. Bring your own skates if you can—the hard
green plastic rental skates with frayed laces do not inspire
gracefulness. Every hour or so the ice is cleared and it's
time for a cup of the most delicious hot chocolate in the
city. I don't know if it's really tastier than any other, but

it seems that way when you are warming your frigid fingers with the heat from the paper cup and watching the Zamboni machine sweep the ice to a glassy smoothness. As the hot liquid travels through you, and the smell of chocolate fills you up, everything seems right with the world.

GINA ROGAK
Director of special events, Whitney Museum of American Art

12.2 Central Park Zoo

Redesigned 1988, Kevin Roche, John Dinkeloo & Associates
Enter at Fifth Avenue and East 64th Street
☎ 212 439 6500; www.centralparkzoo.com
Check the website for hours.

Go to the Central Park Zoo and pay tribute to the seals, then check in with the penguins, and then the polar bears, and your head will be screwed back on properly.

JOHN GUARE
Playwright

Madagascar Giant Day Gecko
Tropic Zone

In this city of egos where everyone's clamoring, "Look at me! Look at me!" there is one exquisite creature that makes a point of invisibility. Its beauty is so shocking that people cry out in surprise when they see it. That is, if they can see it.

It's displayed behind a floodlit window like a priceless piece of jewelry, but finding it amidst the tangle of ferns can take a good twenty minutes. It's not only a master of camouflage, but like the silver mime who works the subway, it rarely moves, clinging to the wall like a wad of chewed gum. Parents tend to spot it first—the electric-green Madagascar giant day gecko that lives in the Tropic Zone of the Central Park Zoo, along with two motionless tomato frogs.

Waiting for this shy and dainty soul to reveal itself takes time. A lot of time. Many don't have the patience and move on to the frolicking penguins and polar bears. But for those who adjust their vision to this miniature stage set, the rewards are exhilarating.

Suddenly, there it is! Glued to the wall beneath a fern! An intensely green lizard with a sprinkling of orange spots on its head and back. It's about a foot long with four hilarious cartoon toes on each foot. Its shiny black eyes are lidless and never flicker. Its only sign of life is a slight pulsing of the stomach. Avert your gaze for a moment, and it's gone. All you see are ferns and the two orange tomato frogs miserably trying to conceal themselves on the leafy green floor.

So there you stand, waiting for just one more glimpse. Now you see it, now you don't—the most ravishing peep show in all of New York City.

TINA HOWE
Playwright

12.4   Balto

1925, Frederick G. R. Roth
West of East Drive and 67th Street and north of the Zoo
www.centralpark.com

One of the statues in Central Park is a bronze of an Alaskan sled dog, a husky named Balto. The big dog seems a little out of place in New York, and his story involves a largely forgotten event in a faraway place.

In January 1925, in the depths of an exceptionally bitter winter, an epidemic of diphtheria broke out in Nome, on Alaska's west coast. The supply of antitoxin serum was soon used up, and with the coast ice-bound and no planes available, it was decided that the best way to get more serum was by dogsled. Twenty teams would be used in a relay that would start from the nearest point reachable by rail—almost seven hundred miles from Nome.

The serum was poured into a cylinder wrapped in a quilt. Each village along the route dispatched its best musher, teamed with the best dogs, to carry the cylinder through its territory. Along the way, temperatures dropped to more than sixty below, wind blew up to eighty miles per hour, and blizzard after blizzard rendered the crude trail invisible. One team was almost stranded on an ice floe. Two dogs froze to death.

The trip took seven days, and when the serum arrived safely in Nome, the story of "the great race of mercy" was widely reported. Nome's best-known dogsled racer, a man named Leonhard Seppala, had carried the serum more than ninety miles—twice as far as any other musher—and his daring wilderness exploits made him a hero to newspaper readers around the country.

In recent years, the success of the Iditarod race, which retraces much of the original route of the serum run, has revived the Seppala legend, and many people assume that Balto was Seppala's lead dog. In fact, Seppala passed over the black husky when he picked his team, preferring a faster dog named Togo. Balto, left behind, was then chosen by Gunnar Kaasen, the musher who wound up completing the final leg of the journey. Thus Balto, not Togo, was around for the photo op when Kassen handed the serum to Nome's doctor.

12

So visit Balto (in the winter, it's better that way), being sure to check for the ironic grin on his bronze mouth—and take your pooch.

SAM POSEY
Race-car driver, artist, and designer

12.5   Central Park Tour

Enter at Fifth Avenue at 67th Street
www.centralpark.com

Throughout Western civilization, public parks have been designed to provide an array of recreational opportunities, and Central Park may be viewed as the pinnacle of this achievement. My favorite walk through this park takes into account the use New Yorkers make of it, in addition to its finest views, its historical highlights, its natural charms, and some of its dramatic twists.

Enter the park from Fifth Avenue at 67th Street, and walk west to the statue of Balto (see p. 260). The statue honors the sled dog that saved Alaska from diphtheria and it has been sat upon by every kid passing by. Proceed westward through the tunnel until you come up onto Literary Walk. Pass Shakespeare and Burns, turn right and head north. This famous walk is lined with a spectacular collection of elm trees and is Frederick Law Olmsted's quintessential Victorian strolling promenade. Cross over 72nd Street, down the magnificent stairs, around Bethesda Fountain, and then bear slightly left to cross Bow Bridge, one of the two finest of the five original cast-iron bridges remaining in the park. Swans, boats, and lovers abound. Once across the bridge, head into the Ramble (see p. 265). Perhaps one of the greatest stopover points for migratory birds, the Ramble also plays host to meandering streams, Adirondack-style rustic benches, and all sorts of people.

Wend your way due north until you come out at Belvedere Castle with its medieval parapets and breathtaking views of the Great Lawn. Check out the Nature Center and ask the rangers some questions. Look carefully fifty yards to the east of the castle on the north side of the transverse: these secret stairs have taken many of the famous and notable—Paul Simon and a president or two—to and from great events. Stroll down around Turtle Pond and the Great Lawn if you have the time. Turn south now and find your way into and through the Shakespeare Garden (see p. 268) and past the Swedish Cottage (see p. 266). If you want to pop out of the park and visit the American Museum of Natural History (my favorite place in New York City), then do so here at 81st Street. Otherwise, stroll down along the west side of the lake, up into Yoko Ono's Strawberry Fields (see p. 265) and pause at the "Imagine" mosaic. Candles and hippies are always here. Continue down past the Sheep Meadow, where city residents get their tan and youngsters meet. Exit at Columbus Circle or head back east if you care to dally at the Central Park Zoo, with its resplendent tropical birds, awesome penguin display, and idiosyncratic polar bears.

ALEXANDER R. BRASH
Chairman, Habitat Committee in the EPA's Harbor Estuary Program

12.6 Bethesda Terrace

1862, Calvert Vaux, designer; Jacob Wrey Mould, sculptor
Mid-park at 72nd Street
www.centralpark.com

The stonework at Bethesda Terrace at 72nd Street merits a close look. Moving east to west, the hand-carved sandstone piers and balustrades flanking the stairs both north and south of the road represent 1) spring, youth, dawn; 2) summer, adolescence, noon; 3) fall, adulthood, afternoon; 4) winter, old age, evening.

JEAN PARKER PHIFER
Architect

12

12.7 Conservatory Water

North of the Fifth Avenue and 72nd Street entrance
www.centralpark.com

Red-tailed hawks

In late spring and early summer, between May and July, the best show in town is at the Model Boat Pond. Along its west shore, facing Fifth Avenue, you'll find people with serious telescopes on tripods aimed up at the twelfth story of a building facing the park just north of 72nd Street. What's up there is a massive, sprawling nest of twigs that tops a long classical arch on the building's façade. The nest—huge and messy, and under the official protection of the National Fish and Wildlife Department—is the home of the red-tailed hawks who have made Central Park their unlikely home. Any of the telescope owners will let you have a look, and you can home in on this beautiful feral family, fierce-eyed, preening, and unbelievably wild. By June the chicks will be clearly visible in the nest, stalking stiffly back and forth, peering out across the park like sentries, waiting for dinner, leading their own unknowable lives before you. Suddenly, into your field of vision, a parent arrives; silent, a rush of reddish feathers, vast smothering wings beating backwards. The chicks make a swarming rush forward, there is a voracious flurry of attention, and dinner is over. The parent moves regally to the edge of the great nest, swivels its neck, gives a pitiless stare out into the park, and sails off again, gliding smoothly out into the upper air. The hawk-watchers cheer.

ROXANA ROBINSON
Author and biographer

12.8 The Still Hunt

1883, Edward Kemeys
East Drive at East 77th Street
www.centralpark.com

Walk down East Drive. On an overhang, find a bronze, life-size statue of a mountain lion, crouched ready to pounce. This Central Park reminder of the wilderness from which Manhattan was carved can have a startling effect on passersby who happen to glance up.

KASSY WILSON
Exhibitions coordinator, Museum of the City of New York

12.9 The Butterfly Habitat

Mid-park at 74th Street

To the left of the Boathouse Restaurant, near where bicycles are rented, is a fenced-in area with flowering wild plants. This is a butterfly habitat, a garden created specifically to attract the winged creatures. Beyond and to your left, up the pathway and then down, is "the point," a place where you can see Bethesda Fountain from the other side of the lake.

MARGOT ADLER
Correspondent, National Public Radio

12.10 **The Ramble**
Between 73rd and 78th Streets
www.centralpark.com

Shunned by many due to its reputation as a furtive and dangerous place by night, the Ramble is Frederick Law Olmsted's vision of primeval New York. Park thickets, untrimmed trees, and apparently unintended streams belie the skilled artfulness of this romantic pre-Gotham fantasy. Rustic stonework and a few ruins are the only hint that this place, like everything else in Manhattan, has been willfully shaped by man.

WALTER CHATHAM
Architect

12

12.11 **Strawberry Fields**
Near Central Park West between 71st and 74th Streets
www.centralpark.com

Enter the park at West 72nd Street and find Strawberry Fields, the oasis planted by Yoko Ono in memory of John Lennon. You can be one of the thousands who have stood for a meditative moment by the Italian mosaic circle inscribed with the word "Imagine." Every year on the night of the anniversary of John Lennon's death (December 8, 1980), several hundred people gather here, holding candles and flowers. They sing every Beatles song they can remember until about one o'clock in the morning, when the police insist that they leave. Strawberry Fields has lovely grass

to lie on, luxurious plantings of trees and foliage, and a
sense of peace that is extraordinary in New York City.
MARGOT ADLER
Correspondent, National Public Radio

12.12 Swedish Cottage Marionette Theater

1876, Manneus Isaeus
Between Delacorte Theater and 79th Street Transverse
☎ 212 988 9093; www.centralpark.com
Reservations are required.

Central Park as a haven from the noise and the intensity
of everyday city life, is no secret. However, the park does
contain little-known features, one of which is the Swedish
Cottage Marionette Theater. Just south of the Delacorte
Theater, at the base of the Shakespeare Garden, one discov-
ers a nineteenth-century Swedish cottage designed originally
as a one-room schoolhouse exhibit by prominent Swedish
architect Manneus Isaeus for the 1876 Centennial Exposition
at Philadelphia. Frederick Law Olmsted was so taken with
it that he paid fifteen hundred dollars to have it shipped
and rebuilt in 1877 in the new park he co-designed in
New York.

Subsequently utilized as public restrooms, a nature study,
and civil-defense headquarters during World War II, in 1947
it became the headquarters and workshop of the Central
Park Marionette Theater, which produced touring shows.
Budget cuts eradicated funding for touring, and the interior
was redesigned in in1973 to include a permanent theater.

Decades of neglect and disrepair threatened the building
with demolition by the early 1990s. The long and distinguished history of delightful productions of children's
classics, in conjunction with the City Parks Foundation,
proved its saving grace. A coalition of private and public
interests raised funds for a $1.5 million renovation in 1997.

Besides a beautiful and historically faithful restoration of
the exterior details, a new proscenium stage and modern
technical facilities now enable the talented staff and visiting
artists to produce what is arguably the finest marionette
theater for children in the United States.

In May 1998, the Swedish Cottage Marionette Theater
reopened to the public with a glorious production of
Gulliver's Travels, followed by equally magnificent presen-
tations of *Jack and the Beanstalk* and *Sleeping Beauty*. At
a ticket price of five dollars, it's one of the true bargains
and secret treasures of New York.

KEVIN JOSEPH ROACH
Set designer

12.13 Bird-watching in Central Park

West 81st Street and Central Park West
For information about bird-watching:
NYC Audubon Society: ☎ 212 691 7483; www.nycaudubon.org
Linnaean Society: ☎ 212 252 2668; www.linnaeannewyork.org
Starr Saphir: ☎ 212 304 3808; 917 306 3808
Parks Department: www.nycgovparks.org

Birding is one of Central Park's best secrets. Indeed, it's
considered one of the fifteen most extraordinary birding
sites in the United States during spring and fall migrations.
That's because birds—more than two hundred and seventy
species—come to the park as they cross the Atlantic flyway.
Most New Yorkers believe the park belongs only to people,
pigeons, rats, and squirrels, but it turns out that suburbs
do not provide migrating birds with enough cover from
predatory hawks, so Central Park, with its seed-bearing
trees and forested areas, has become a haven for hundreds
of thousands of birds to rest and feed during their long
migratory flights.

A host of organizations, including the Audubon Society,

the Linnaean Society, and the Parks Department, lead bird-walks, and this is the best way to get a feel for birding in the park, especially since the best birding site, the Ramble, is a maze of complex paths in which it is easy to get lost. My favorite guide is Starr Saphir, who has been doing these walks for years, and even the total amateur, armed with a pair of binoculars, will see miraculous things in a couple of hours. I've lived near the park for fifty-two years, yet before I met Saphir, I had never seen a scarlet tanager, or a green heron, or twenty species of warblers.

The birding log, a diary in which expert birders record what they've seen in the park that day, can be found at the Boathouse Restaurant (where you can also get your morning coffee). Other animals and flowers are often included as well, and if you read back through the year's entries, you'll be amazed at the exuberant life of the park.

MARGOT ADLER
Correspondent, National Public Radio

12.14 The Shakespeare Garden

c. 1915
West 79th Traverse near Belvedere Castle

Each flower of this literary maze is mentioned in one of Shakespeare's poems or plays. The medley of herbs and flowers brings the Bard's works into a very beautiful and amazing tangle of winding green and varicolored swirls. This small garden offers lovely benches to sit amidst the poetry of posies and read Shakespeare's sonnets.

KAREN MOODY TOMPKINS
Artist

12.15 Delacorte Theater

1962, Eldon Elder
Mid-park, enter at Central Park West and West 81st Street or
Fifth Avenue and East 79th Street
☏ 212 539 8750; www.publictheater.org

In 1962, after a contentious dispute with Robert Moses
—the undisputed czar of public construction in New York
City for about thirty years—the enterprising theatrical
producer Joseph Papp obtained permission to perform
Shakespeare plays in the middle of Central Park. He set up
a group of bleachers and established free "Shakespeare in
the Park," which soon became a desirable summer attraction in New York (June through August). The unbeatable
Mr. Papp secured the promise of a check from George
Delacorte for the construction of a real amphitheater to be
built in lieu of the bleacher arrangement.

12

Unfortunately, a new mayor, less prone to cultural
fantasies than his predecessor, turned down the proposal
for a structure that would have remained through the ages,
though the design had already been approved by his own
commissioner of parks. Joe Papp's persistence eventually
forced the mayor to permit the creation of a two-thousand-
seat amphitheater, provided its wood appearance and main
platform construction marked it as a "temporary" structure.
The amphitheater has now stood for twenty-four years,
and though it requires yearly repairs, it is much enjoyed by
the community.

If one is willing to queue for them, free tickets are available only on the day of performance at either the Delacorte
Theater or the Public Theater (425 Lafayette Street). Senior
citizens have a less crowded queue of their own in front of
the Delacorte box office.

GIORGIO CAVAGLIERI
The late Giorgio Cavaglieri was an architect.

North End of Central Park
Above the 96th Street Transverse

Most people vaunt the pleasures of Central Park, but few have ventured to its northern end. Once feared as a haven of crime, now the only thrills that await visitors (during the daytime) are the mise-en-scène of raw rock, tight crevices, rushing water, and ruins of a fort that served in the War of 1812. Olmsted's attempts to make a veritable portrait of the natural world, running the gamut from the pastoral to the sublime, can only be fully savored by those who push into the undercrofts of the bridges and passages he created in the "wild" northern end above 100th Street. Calm your nerves afterwards in the refinements of the Conservatory Garden.

BARRY BERGDOLL
Philip Johnson Chief Curator of Architecture and Design,
The Museum of Modern Art

12.17 ### Conservatory Garden
1936, Gilmore D. Clarke, Thomas D. Price & M. Betty Sprout;
1983, redesigned by Lyndon B. Miller
Enter at Fifth Avenue between East 104th and East 105th Streets
www.centralpark.com

Central Park offers many pleasures, but none so unexpectedly delightful as the Conservatory Garden. Perhaps because most visitors frequent the southern end of the park, it comes as a complete surprise to walk through the ornate iron gate that once guarded Cornelius Vanderbilt's mansion on Fifth Avenue and 58th Street, and find yourself in this elegant time warp. There are three gardens, each in a different style. The south garden (my favorite) is done in informal English, themed to Frances Hodgson Burnett's children's classic *The Secret Garden*. Narrow slate paths bordered by exquisite plantings draw you to the center, where a tree-shaded lily pond, watched over by a bronze pair of children, attracts many birds.

The center garden is classic Italian, with its long mani-cured lawn leading to a dramatic, unadorned fountain spouting its single, geyser-like spray. In the background, a terrace of yew and spiraea lead upward to an arbor covered in Chinese wisteria, most beautiful in spring when it is overrun by purple blossoms.

The North Garden, with its shallow pool featuring a trio of dancing nymphs in its center, is French. Enter from one of its four arbors, covered with white-and-pink-tinted roses. This garden offers dazzling displays of tulips in spring and chrysanthemums in the fall. Come on a beautiful day and be prepared to stay a while.

LORRAINE B. DIEHL
Writer

12

I treasure the formal, symmetrical walks of the Conservatory Garden at 105th Street in Central Park. The fountains and their quiet, enclosed surroundings are a sheer joy, especially the fountain in the North Garden, where nymphs combine innocence and hedonism in a perfect, idiosyncratic picture of happy youth in motion.

MARIA ARRILLAGA
Writer and professor

Amidst the magnitude of the city, you can sit in relative quiet, hearing only the drips of water from the garden's nymph fountain. For its breadth of flora and generous and strategically placed benches, the garden still feels like an undiscovered treasure. It is the perfect afternoon spot and a great gateway to the newly restored Harlem Meer.

CLARE BELL
Program manager, Roy Lichtenstein Foundation

Andrew Haswell Green

12.18 **Andrew H. Green Bench**
1929, John H. Van Pelt & Margaret Van Pelt
Near East Drive at 105th Street
www.centralpark.com

2.12 **The Consolidation of Greater New York Sculpture**
1906, Albert Weinert
In the Surrogate's Court Building
Chambers Street vestibule
31 Chambers Street

Andrew Haswell Green is a personal—and utterly forgotten—hero of mine. He's sometimes described as the Robert Moses of the nineteenth century, yet hardly anyone knows his name. He supervised the creation of Central Park, rescued the city from bankruptcy after the Boss Tweed scandals, and helped create the Metropolitan Museum of Art, the Bronx Zoo, the Museum of Natural History, Riverside Park, and the New York Public Library. But most importantly, he was the man who championed the 1898 consolidation of the five boroughs into the New York City that exists today. That triumph earned him the title "The Father of Greater New York." After nearly five decades of selfless public service, the eighty-three-year-old Green was shot dead on the front steps of his home in a case of mistaken identity.

All that exists in the city to honor his memory is a forlorn stone bench in Central Park that's not even listed on most park maps. The original five trees that surrounded the bench—each one representing a borough—succumbed to Dutch elm disease decades ago, so in 1998 the Parks Department rededicated the bench and planted new saplings.

Green's greatest accomplishment, the consolidation, is almost as forgotten as he is. But just inside the entranceway of the Surrogate's Court Building you'll find a monument that marks the event, a sculpture titled *The Consolidation of Greater New York*. Allegorical Ms. Brooklyn is shown reaching out to allegorical Ms. New York, a union that, I can assure you, was easier to render in marble than in real life.

MICHAEL MISCIONE
Manhattan Borough Historian

12.19 The Pumpkin Float at Harlem Meer

Northeast corner of park
www.centralparknyc.org

On most days at the Harlem Meer you can find children fishing with long poles and bread dough. But if you come on a Sunday shortly before Halloween, you can watch as hundreds of children bring carved pumpkins with candles inside and float them on wooden rafts on the Meer—a magical site as darkness falls.

MARGOT ADLER
Correspondent, National Public Radio

12

UPPER WEST SIDE

12.20 Lincoln Center for the Performing Arts

West 62nd to West 66th Street between Columbus
and Amsterdam Avenues
www.lincolncenter.org

Sit on the rim of the plaza fountain and feast your eyes
and mind on the monumental cluster of buildings devoted
to the performing arts. Next, move to the North Plaza and
contemplate the glorious Henry Moore in a reflecting pool.
GEORGE WEISSMAN
*The late George Weissman was president of Phillip Morris
Companies and board chairman of the Lincoln Center for the
Performing Arts.*

North Plaza
1965, Dan Kiley

One of the most restful places in the Upper West Side is the
little park, designed by the legendary landscape architect
Dan Kiley, in front of the Vivian Beaumont Theater at
Lincoln Center. Shade trees and a large reflecting pool set off
two Henry Moore sculptures, and the three huge glass walls
that appear to support Eero Saarinen's simple and graceful
theater building shimmer with the light off the pool. From
early morning until the crowds pour out from the various
Lincoln Center attractions, it's a fine place to bring a snack
or just sit and collect your thoughts.
GREGORY MOSHER
Theater director and producer

12.21 Arts for Transit: *Artemis, Acrobats, Divas and Dancers*

1998, Nancy Spero
66th Street-Lincoln Center subway station
www.mta.info

My current favorite piece of subway art is Nancy Spero's *Artemis, Acrobats, Divas, and Dancers*, twenty-two multi-colored glass mosaic panels on either side of the train tracks at Lincoln Center. All the figures are women—diving, dancing, running, playing musical instruments, performing acrobatic feats, rollerskating. They are culled from classical and contemporary sources and are the perfect introduction to the performing arts center directly above. On the downtown platform, the mythological figure Diva repeats, sometimes large, sometimes smaller, but always sheathed in royal golds and crimsons and attended by other, more delicate, goddesses and warriors. The mosaicist, Peter Colombo, who worked on this project for three years, possibly has cut the finest, most detailed smalti since ancient times. His mixes of tiny colored glass tesserae sparkle brilliantly among the surrounding stretches of larger, more solidly colored glazed ceramic mosaic tiles. Thin bands of Naples yellow, Etruscan red, and cobalt blue cleverly flow from section to section, uniting them while elucidating individual passages.

JOYCE KOZLOFF
Artist

12

West 67th Street Studios

12.22 **Hotel des Artistes**
1918, George Mort Pollard
1 West 67th Street between Columbus Avenue and Central Park West
Not open to the public.

12.23 **2 West 67th Street**
1919, Rich & Mathesius
2 West 67th Street between Columbus Avenue and Central Park West

12.24 **Central Park Studios**
1905, B.H. Simonson and Pollard & Steinam
15 West 67th Street between Columbus Avenue
and Central Park West

12.25 **Atelier Building**
1905, B.H. Simonson and Pollard & Steinam
33 West 67th Street between Columbus Avenue
and Central Park West

12.26 **39 West 67th Street**
1907, Pollard & Steinam
39–41 West 67th Street between Columbus Avenue
and Central Park West

West 67th Street, just off Central Park West, harbors
one of the most remarkable urban environments in Manhattan. The high façades lining the narrow street primarily
belong to apartment buildings, many created as artists'
studios. George Mort Pollard designed the finest of them,
particularly the neo-Gothic Hotel des Artistes (No. 1). The
windows of its façade, like No. 2 across the street, reveal
the double-height spaces inside intended for painters. The
Hotel des Artistes was built by a syndicate of artists as a
studio and apartment building; the artists rented half the
building to nonartists and realized enough of a profit that
there was a rush to erect similar buildings. Among them
were: the Central Park Studios (No. 15); the Atelier Building
(No. 33), whose lobby features some of the finest period
Gothic detailing; and 39–41 West 67th, which has a stack
of bay windows on the street façade made of sheet metal,
rather than masonry. Among the tenants of the lavish spaces
above were Isadora Duncan, Norman Rockwell, Alexander
Woolcott, Noël Coward, Fannie Hurst, and John V. Lindsay.
   Fortunately, recent additions to the street, including
two studios for ABC Television (149 Columbus Avenue)

designed by Kohn Pederson Fox in 1978, respect the scale
of their neighbors and maintain the tight environment.

PETER J. HOLLIDAY
Historian of classical art and archaeology

12.28 **Dakota Apartments**
1884, Henry J. Hardenbergh
1 West 72nd Street at Central Park West
Not open to the public.

When I was a kid trying to escape the monotony of Flatbush,
I'd take the D train across the bridge each Saturday to
the place I really belonged: Manhattan. Despite all the
mysteries and glories I discovered, I remember the rush I got
walking up Central Park West and coming upon that behemoth of a building for the first time, that German Gothic/
French Renaissance/English Victorian cacophony called the
Dakota. Of course, I didn't know the architectural styles
when I was fifteen. I only knew this wasn't Brooklyn. This
wasn't Flatbush. This was glamour. This was sophistication.
This was Manhattan. Although half-shutters mask the first-
floor windows, you can still peer into an apartment or two,
now as then; I was dazzled by the enormous rooms, and the
spectacular architectural details. I remember wondering,
"Who lives here? What kind of people can be surrounded
by this luxury?"

Of course, this was before December 8, 1980, when John
Lennon was killed outside the building. Now, tourists come
by the score to pay their respects or gawk. But when I first
discovered the building, its pop-culture claim to fame was
that it was where *Rosemary's Baby* was filmed.

The Dakota was designed by Henry Hardenbergh, who
also designed the Plaza Hotel. Legend has it that it was
called the Dakota because it was so distant from the then-
urban hub. About ten years ago the grime of New York
City was sandblasted away and now, instead of the black

sooty color I remember, it's a camel-hair tan. It seemed more gothic, more foreboding with the dirt, but I still can look at it for hours in amazement: the moldings, the terracotta panels, the corner pavilions, and the storybook gables and roofing.

Don't try to penetrate its courtyard. The ever-present guard knows exactly who should be there and who shouldn't. The apartments are for Yoko, Betty, Rex, and their friends. But we mortals can still marvel at the magnificence. I've lived on the Upper West Side for more than twenty-five years, but every time I walk down 72nd Street I become the fifteen-year-old from Brooklyn, gazing up in amazement at my favorite building in New York.

GLEN ROVEN
Composer

`12.30` Steps on Broadway

2121 Broadway at West 74th Street
☎ 212 874 2410; www.stepsnyc.com

While most New Yorkers and visitors find the ballet at Lincoln Center the finest in spectator sports, I prefer to participate in this incredible art form. On any given day there are numerous marvelous classes to take at Steps, a dance studio fortuitously located upstairs from Fairway Market at 74th Street and Broadway. There is no more heavenly spot in New York; upstairs the sounds of *Don Q* or *Swan Lake* or *La Bayadère* treat your ears, and downstairs there is the heady symphonic perfume of basil and figs and olives. At Steps, anyone who is qualified and has training may pay for a ticket and take a class.

Classes are taught by seasoned ballet masters from all parts of the globe, and in many classes the positions, steps, and instructions are given in French, the universal language of ballet. On any given day, the higher-level classes might include visiting professionals and hopefuls. The reward after an hour and a half of focused class is the last exercise, when the dancers leap across the floor to a selection of the pianist's choice. Afterwards, everyone runs down the stairs to Fairway to pick up dinner before going home or to the ballet or back out into the streets of the city.

JANE TUCKER VASILIOU
Vasiliou & Co.

12.31   ## New-York Historical Society
1908, York & Sawyer; 1938, addition of north and south wings by Walker & Gillette; 1990s, restoration by Beyer Blinder Belle
170 Central Park West between West 76th and West 77th Streets
☎ 212 873 3400; www.nyhistory.org
Closed Sundays and Mondays.

Henry Luce III Center for the Study of American Culture
2000, Beyer Blinder Belle
Fourth floor

12

This is an institution that has been overlooked and eclipsed by other New York institutions such as the Museum of the City of New York and the Met. It has recently been brought back to new life by former New York City Parks Commissioner Betsy Gotbaum. She has gone through their many collections of artworks related to old New York families and furnishings—including paintings, sculpture, furniture, household tools, and decorative objects, much of it stored and unseen for many years but now on display in the wonderful new Henry Luce III Center for the Study of American Culture—and also found the funding so that this great institution could be ready for the twenty-first century.

MARIO BUATTA
Interior decorator

Although many residents and visitors to New York City may be familiar with the New-York Historical Society and its various exhibitions, few seem to know about the Luce Center on the building's fourth floor. It's like the city's attic, with an amazing collection of Americana, including a piece of George Washington's coffin, a barrel used for the opening ceremonies of the Erie Canal in 1825, Duncan Phyfe's tool chest, a collection of a hundred and thirty-two Tiffany lamps, and thousands of other objects and artworks. While much of the material has little more than an accession number, there are wall displays with more information and computer stations set up throughout the gallery where visitors can search through a database of the museum's collection for greater detail. It is a pleasure just to walk around and look at the things that catch your eye and, best of all, you can pick up an engaging audio guide that is offered for free. Anyone interested in American history will find this a treasure trove.

THORIN TRITTER
Historian

Reading Room
Second floor

The Reading Room of the New-York Historical Society is the portal to one of the great institutional repositories for the city's secrets. The library's marvelous collections of broadsides, newspapers, sheet music, and documentation about the history of New York City hotels have been assembled over the course of nearly two hundred years, and capture the textures of everyday existence now hidden under the strata of New York's various past lives. These, too, are represented and preserved in the society's stacks and drawers: the turbulent geological prehistory, the Dutch, English, and Revolutionary periods, the great fires, the slave trade and brutal repression of African-American

revolts, mercantile expansion and the Civil War, the influx
of immigrants and the consolidation of Greater New York
at the end of the nineteenth century, and the whole history
of the twentieth. Little known to the general public—to
which it is open—or even to those who tour the galleries
on the first and second floors, or the Henry Luce III Study
Center on the fourth, the library is a mecca, and a home
away from home for scholars who return day after day to
mine its archives of books, letters, manuscripts, maps,
prints, drawings, and photographs.

BARNET SCHECTER
Historian and author

New York's Royal Governor

12.31 **New-York Historical Society**
170 Central Park West between West 76th and West 77th
Streets
☎ 212 873 3400; www.nyhistory.org
Closed Sundays and Mondays.

1.3 **Admiral's House**
1708
Governors Island
www.govisland.com
Not open to the public.

1.10 **Trinity Church**
1846, Richard Upjohn
Broadway at Wall Street
☎ 212 602 0800; www.trinitywallstreet.org

Edward Hyde, Lord Cornbury, first cousin to England's
Queen Anne, whom he "mightily resembled," was New

12

York's royal governor from 1702–1708. Although the occasional historian will dismiss this as vile anti-Royalist gossip, he was also fond of showing up—at work and at play—in women's clothing. Reputedly, after nights of drinking, he would stumble onto the wooden ramparts of the colony's fort and accost soldiers, who mistook him for a tipsy wench. He would give them a tug on the ear (apparently his favorite body part) and rush off shrieking. Among Cornbury's many achievements during his stay here was the introduction of horse racing to America. Here, for your amusement and instruction, are city landmarks trodden, in an elegant pair of pink slippers, by His Lordship.

The New-York Historical Society owns a portrait, reputedly of Cornbury, wearing a low-necked blue silk dress with a hoopskirt and fitted bodice. The canvas is in the style of itinerant painters of the day, who would bring "blanks"—ready-made portraits lacking only the head—to the homes of prospective customers.

Cornbury's arms and hands—swanlike and ivory—are an ill match to his face with its heavy jowls, protruding lower lip, and self-satisfied expression. The society also owns an agonized letter, on parchment, that Cornbury wrote to his father while still in England, begging him to liquidate his debts.

Governors Island, in New York Harbor, contains Lord Cornbury's second great achievement, after horse racing. He persuaded the colonial legislature to grant him the huge sum of fifteen hundred English pounds to fortify the harbor against "French privateers." Two years went by without the appearance of the proposed battlements. People did notice, however, that much of the primeval timber on the northeast end of Nutten's Island had been felled, and a grand mansion of imported brick—a fabulously expensive material in seventeenth-century America—was going up.

From its description in the annals of the New York legislature, one expects something the size of the New York Public
Library's 42nd Street branch, but to our standards, the house
is disappointingly small, and looks to have been resurfaced
by Garden State brickface.

City Hall Park was the site of Debtor's Prison, an unheated
plank structure in back of the tavern that then served as
City Hall. Cornbury found his way into this accommodation
in 1708 when, upon the death of Queen Anne, the colonial
legislature and an army of other creditors descended upon
him. He did not emerge until 1709 when his father's death
simultaneously made him the Third Earl of Clarendon and
economically solvent.

Trinity Church, on lower Broadway facing Wall Street,
received its land (and the contiguous parcels on which many
of the houses of commerce now rest) as a royal grant from
Cornbury. Burned by the British during the Revolutionary
War, it, too, has been rebuilt. Cornbury's wife, a wealthy
Irish heiress named Katharine O'Brian (to whose funeral
Lord Cornbury is reputed to have worn a dress), is still
buried there, apparently forgotten.

KATHRYN NOCERINO
Poet and writer

12.32 American Museum of Natural History

Central Park West at 79th Street
212 769 5100; www.amnh.org
Open daily.

Holden Caulfield's Tour of the Museum of Natural History

Ask any child in New York City. Whether it's the girl with
the skates in J. D. Salinger's 1945 novel *The Catcher in the
Rye* or a contemporary kid whizzing by on Rollerblades,
the answer will be the same: "the museum" means the
American Museum of Natural History. Tracing the history

of life and matter from the very beginning of time, the museum also contains the personal history of countless children, some of whose earliest memories have been formed in its shadowy halls.

One such child was Holden Caulfield himself. In Miss Aigletinger's fourth grade, he used to visit the museum "damn near every Saturday." "I knew that whole museum routine by heart," he tells us, recollecting with great nostalgia.

A teacher myself, I imitate Miss Aigletinger. Every year, when my seventh graders read *The Catcher in the Rye*, I take them to the Museum of Natural History to retrace Holden's path. We steer clear of the newer exhibits—the Hall of Biodiversity, the glassy new Rose Center—and explore the older, dustier recesses of the museum that seem never to change. As if on a treasure hunt, the kids try to find the same Indians, the same dioramas, the same "glass cases" that Holden describes in such vivid detail. Take this tour with us, guided by Holden's voice, and see how you score on the quiz that follows.

What to bring:

- J. D. Salinger, *The Catcher in the Rye*. (Remember, this is a literary pilgrimage and the book is our map.)
- A pen or pencil
- A handful of marbles
- Candy or gum for optional smuggling into the Imax theater. Just don't get caught.

Start at the main entrance on Central Park West, where the building sprawls like a fortress across from the trees. Passing the triumphal statue of Theodore Roosevelt, go up the stairs and into the rotunda, where the lofty ceiling echoes with the shouts and shrieks of school groups, tourists, and disgruntled babies. Read the four inscriptions on the walls.

Go down the stairs to the first floor, make a left and

walk through the museum shop to the Imax theater. Built in 1995, it is not the same auditorium that Holden remembers, but with its huge screen, squeaky chairs, and enveloping darkness, it still feels like you are in "the only nice, dry, cozy place in the world." If you like, you can chew on some squashed gumdrops you've kept hidden in your pocket.

Proceed to the Hall of Northwest Coast Indians that Holden remembers as "a long, long room and you were only supposed to whisper." No such rule is instituted today, but it doesn't need to be. Full of monstrous, huge-eyed totem poles, cruel spears, life-size dioramas of bear dances and shamans, the room is so vast with mystery and shadow that speaking aloud feels disrespectful. If you have dramatic flair, however, drop your handful of marbles on the stone-and-mosaic floor so that they "make a helluva racket."

12

Look carefully at the first display case on your left. Various members of the Kwakiutl tribe are performing domestic tasks, and near the corner is the source of one of Holden's earliest erotic memories. There was "this squaw weaving a blanket," he confides, who was "sort of bending over, and you could see her bosom and all. We used to sneak a good look at it. . . ." She is, in actuality, not weaving a blanket, but her bosom is indeed showing if you sneak a good look at it.

Exit the Northwest Coast Indians and you'll be confronted by the gigantic Haida Indian canoe. Holden is right when he says it's "about as long as three goddamn Cadillacs in a row, with about twenty Indians in it." Circle the canoe a couple of times to take in its size—the entire boat was carved out of a single red cedar—and to appreciate all the poses, masks, and weapons of the chief, oarsmen, and attending medicine men. At the center of the prow, find the "witch doctor," or shaman, in the wolf-headed mask; he is Holden's favorite.

Unfortunately, some of the exhibits have been removed since Salinger's time. The lone Eskimo that Holden describes fishing so intently at his ice hole no longer exists, nor do some of the dioramas with the birds flying south. But you can still find a few, painted in illusionistic perspective, as well as deer "with their pretty antlers and their pretty skinny legs." Spend some time in the great mammal exhibits on the first and second floors (just retrace your steps back to the staircase) and wander through the forests and veldts with their flora and fauna captured in place and time. "You could go there a hundred times and . . . nobody'd be different. The only thing that would be different would be you."

Quiz:

1. What are the titles of each of Teddy Roosevelt's inscriptions?
2. In which inscription does Roosevelt mention "game boys"?
3. In Miss Aigletinger's class, you were supposed to hold hands with your partner. What was the name of Holden's partner and why didn't he like holding hands with her?
4. What does Holden remember about candy and gum in the auditorium?
5. What was the Kwakiutl Indian really doing?
6. Holden calls the Haida Indian canoe a "war canoe," but the craft is actually built for a ceremonial feast. What is the feast called?
7. How many Indians are in the canoe exactly?
8. How many fish has the Eskimo caught?
9. What happens when you look upside down at the birds flying south?
10. After speaking to the little girl, what part of the museum does Holden visit?

Answer Key:

1. Youth, Manhood, Nature, and the State . . . . 5 points
2. Youth . . . . 5 points
3. Gertrude Levine. Her hands
   were sweaty or sticky . . . . 10 points
4. They made the auditorium smell nice,
   like it was raining outside . . . . 10 points
5. She is shaving cedar bark for a paddle . . . . 10 points
6. A potlatch . . . . 10 points
7. Seventeen . . . . 10 points
8. Two . . . . 10 points
9. They look like they're in an even
   bigger hurry to fly south . . . . 10 points
10. Trick question. He changes his mind
   and decides not to go in . . . . 20 points

Scoring Guide:

12

0–35   You are a worse student than Holden. Reread the
        book at once!

40–65   Mediocre at best. Go hang out with Ackley, or even
        worse, Stradlater.

70–85   Not bad. Take a break and listen to "Little Shirley Beans."

90–100 You are an expert! Treat yourself to Holden
        Caulfield's tour of the "toons" at the Metropolitan
        Museum of Art.

JANE AVRICH
Writer and teacher

12.33   Riverside Park
1873, original design by Frederick Law Olmsted
Riverside Drive to the Hudson River between West 72nd
and West 158th Streets
www.nycgovparks.org

It is little recognized among tourists that Riverside Park is
the gateway to one of the most spectacular views in New
York City. Enter the park at 90th Street. Proceed down the
hill, past the playground with the hippo. Straight ahead,
down a seemingly neglected set of steps, through the tunnel (the traffic from the West Side Highway exit is on your
right), and there you have an incredible Hudson River
view. On your right stands the George Washington Bridge
and on your left is downtown Manhattan, accessible now
via a bicycle path that runs along the Hudson River. Before
you stretches the river, and past that, New Jersey.
NADINE ORENSTEIN
*Curator, Prints and Drawings Department, The Metropolitan
Museum of Art*

A good place to enter is at 72nd Street, which forms the
southern end of the park. Standing sentry here is a statue
of Eleanor Roosevelt, a patron saint of the liberal Upper
West Side. Walk west through the arch that leads under
the West Side Highway and you'll find yourself facing the
majestic Hudson River. The walk along the river is one of
the most bracing in the city, and the view north toward
the George Washington Bridge is stunning. A short stroll
will bring you to the 79th Street Boat Basin, home to an
eccentric community of houseboats. During summer
months, you can watch the sun set over a beer and burger
at the Boat Basin Cafe (seasonal, ☎ 212 496 5542;
www.boatbasincafe.com), though be warned that in the

evening the place becomes a singles zoo. Walking farther north, you'll find a path leading back under the highway and into the park proper, where joggers, dog walkers, parents with strollers, and other Upper West Side types abound.
MICHAEL MASSING
Journalist and writer

12.34 **Barney Greengrass**
541 Amsterdam Avenue between West 86th and West 87th Streets
☎ 212 724 4707; www.barneygreengrass.com
Closed Mondays.

An Upper West Side landmark, Barney Greengrass looks much as it did when it moved here from Harlem in 1929, and the Greengrass family still runs it. Here you can get oversized platters of bagels, cream cheese, lox, and whitefish; the specialty is eggs scrambled with nova and onions. At weekend brunch, the place is packed, so be prepared to wait, but it's worth it for a taste (literally) of the old Jewish Upper West Side. (The giant apartment building across the street, the Belnord, was once home to Isaac Bashevis Singer, the Yiddish writer.)
MICHAEL MASSING
Journalist and writer

A genuine New York fixture—three generations, ninty-plus years in business, more than seventy in the same location—Barney Greengrass is the place to experience one of New York's ur-cuisines: the salty-sweet-smooth salmon, sturgeon, and whitefish that are the product of the long Jewish love affair with smoked fish. Who eats at Barney's? Mavens. Old-timers. Upper West Side families, returnees from the huge New York diaspora, Philip Roth characters (see *Operation Shylock*), Philip Roth himself, and now, you. A good—and traditional—place to start is the scrambled eggs with lox and onions, but for my money, true perfection lies in the lox and kippered salmon with onion, tomato, and scallion cream cheese. I recommend having it on a toasted everything bagel, but no matter what bagel you choose, you'll be in smoked-fish heaven.

MARTHA SCHULMAN
Writer and teacher

London Mimicry

12.35   **Pomander Walk**
1921, King & Campbell
West 94th Street to West 95th Street between Broadway and West End Avenue

11.28   **Henderson Place**
1882, Lamb & Rich
East 86th Street between York and East End Avenues

New York's signature architectural style is the imaginative towers of the skyscrapers built during the first third of the twentieth century. At ground level, you have either the very plain brownstone Edith Wharton so detested, or buildings that echo the cities of Europe, most often London.

My favorite bit of this architectural mimicry is Pomander Walk, built in 1921 and named for a popular Broadway play of the time. This easy-to-miss thoroughfare, which runs parallel to Broadway and West End Avenue between 94th and 95th Streets, was, like the play, named for a tiny street in the London suburb of Chiswick.

Although the gates have been closed since 1986, on a recent sunny morning it took literally no more than two minutes before a resident, on her way back from shopping, let me in. Up a flight of a dozen steps is an enchanted streetlet, its scaled-down Tudor houses apparently modeled after the sets of the long-forgotten play. In front of each house is a well-tended garden in the English country style. Looking up, you see window boxes with hanging flowers that enhance the overall theatricality.

New York is a much more sociable city than it is given credit for being, but Pomander Walk seems incredibly like some small town where everybody knows everybody else.

Pomander Walk has an architectural cousin across town on East 86th Street, just around the corner from Gracie Mansion. Henderson Place, which runs only half a block, has a row of red brick townhouses in Queen Anne style. What distinguishes them from so many other imitations of London is the fact that they do not seem full size. The miniaturization gives them a sweet theatricality. (Not surprisingly, the Lunts lived here for many years.)

These elegant houses face an undistinguished modern apartment building, so they do not have the enveloping enchantment of Pomander Walk. But they are a reminder of the kind of imagination New York developers used before their only consideration was how high, and thus, how lucrative.

HOWARD KISSEL
Art and theater critic, and author

12.37 Wang Chen's Table Tennis Club
2628 Broadway between West 99th and West 100th Streets
☎ 212 864 7253; www.wangchenttc.com

Wang Chen proudly claims to be the only place in Manhattan where one can play the "official" version of table tennis. Walk in and the differences between the official version of the game and the Ping-Pong of your youth immediately become apparent. The official-sized tables are considerably smaller than the Ping-Pong tables in basements and frat houses across America. The players of the official game bend at the waist and hold their arms at seemingly painful, crooked angles in their quest for the perfect spin with which to launch the balls across the net. As a result, the best players look like extraordinarily well-muscled marionettes as they lurch for-wards and back, hitting balls to each other.

Go during the day and you may see Nigerian businessmen conducting deals in the Yoruba language over games of table tennis, or the associates from a major New York investment bank on a corporate outing.

Go in the evening and you may be able to watch Renata Pulochova, who once played on the Czech national table tennis team, Wang Chen, once the No. 4 female table tennis player in the world, George Brathwaite, who was one of the "Ping-Pong diplomats" to China in 1971, or an up-and-coming table tennis star.

Or sign up for a lesson—my instructor spent much of my lesson asking me to "move, please move," praising me on those rare occasions when I actually did move with, "Thank you. Very good!" My friend, considerably more energetic than I on that particular evening, actually received instruction on how to spin the ball.

Or simply go and play a game or two, while steeping your-self in the table tennis subculture surrounding you. Or if you don't want to play, go to watch anyway.

KATE HARTNICK ELLIOTT
President, Hartnick Consulting

A Summer Evening in Riverside Park

12.36 **Riverside Park Tennis Courts**
Riverside Park at West 96th Street
☎ 212 978 0277; www.riversideparkfund.org
Open April to November.

12.39 **Hudson Beach Cafe**
Riverside Park at 105th Street
☎ 917 370 3448; pdohurleys.com
Closed in the winter. Check website for schedule.

Take a stroll along the promenade. Stop at the community gardens at 89th Street, and enjoy the Upper West Side's interpretation of an English country garden. Drop down to the river's edge at 95th Street, and continue to the public tennis courts on 96th Street. Play here at sunset, with a river breeze. When your game is finished, follow the sounds of salsa music to the Hudson Beach Cafe on 105th Street in Riverside Park, where Puerto Rican and American flags are displayed proudly above the bar. Dance, have a margarita, and toast the city for nights like this.

GEORGIA O'NEAL
Owner, Tree and Leaf Farm

12.38 Firemen's Memorial
1913, Attilio Piccirilli, sculptor; H. Van Buren Magonigle, architect
Riverside Drive at West 100th Street

12

At the funeral service for Deputy Chief Kruger in 1908 (he died at a fire on Canal Street), Episcopal Bishop Henry Potter called for the erection of a monument to honor the heroism of New York City firefighters. Newspapers throughout the city took up the bishop's plea, and a few years later the Firemen's Memorial was dedicated, high on top of Riverside Drive, in beautiful park-like surroundings: a quiet, somber setting amidst the hustle of Broadway and near Columbia University only a few blocks away. The inscription on the monument reads, "To the men of the Fire Department of the City of New York who died in the line of duty, soldiers in a war that never ends, this memorial is dedicated by the people of a grateful city." Each October, memorial services are held here by the department. Completely refurbished in 1991, this monument is for firefighters a sacred and honored place, and for New Yorkers, a reminder of the price paid for their safety.

THOMAS VON ESSEN
Former New York City Fire Commissioner

12.40   Nicholas Roerich Museum

1898, Clarence F. True
319 West 107th Street between Broadway and Riverside Drive
☎ 212 864 7752

This is a fabulous museum in a charming town house displaying the work of the rather mystical Russian artist Nicholas Roerich. Many of the paintings reflect his intense spirituality and deep passion for art.
KAREN MOODY TOMPKINS
Artist

12.41   Riverside Park Above West 96th Street

There is, of course, that pesky problem of the West Side Highway directly to one side, but the beauty of this particular unsung river path is that it maintains a distinctly nonlandscaped feel. There are no railings, no gardens, no restaurants—only a straight shot up the west side of Manhattan along the river, the George Washington Bridge ahead in the distance, and the rocky coastline of New Jersey to espy on the other side. If you're a serious runner—as, say, in training for the New York City Marathon (which is worth doing at least once)—you can run over the bridge for a truly magnificent view.
KATHLEEN DEMARCO VAN CLEVE
Author, screenwriter, and film producer

Olde New Yorkese

New York City's blend of immigrants, émigrés, transients, and natives has produced a lexicon that is pleasantly peculiar to New York City. From the beginning of this urban city-state, new and different languages were heard on the street; according to one historian, in 1626, eighteen different languages could be heard in the village of Nieuw Amsterdam.

However, with the changes wrought by assimilation, technology, economics, immigration patterns, politics, mores, and the city's own ever-changing atmosphere, some words and phrases are either disappearing or becoming as archaic and obscure as Shakespeare's "yclept." Here are some favorites that are fast disappearing from New York's vocabulary:

On Line: When the Internet was just a twinkle in Thomas Watson's eye, New Yorkers wanting to gain admission to Radio City Music Hall or buy tickets for the latest Broadway hit stood on line. The rest of the country stood "in line."

Egg Cream: This ambrosia-like beverage contains neither eggs nor cream. The traditional version of this drink, inhaled in candy stores and luncheonettes throughout the five boroughs, consisted of tooth-rattlingly cold milk, chocolate syrup, and soda water. With the disappearance of soda fountains—the seltzer of soda water spigots was critical to the true egg cream—the beverage and the name are rapidly slipping into memory.

Candy Store: Not to be confused with Godiva, Perugina, or even Fanny Farmer. A true candy store was a neighborhood institution, selling newspapers, cigarettes, and other tobacco products, candy bars, bulk penny candy, and school supplies. A good candy store also had a soda fountain where one could be refreshed with a two cents plain, an egg cream or, in season, a lime rickey, or a Mello Roll.

LEE GELBER
Urban historian and tour guide

CHAPTER 13

MORNINGSIDE HEIGHTS

HARLEM

Morningside Heights & Harlem

MORNINGSIDE HEIGHTS

13.1 **Hungarian Pastry Shop**
1030 Amsterdam Avenue between West 110th and
West 111th Street
☎ 212 866 4230

🍴🍷 Slotted into the ground floor of an anonymous apartment
building on Amsterdam Avenue just below 111th Street,
the Hungarian Pastry Shop is one of the sweetest retreats
in the city. Despite its generic name, and with no decor
to speak of, it's been a bastion of the Columbia University
neighborhood for at least a quarter of a century. You give
your order at the front counter along with your first name,
which a waitress then circulates about five minutes later.
Usually she misreads her own handwriting, so whose order
she has is always a matter of interpretation (Mel? Bill?
Cal?). This is neatly appropriate for a place in which the
table reading is as likely to be Derrida as *The New York
Post*. But the real secret to the Hungarian Pastry Shop's
success is the pots of mediocre coffee with which you can
refill your initial overpriced order as frequently as you
wish—for hours or, as seems the case of some perennial
students, decades. Thus the place has probably fueled more
Ph.D.'s than any institution in the hemisphere.

One fringe benefit of the Hungarian Pastry Shop is
its view across the avenue to the gardens of the Cathedral
of St. John the Divine and especially the so-called Peace
Fountain. Hands down the ugliest public sculpture in
New York, it rises massively from a placid marble pool
to a bulging man-in-the-moon face from which a gigantic
winged figure, who appears to be strangling a gazelle,
emerges while huge bronze crab claws drip over the edge.
Local rumor has it that the sculptor donated a million

dollars to the cathedral—in the days when that was real money—in return for the permanent display of his well-intended statement of universal amity gone grotesquely awry. So be it; the thing is so awful you can't help but admire it as you pour a cup of coffee and return to your reading.

MELVIN JULES BUKIET
Author and literary critic

13.2 Cathedral Church of St. John the Divine

1892–1911, Heins & La Farge; 1911–1942, Cram & Ferguson
1047 Amsterdam Avenue at West 112th Street
☎ 212 316 7540; www.stjohndivine.org

On the hillside of Morningside Heights stands the Cathedral of St. John the Divine, unfinished more than a hundred years after the first stone foundations were laid in 1892. The Episcopal diocese purchased this lot north of 110th Street in the 1880s and began planning a cathedral that would rise above the city and be visible throughout the island of Manhattan. It was to be like Paris's Sacré-Coeur. That was before skyscrapers began to sprout on the city's grid. Today, the cathedral is largely hidden from view, unless you're right in front of it, but it's well worth a visit. Even incomplete, it's the largest church in America and one of the largest cathedrals in the world. Its main vault, standing one hundred and twenty-four feet high, is more than six hundred feet long and could hold two football fields in a row. Along the edge of this expanse, individual niches filled with sculptures, stained glass, and historical artifacts catch the eye.

After viewing the interior, walk around the outside to see the results of changing architectural tastes. The Episcopal diocese initially chose a Romanesque and Byzantine plan by Heins & La Farge, which was used for the sanctuary and choir. In 1911, however, the church, concerned with changing tastes, chose Ralph Adams Cram as its new architect and

13

adopted a Gothic Revival design to complete the building. This shift is visible inside the building, but even more from the street along the north side, where you can see the rounded Romanesque choir next to Gothic flying buttresses.

To get the full experience of the cathedral, take advantage of the Vertical Tour, which is offered periodically. This guided walk takes you a hundred and twenty-four feet up stone spiral staircases onto the roof of the cathedral. As you ascend through the walls of the building, you get close-up views of gargoyles, and other ornamentation, that are barely visible from the floor below. At the "summit," there are spectacular views down to the city below. From there you get a sense of the geography that made the site so attractive to its planners.

THORIN TRITTER
Historian

The guidebooks will tell you that it is the largest Gothic cathedral in the world, that the Statue of Liberty could stand upright in the nave, that the figure of Christ in the rose window is six feet tall, but more telling for me is that at most times of the day you can't see the ceiling. It's that far away. The impression is that heaven has somehow been included in the congregation.

CYNTHIA ZARIN
Poet and writer

Believe it or not, one of the largest cathedrals in the world sits across from a funky Hungarian coffee shop at the edge of Harlem. Pass through St. John's Portals of Paradise under the gaze of Moses, John the Baptist, and thirty other limestone figures from the Old and New Testaments and feel the transformation take place as you enter sacred space. Though the cornerstone was set in 1892, like much of New York, the cathedral is still a construction site—its scaffolded stone towers are not yet finished. But the magnificent

breadth of the room inside inspires a sense of utter completeness and can convince even the faithless to believe. The first time I walked the length of the vaulted nave to the great choir and looked up at the dome one hundred and seventy-seven feet above, I got weak in the knees. The Statue of Liberty could stand on her toes and still fit underneath. Built as a sanctuary for faiths of all nations, the cathedral has seen the Dalai Lama, as well as Sufi masters, Zen *roshis*, and rabbis, lead prayer services. This is the place to surrender to your higher power or to the simple need for refuge from the chaos of urban life.
RENEE SHAFRANSKY
Psychotherapist, writer, and film producer

13.3   ## Columbia University
1897, McKim, Mead & White
West 114th Street to West 120th Street between Broadway and Amsterdam Avenue; entrance at West 116th Street and Broadway
☎ 212 854 4900; www.columbia.edu
Columbia offers regularly scheduled tours of the campus and its buildings.

13

Buell Hall/Maison Française
1885, Ralph Townsend
Central campus, south of St. Paul's Chapel

Low Memorial Library
1897, McKim of McKim, Mead & White
Central campus, north of West 116th Street (College Walk)

St. Paul's Chapel
1907, Howells & Stokes
North campus, east of Low Library

Avery Hall
1912, McKim, Mead & White
North of St. Paul's Chapel

Alma Mater
1903, Daniel Chester
Central Campus, on the steps in front of Low Library

Columbia University is one of the oldest and largest institutions of higher education in America. Its Morningside Heights campus, designed by McKim, Mead & White, is one of the great urban spaces in New York and complements the university's prestige.

The history of the university's founding and expansion reflects the growth of the city. Chartered in 1754 as King's College, the fledgling institution quickly outgrew its original home on a site adjacent to Trinity Church. In 1760, it moved to a three-acre site near Park Place (then named College Place). By 1810, the city had begun to close in on the openness and greenery of that site: there were concerns about the noise from the city's nearby port, and the area was gaining notoriety for prostitution. Columbia College (patriotically rechristened after the Revolution) therefore acquired the failed Elgin Botanical Gardens, about twenty acres just north of 47th Street and fronting Fifth Avenue. As the city continued to expand northward, this landholding proved to be one of Columbia's most profitable investments, leased after 1929 to Rockefeller Center until it was sold in 1987.

In 1857, the trustees applied the proceeds of the sale of the College Place property to acquiring the grounds of the Deaf and Dumb Asylum located at 49th Street between Madison and Fourth (Park) Avenues. That institution's buildings were to serve as temporary quarters until a new campus could be built on the Botanical Garden site, just a block away, but the Civil War and volatile economy in its aftermath delayed such plans. After forty more years, the phenomenal growth of Manhattan above 42nd Street, especially the arrival of the railroad into Grand Central and the northern push of speculative residences and commerce, made the conditions at 49th Street increasingly untenable. In addition, Columbia determined to expand along the model of a Germanic research university, as several other American institutions did during the ninteenth century. In 1891, the newly constituted Columbia University acquired the grounds of the Bloomingdale Insane Asylum in Morningside Heights (an irony generations of students and professors have relished). Construction began in 1897.

PETER J. HOLLIDAY
Historian of classical art and archaeology

One of the few great contributions of City Beautiful planning to New York City, the Columbia University campus is a permanent testimony to the impact of Chicago's ephemeral White City of 1893 (the World's Columbian Exhibition), from which master planner Charles Follen McKim was freshly graduated. At the same time, it is a place richly suggestive of the inherent tension between the Beaux Arts processional planning that captured the American civic imagination in the late ninteenth century and the nearly relentless grid of the Commissioner's Plan of 1811, which was laid out to the northern tip of the island even before building had reached the island's frontier.

When Columbia acquired the pastoral site of the old Bloomingdale Asylum (the quaint brick villa known today as Buell Hall/Maison Française just to the east of Low Library is the only remnant), McKim seized the opportunity to build on the four blocks uninterrupted by cross streets to compose in brick, limestone, and granite a vision of the American research university as a grand forum. Though he dreamed of an axial approach to its great central axis, and even a vista from the upper terrace of this academic sanctuary of the city to the south, neither the grid nor the city's vertical drive allowed that. Rather, we come obliquely upon the Pantheon-esque centerpiece of it all, Low Library

(1895–1897). Approached across a grand forecourt paved with deep-red bricks laid in a herringbone pattern to recall the floor of the Roman Forum, McKim's great outdoor room comes alive on warm fall or spring days, when the stairs become the bleachers for this civic stage. Students, faculty, and neighbors of all ages chat, distribute pamphlets, exchange footballs, or hurry upward to the grand plateau on which McKim arranged a backdrop of redbrick classroom buildings, accented by a trio of cupolas of the library, the student center, and the chapel. Be sure to go before 5 p.m., when the great bronze doors of Low Library close, for the interior, even without its grand central desk and concentric reading tables reminiscent of the old British Museum and the Library of Congress, is one of the most solemn Beaux Arts interiors in New York.

For decorative subtlety and even technological innovation, McKim's former employees, Howells & Stokes, outdid the master in St. Paul's Chapel (1903–1905). In their use of the recently patented thin-tile vaults of the Guastavino system (you saw some in the IRT subway as you arrived), they elevated this new technology to new aesthetic heights in the dome, vaults, galleries, and even stairways of this richly textured sanctuary. The small spiraling stair, visible by entering the right side door off the narthex porch of the chapel, is a veritable primer in how this medieval Spanish technique revolutionized American building circa 1900. Take a peek into Avery Library, one of the great repositories of architectural books anywhere in the world. And maybe before you leave school you'll discover Columbia's most famous secret—as hundreds of first-year students do each autumn—by gazing between the folds of the statue of Alma Mater, Daniel Chester French's great enthroned matron who presides over the whole scene.

BARRY BERGDOLL
Philip Johnson Chief Curator of Architecture and Design,
The Museum of Modern Art

13.4 **Riverside Church**

1930, Allen & Collens and Henry C. Pelton
490 Riverside Drive between West 120th and
West 122nd Streets
☎ 212 870 6700; www.theriversidechurchny.org

Laura Spelman Rockefeller Memorial Carillon

Unconcerned with the liability insurance that transformed
the Empire State Building observation deck into a rat cage,
the carillon at Riverside Church provides the best chance
to ascend one of the city's spires and gaze out over the city.
An ecclesiastical office building disguised as a cathedral,
the tower offers a bank of elevators in place of the winding
spiral stair.
SEBASTIAN HARDY
Urban planner

13

13.5 **Sakura Park**

1934, Olmsted Landscape Architecture Firm
West 122nd Street between Riverside Drive and
Claremont Avenue
www.nycgovparks.org

Sakura Park, one of New York's prettiest and least-known
parks, at first seems little more than an annex of Riverside
Park, which it adjoins at the northern tip of Morningside
Heights. But spend a few minutes here and you'll realize that
it has a peaceful, melancholy charm all its own. Situated
directly across Riverside Drive from Grant's Tomb, elevated
slightly from the street, filled with benches, big trees, and a
gazebo, it's a perfect place to rest your feet, eat your lunch,
or simply contemplate the teeming city that lies beyond.
RACHEL WETZSTEON
*The late Rachel Wetzsteon was a poet and the author of three
collections of poems, including* The Other Stars.

13.6 General Grant National Memorial (Grant's Tomb)
Riverside Drive at West 122nd Street
☎ 212 666 1640; www.nps.gov

General Grant National Memorial Bench
1973, Pedro Silva and Cityarts Workshop, with Phillip Danzig

These colorful, tile-covered benches stretch four hundred and fifty feet along both sides and the rear of the solemn mausoleum to the general and president, and his wife. They were completed in 1973 as a community folk art appreciation of Grant's role in preserving the nation in 1865. More than two thousand people volunteered to complete the benches.

PHILLIP DANZIG
The late Phillip Danzig was an architect and a muralist.

13.7 Amiable Child Monument
Riverside Drive and West 123rd Street
www.nycgovparks.org

On July 15, 1797, a small child fell to his death from the edge of the cliffs overlooking the Hudson River. Just north of Grant's Tomb, on the edge of Riverside Park, is a fenced enclosure surrounding a stone monument, "Erected to the Memory of an Amiable Child, St. Claire Pollock, Died 15 July 1797 in the Fifth Year of His Age."

GERALD WEALES
Author and Emeritus Professor of English, University of Pennsylvania

13.8 Riverside Drive Viaduct
1901, F. Stewart Williamson, engineer; rebuilt 1987
West 125th Street and the Hudson River

The viaduct at 125th Street at the Hudson River is a little-known but elegant metal bridge structure.

M. PAUL FRIEDBERG
Landscape architect

HARLEM

13.9 **Lenox Lounge**

288 Lenox Avenue (Malcolm X Blvd.) between West 124th
and West 125th Streets

☎ 212 427 0253; www.lenoxlounge.com

The Cotton Club and Savoy are long gone, but this legendary lounge remains and has played host to Bird and Billie
(Holiday), Miles Davis (with Malcolm X watching), and a
thousand other jazz journeymen. This joint is living history
and I get the chills just thinking about what went down
here. The famous back room is where you can hear some
young cats wail, while the hard, loud, long front bar is
jammed with a rainbow coalition of locals mixed with up-
and downtowners. The original Art Deco decor, complete
with zebra-striped walls and padded leather ceiling, has been
over-restored. I miss the sixty-year-old nicotine-blackened
ceiling and the sconces falling off the walls.

FREDERIC SCHWARTZ
Architect

13

13.10 **The Studio Museum in Harlem**

144 West 125th Street between Lenox Avenue (Malcolm X
Blvd.) and Adam Clayton Powell Jr. Blvd.

☎ 212 864 4500; www.studiomuseum.org

Closed Mondays, Tuesdays, and Wednesdays.

The least ivory-tower museum in town, the Studio Museum
in Harlem has both serious historical exhibitions and
contemporary artists at work in studio areas of the building.
There is an outdoor space for art and a sense of interaction
and porousness between the museum and the community.
After visiting the Studio Museum, have lunch at Sylvia's.

REBECCA SMITH
Artist

13.11 Sylvia's Soul Food Restaurant

328 Lenox Avenue (Malcolm X Blvd.) between West
126th and West 127th Streets
☎ 212 996 0660; www.sylviassoulfood.com

In the heart of Harlem, Sylvia's (now seating and serving
four hundred and fifty) has been a soul food institution
since 1962. Sylvia and her husband, Herbert Wood, met in
a beanfield when they were kids and they've been together
ever since. Stick to the basics like the ribs, fried chicken,
collard greens, and sweet-potato pie. Go late at night to
bypass the tour buses or try the gospel brunch after Sunday
services at the Abyssinian Baptist Church.
TRACEY HUMMER AND FREDERIC SCHWARTZ
Writer and Architect

13.16 Abyssinian Baptist Church

1923, Charles W. Bolton & Son
132 Odell Clark Place (West 138th Street) between Adam
Clayton Powell Jr. Blvd. and Lenox Avenue (Malcolm X
Blvd.). Visitors should use the entrance on the corner of
West 138th Street and Adam Clayton Powell Jr. Blvd.
☎ 212 862 7474; www.abyssinian.org
Only open to the public for the 11 a.m. Worship Service on
Sundays. Check the website for hours, as the service is
sometimes closed to the public.

The ashlar neo-Gothic stone church became famous for its
prominent ministers, notably Adam Clayton Powell Sr. and
his son Adam Clayton Powell Jr., the first black congressman
from New York City. Founded in 1808 by black worshippers
who wanted independence from the First Baptist Church, the
congregation took a name associated with ancient Ethiopia.
The city's second-oldest black church took more than a

century to move north to Harlem, as did the city's downtown "Little Africa" population.

CHRISTOPHER PAUL MOORE
*Historian, author, and research coordinator, New York Public
Library's Schomburg Center for Research on Black Culture*

Harlem Stroll

13.12 **Schomburg Center for Research in Black Culture,
The New York Public Library**
1980, Bond Ryder Associates
515 Lenox Avenue (Malcolm X Blvd.) at West 135th Street
📞 212 491 2200; www.nypl.org
Closed Sundays and Mondays.

13.13 **Harlem Y.M.C.A.**
1932, James C. Mackenzie Jr.
180 West 135th Street between Lenox Avenue (Malcolm X
Blvd.) and Adam Clayton Powell Jr. Blvd.
📞 212 912 2100; www.ymcanyc.org

13.14 **Strivers' Row**
West 138th and West 139th Streets between Frederick
Douglass Blvd. and Adam Clayton Powell Jr. Blvd.

13.15 **Countee Cullen Branch, The New York Public Library**
1942, Louis Allen Abramson
104 West 136th Street between Adam Clayton Powell Jr.
Blvd. and Lenox Avenue (Malcolm X Blvd.)
📞 212 491 2070; www.nypl.org
Closed Sundays.

13.16 **Abyssinian Baptist Church**
1923, Charles W. Bolton & Son
132 Odell Clark Place (West 138th Street) between Adam
Clayton Powell Jr. Blvd. and Lenox Avenue (Malcolm X
Blvd.). Visitors should use the entrance on the corner of

13

West 138th Street and Adam Clayton Powell Jr. Blvd.
☎ 212 862 7474; www.abyssinian.org
Only open to the public for the 11 a.m. Worship Service on
Sundays. Check the website for hours, as the service is
sometimes closed to the public.

Near the geographic center of Harlem stands the New
York Public Library's Schomburg Center, one of the world's
great research facilities for studying African-American and
African life and culture, and a mecca for the curious about
Harlem and the fabled 1920s Harlem Renaissance. A
modern three-story complex, it incorporates a landmark
building as well as the Countee Cullen Library, the site of
heiress A'Lelia Walker's mansion and literary salon known
as the Dark Tower. One half-block west on 135th Street is
the Harlem Y.M.C.A., temporary home of Langston Hughes
and Claude McKay. Walk three blocks north on the west
side of Seventh Avenue and you come to Strivers' Row,
two streets of elegant turn-of-the-century Italianate houses
designed by architect Stanford White. Half a block east,
down 138th Street, is the historic Abyssinian Baptist Church.
    If you are less adventurous, a few steps from the IRT
Seventh Avenue express subway exit at 135th Street will put
you inside the lobby of the Schomburg Center. Sign the
visitor's register and, comfortably indoors, you can begin to
satisfy an hour's curiosity or a lifetime's scholarly interest.
For the sightseer, a tour is recommended before a leisurely
visit to the several exhibition galleries. One can also attend
a lecture, film screening (some are free), or performance in
either of two theaters. Peek into the sculpture garden on
your way to browse in the gift shop for that hard-to-find
book. A walk through the large, sunlit lobby of the
Langston Hughes Auditorium is essential. Its terrazzo and
brass-strip floor, designed by Houston Conwill, illuminates
the Langston Hughes poem "The Negro Speaks of Rivers."
Beneath the center of the floor rests the poet's ashes.

Before you leave, stand at that spot in the center of Harlem and read the inscription: "My soul has grown deep like the rivers."

RAYMOND R. PATTERSON

The late Raymond R. Patterson was a poet and Professor Emeritus at City College of New York.

13.13 Harlem Y.M.C.A.

1932, James C. Mackenzie Jr.

180 West 135th Street between Lenox Avenue (Malcolm X Blvd.) and Adam Clayton Powell Jr. Blvd.

📞 212 912 2100; www.ymcanyc.org

On this important thoroughfare stands a proud institution that has been a beacon for the community since the first Harlem Renaissance. Opened in 1933, the eleven-story neo-Georgian Harlem Y.M.C.A. received landmark status in 1999. As one of the country's major African-American Y.M.C.A.'s, its handsome halls and rooms, with their original tiles, wooden doors, and carved ceiling beams, have embraced countless children and adults, nurtured great talents, and sheltered many aspiring souls. Renowned writer Langston Hughes stayed in its residence; Paul Robeson, Harry Belafonte, Ossie Davis, and Ruby Dee, among others, graced its Little Theater program for more than forty years; major artist Aaron Davis painted a still-extant wall mural, *The Evolution of Negro Dance*, during the Great Depression; and revered baseball hero and one-time Y member Jackie Robinson lives on in the youth center named for him opposite the main Y.M.C.A. building.

Sharing the block with two other major community institutions—Harlem Hospital and the Schomburg Center for Research in Black Culture (see p. 309)—the Y.M.C.A. is a key player in the second Harlem Renaissance, now underway.

PAMELA BAYLESS

Writer and communications consultant

13

13.17 Mother African Methodist Episcopal Zion Church

1925, George W. Foster Jr.
140 West 137th Street between Adam Clayton Powell Jr.
Blvd. and Lenox Avenue (Malcolm X Blvd.)
📞 212 234 1545; www.amez.org
Open to the public for services only.

Organized in 1796 by black worshippers who withdrew
from the John Street Methodist Church in lower Manhattan,
the Mother A.M.E. Zion Church is the city's oldest African-
American church and, as its name implies, the "mother"
church of the international A.M.E. Zion denomination.
Designed by George W. Foster Jr., one of the first black
architects in the United States, the neo-Gothic stone church
is the sixth edifice and location for the congregation, which
started in a house neighboring the eighteenth-century
African Burial Ground (see p. 43) and moved gradually up
to Harlem in the 1900s.
CHRISTOPHER PAUL MOORE
*Historian, author, and research coordinator, New York Public
Library's Schomburg Center for Research on Black Culture*

13.18 St. Nicholas Park

West 128th to West 141st Street between St. Nicholas Avenue
and St. Nicholas Terrace
www.nycgovparks.org; www.stnicholaspark.org

Commemorating colonial New Amsterdam's patron Saint
Nicholas, who through local writers Washington Irving and
Clement Clarke Moore and local artist Thomas Nast became
our beloved Santa Claus, the frontier-like park is my family's
favorite Christmas holiday spot. Built in 1906 to the designs
of landscape architect Samuel Parsons on a massive, rocky
outcrop following the rugged and hilly topography of
northern Manhattan, the park's development and the construction of the elevated rapid transit line made this section
of Harlem a fashionable residential district at the turn of

the century. In the park is "The Point of Rocks," where George Washington commanded and observed the Battle of Harlem Heights in 1776. During the seventeenth century, the steeple of Manhattan's first permanent church (built in 1642 and popularly called the St. Nicholas Church by the children of the Roosevelts, Stuyvesants, and my grandcestor Nicholas Manuel) could be seen from the point nine miles south in downtown Fort Amsterdam. New York City may not look like the North Pole, but it is the birthplace of Santa Claus!

CHRISTOPHER PAUL MOORE
Historian, author, and research coordinator, New York Public Library's Schomburg Center for Research on Black Culture

13.19 Riverbank State Park

1991, Richard Dattner & Associates
West 137th to West 145th Street, west of the Henry Hudson Parkway; entrance on West 145th Street
Park: ☎ 212 694 3600; Pool: ☎ 212 694 3666
www.nysparks.state.ny.us

My favorite pool in New York is the splendid fifty-meter pool at Riverbank, over the Hudson River at 145th Street in Harlem. This is part of an extraordinary recreational and cultural complex that is virtually unknown to most New Yorkers.

OLIVER SACKS
Neurologist and author

Henry
Hudson
Bridge

*Spuyten
Duyvil*

Bro
B

W 218th St

Inwood

Isham St

Inwood

Inwood
Hill
Park

W 207th St

W 204th St

Payson Avenue
Cooper St
Broadway
Academy St

Dyckman St
Thayer St
Arden St
Sickles St
Ellwood St

Nagle Avenue
Tenth Avenue
Ninth Avenue

Fort
Tryon
Park

High
Bridge
Park

Margaret Corbin Dr

Hillside Avenue

Amsterdam Avenue

*Hudson
River*

W 192nd St
W 190th St
W 189th St
W 188th St
W 187th St

W 186th St
W 185th St
W 184th St
W 183rd St
W 182nd St
W 181st St
W 180th St
W 179th St

Cabrini Blvd

Cabrini Blvd

Pinehurst Av
Ft Washington Avenue
Overlook Ter
Bennett Avenue
Wadsworth Avenue
Broadway
St Nicholas Avenue
Laurel Hill Ter

West Side Hwy (Henry Hudson Pkwy)
Riverside Drive

George
Washington
Bridge

I-95

W 178th St
W 177th St
W 176th St
W 175th St

Fort
Washington
Park

West Side Hwy (Henry Hudson Pkwy)

Haven Avenue
Riverside Drive
Ft Washington Avenue
Audubon Avenue
Amsterdam Avenue
Edgecombe Av

W 174th St
W 173rd St
W 172nd St
W 171st St
W 170th St
W 169th St
W 168th St
St Nichols W 167th St
Av W 166th St

High
Bridge
Park

W 165th St
W 164th St
W 163rd St
W 162nd St
W 161st St
W 160th St
W 159th St
W 158th St
W 157th St
W 156th St

Broadway

Jumel Ter

Audubon Ter

CHAPTER 14

INWOOD, FORT GEORGE, WASHINGTON HEIGHTS & AUDUBON

INWOOD, FORT GEORGE, WASHINGTON HEIGHTS & AUDUBON

14.1 ## Hispanic Society of America

1908, Charles Pratt Huntington
Audubon Terrace: Broadway between West 155th and
West 156th Streets
☎ 212 926 2234; www.hispanicsociety.org
Closed Mondays.

The Hispanic Society has far and away the best museum and
library in this country for the study of Spanish culture. The
fact that the society is in one of the most culturally vibrant
cities in the world, in a neighborhood that is almost entirely
Spanish-speaking, and yet is largely unknown, simply makes
it more intriguing. The grand Beaux Arts terrace that it occupies on Broadway between 155th and 156th Streets serves
as a reminder of how swiftly this part of Manhattan evolved
over the twentieth century.
WILLIAM AMBLER
Curator

The Hispanic Society of America was hugely popular at
first. In 1909, when it opened a big show devoted to
Valencian Impressionist Joaquín Sorolla, it obliged a total
of one hundred and fifty thousand visitors by staying open
until 11 p.m. At the time, *ARTnews* reported that the
exhibit "won the most emphatic popular success ever known
in the history of art in New York." Today, however, you
might feel as though you're in a dark ducal home in a
Spanish province, about fifty years ago.
   The Hispanic Society sits on a recessed courtyard off
Broadway between 155th and 156th Streets in a bustling,
mostly Dominican neighborhood. It has changed very little
since it was founded in 1904 by Archer Milton Huntington,

who used the family fortune (shipbuilding and the Central Pacific Railroad) to acquire the best collection of Spanish art, books, and manuscripts in the United States.

He bought objects chronicling the panorama of Spanish history, from paleolithic stone tools to modern Catalan porcelain, rare Roman glass vessels and ivory combs, silken textiles woven in Moorish patterns, intricately illuminated medieval Bibles, and some of the best lusterware you will see anywhere. And he amassed paintings by masters including El Greco, Velázquez, and Zurbarán. Principal among the major works is Goya's portrait of his alleged mistress, the Duchess of Alba, who flaunts a ring with the artist's name on it.

Huntington also bought a parcel of farmland from the naturalist John James Audubon, with the intention of creating an acropolis on the Upper West Side. Known as the Audubon Terrace Historic District, it includes buildings for the American Numismatic Society, the American Academy of Arts and Letters, and one for George Gustave Heye, whose great collection of Native American art has since been transplanted downtown to the Smithsonian's National Museum of the American Indian (see p. 17). The inner court of the Hispanic Society, in the style of the Spanish Renaissance, looks like a palace and was, in fact, inspired by the Vélez Blanco Castle in the province of Almería. Sculptures of El Cid, Don Quixote, and Boabdil, the last Moorish king of Granada, by Huntington's wife, Anna Hyatt Huntington, adorn the outdoor space.

14

ROBIN CEMBALEST
Executive editor, ARTnews

This is a neglected museum with some fine Old Master paintings.
VICTORIA NEWHOUSE
Architectural historian and writer

14.2 Morris-Jumel Mansion

1765
65 Jumel Terrace between West 160th and 162nd Streets
📞 212 923 8008; www.morrisjumel.org
Closed on Mondays and Tuesdays (except by appointment).

This house, on a rise overlooking Harlem Valley, was built in 1765 for Roger Morris, an English colonel. During the American Revolution it was used as General George Washington's headquarters. In 1810 it became the residence of Stephen and Eliza Jumel, who decorated it in the French Empire style. After the death of her husband, Eliza married former vice president Aaron Burr, the man who had shot Alexander Hamilton in a duel years before. Eliza had been a prostitute in her youth and had amassed a fortune that Burr managed to squander in bad investments. She sought a divorce from Burr in 1834, and he died two years later, on the day the divorce was granted. Eliza remained in the house until her death in 1865.

Today the house is open to the public as a museum, with period furniture in all the rooms. Entering the house is like stepping back into the nineteenth century. It is a true part of American history, with ties to President George Washington and Vice President Aaron Burr.

CELEDONIA JONES
Manhattan Borough Historian Emeritus

Women Who Soared the Heights

14.9 Fort Tryon Park

1935, Frederick Law Olmsted Jr.
West 192nd Street to Dyckman Street between Broadway and Riverside Drive
www.nycgovparks.org

14.10 **St. Frances Cabrini Shrine**
701 Fort Washington Avenue at West 190th Street
☏ 212 923 3536; www.mothercabrini.org

14.11 **New Leaf Restaurant and Bar**
1 Margaret Corbin Drive in Fort Tryon Park
☏ 212 568 5323; www.newleafrestaurant.com
Closed Mondays.

14.5 **Bennett Park**
West 183rd to West 185th Street between Fort Washington
and Pinehurst Avenues
www.nycgovparks.org

The rock layer of Manhattan schist that forms the solid
foundation for the city's famous skyscrapers runs the full
length of the island and is highest at the northern end.
Motorists on the George Washington Bridge and Henry
Hudson Parkway will notice the sheer faces of cliffs in
the section of upper Manhattan called Hudson Heights.
Possibly inspired by its geological supremacy as the highest point in the city, Hudson Heights has long been home
to women who soared to great heights themselves.

At the time of the American Revolution, upper Man-
hattan was the home of farmers who were mostly Tory
sympathizers. Our boys lost big time at the battle of Fort
Washington in 1776, fought in what is now Bennett Park.
(The site is bordered by Hudson View Gardens, New
York City's first cooperative apartments.)

The ramparts of the fort are outlined in granite blocks,
and include the site of the highest natural point in Manhattan (two hundred and sixty-eight feet above sea level).
A plaque on Fort Washington Avenue relates the details
of the battle, but not the story that a turncoat informed
the British of the placement of patriot guns. George

14

Washington watched the capture of twenty-eight hundred troops from the New Jersey side of the Hudson. The captured patriots were marched to lower Manhattan and placed in the notorious prison ships in the harbor downtown.

Among the wounded from the Battle of Fort Washington was Margaret "Captain Molly" Corbin, a camp follower who had accompanied her husband, John, who served in the patriot army as a matross, loading and swabbing the cannon. When John was killed, Molly took his place. Left for dead after suffering severe wounds to her arm and face, Molly was found and transported by the patriots to Philadelphia. She survived, but never fully recovered from her wounds. In 1779, she was made part of the Invalid Corps—soldiers who had been disabled fighting for freedom—and received a lifetime half-pension for the wounds she suffered. But her lifestyle did not inspire D.A.R. types to promote her as a figure of feminine patriotism as they did her more genteel Revolutionary sister, Molly Hays McCauley (Molly Pitcher), with whom she often is confused. It appears that our Molly was a hard-drinking girl.

Molly Corbin, first heroine of the American Revolution, is buried in West Point, just up the Hudson River, but she is commemorated by various sites in upper Manhattan. Going uptown a few blocks, you'll come to a traffic circle before the park entrance—Margaret Corbin Plaza. The spot from which her statue was stolen years ago by some enterprising New Yorkers now has a carved wooden sign announcing the entrance to Fort Tryon Park.

Fort Tryon Park is named after the last English civil governor of New York—a bit of a kick in the face for our guys and Molly. But pro-British feelings were at a high in 1935, when park renovations were completed and Rockefeller gave the land to the city. A plaque along the paved road near the site of the battle attests to Molly Corbin's contribution to the Revolution.

Just south of Margaret Corbin Plaza is the St. Frances Cabrini Shrine. The shrine, adjacent to Mother Cabrini High School, houses the relics of the saint known commonly as Mother Cabrini. In the chapel is a large mosaic relating the story of Mother Cabrini's life and works. She was born in Italy on July 15, 1850, and originally wished to become a missionary in China, choosing the name Frances Xavier for the martyred saint. After visiting Rome to request permission to travel to China, she was instructed by Pope Leo XIII, "Not to the East, but to the West." Mother Cabrini was sent to America. Here she cared for the immigrants flooding into New York who had neither social services nor access to the sacraments. She established schools, hospitals, orphanages, and nursing homes throughout the city. Mother Cabrini became an American citizen in 1909 and was canonized as "Mother of the American Immigrant" in 1946—the first American saint.

14

Mother Cabrini's relics are housed in a crystal coffin directly under the altar. It is a bit startling to see the relics of this pint-sized nun close up. Mother Cabrini is wearing the black habit of the nuns of her order, the Missionary Sisters of the Sacred Heart of Jesus. The chapel is crammed full of votive offerings and plaques thanking the saint for her intercession in granting miracles, and mementos from her life are displayed in the glass cases lining the gift shop. There are photos, medals, articles of clothing, and even the springs from her dentures. The nuns can be persuaded to open the cases to allow the faithful direct access to the saint's ribbons.

Saint Cabrini's feast is November 13. Every year the chapel celebrates with eight masses in five languages. An annual birthday celebration on July 15 includes masses in

English, Spanish, and Creole, as well as a children's carnival to which all Hudson Heights children are invited.

St. Frances Cabrini Shrine is located on a cliff overlooking the Hudson River at a site chosen by Mother Cabrini herself. As she drove her buggy to what was then a remote corner of New York City, she stopped there to rest her horses and enjoy the view. Much like those who visit here today, Mother Cabrini found great peace of mind in contemplating the magnificent view over the Hudson River and the Palisades. She purchased the property and opened Sacred Heart Orphan Asylum, a boarding school for girls. Now known as Mother Cabrini High School, the school continues to educate young Catholic women and was named a Blue Ribbon School by President Clinton in the year 2000, a hundred years after its founding.

World War II brought such an influx of German Jews to Hudson Heights that it became known as "Frankfurt on the Hudson." Today it is one of Manhattan's nicest residential neighborhoods, attracting families with small children as well as sizable Polish and Russian immigrant populations. It is not unusual to visit the famous Heather Garden of Fort Tryon Park and find young mothers who speak Spanish, Russian, or Polish seated beside older ladies chatting in German and Yiddish. Each may have a tale of courage to relate.

Visitors to Hudson Heights should be on the lookout for families of yellow hawks, which can occasionally be seen resting after their return from hunting in the thick woods of Fort Tryon Park. Human visitors looking for a place to rest and a bite to eat should head for New Leaf Restaurant in the Heather Garden, or bring a picnic and sit at the chess tables in Bennett Park. Here, you can enjoy the views and contemplate the scene where Molly Corbin made history as America's first heroine of the Revolution.

KIM DRAMER
Art historian

14.3 ## Jeffrey's Hook Lighthouse

1880
West 178th Street and the Hudson River under the east tower
of the George Washington Bridge
Tours only, spring through fall: ☎ 212 304 2365;
www.nycgovparks.org

The cast-iron Little Red Lighthouse was originally the
North Hook Beacon from 1880 to 1917 in Sandy Hook,
New Jersey. In 1921, ten years before the George Washington
Bridge was built, it was moved to this spot, known at the
time as Jeffrey's Hook. After the erection of the bridge,
the lighthouse's beacon was no longer required, but it was
saved from auction by letters from young readers who
loved the classic children's book *The Little Red Lighthouse
and the Great Gray Bridge*.

JAMES BOORSTEIN
Architectural conservator and artist

14

14.4 ## George Washington Bridge

1931, O.H. Ammann (engineer) & Cass Gilbert (architect)
West 178th Street and Fort Washington Avenue (Manhattan)
to Fort Lee (New Jersey)
www.panynj.gov

Wear your sneakers, walking shoes, or hiking boots. Whatever your walking pleasure, New York has myriad unique
places—parks, gardens, bridges, and boardwalks in which,
on which, and over which to walk. And well within an
hour of the city you can hike through wilderness and sand
dunes or even climb stone faces.

One of the most exciting city walks is crossing the George
Washington Bridge into New Jersey. From the bridge's
north walk you can see upstream to the mountains along
the Hudson River and watch the river's swift tidal current
rush below your feet. Behind you are cars, buses, and trucks,

and beyond them, the city's towers, but for a few moments in mid-span, you feel as free as the seagulls above you.
ESTELLE GILSON
Writer, journalist, and translator

If your time in New York has not humbled you, then a trip to the base of the George Washington Bridge might. Rising six hundred and four feet above the water, the most influential twentieth-century suspension bridge was completed in 1931; the lower level was added thirty years later, making it the world's only fourteen-lane suspension bridge. Le Corbusier famously described it as "the most beautiful bridge in the world."

To understand why, try examining its underbelly. There is a perfect point, directly under the roadway, where the lines of the span and the towers converge and everything falls—abstractly, serenely—into place.

When you get there, notice the two granite abutments that project well beyond the metal structure, just a few feet from the water. These were designed as the pedestals for the granite cladding designed by Cass Gilbert. The stone covering was abandoned, however, during the Depression, leaving the bridge's intended skeleton exposed. The commissioners and the public came to appreciate the Modernist view of the bridge's elegant structure, and over the years, it achieved iconic status. Beginning in 2001, the steel towers were illuminated for special occasions.

Before you leave, take some time to enjoy the Hudson River views. To the south, Manhattan arcs toward the east, allowing a view of the tall Riverside Church tower, seemingly nestled beside the Statue of Liberty and the skyscrapers of downtown. To the north are Manhattan's northern tip, the great Palisades, and the majestic, lazy Hudson, all looking amazingly rural.
JAMES BOORSTEIN
Architectural conservator and artist

Hudson Heights Stroll

14.6 **Hudson View Gardens**
1925, George F. Pelham
116 Pinehurst Avenue between West 183rd
and West 185th Streets
☎ 212 923 7800; www.hudsonviewgardens.com

14.8 **Birthplace of Maria Callas**
689 West 184th Street between Broadway and Bennett Avenue

14.7 **Castle Village**
1939, George F. Pelham II
120-200 Cabrini Boulevard between West 181st
and West 186th Streets
www.castlevillage.com

14.9 **Fort Tryon Park**
1935, Frederick Law Olmsted Jr.
West 192nd Street to Dyckman Street between Broadway
and Riverside Drive
www.nycgovparks.org

14

Upper Fort Washington Avenue begins at the George Washington Bridge in Manhattan. As you proceed north, you'll see Hudson View Gardens, a Tudor-style co-op apartment complex built in the 1920s. One street over is Castle Village, another co-op built over the Hudson in the 1930s. Beginning at 184th Street, several 1930s Art Deco-style apartment buildings remain. The brick Romanesque building at No. 689, now a co-op, was once a hospital where it's said that Maria Callas was born. Fort Washington Avenue ends at Fort Tryon Park, one of the city's most beautiful, with gorgeous views of the Hudson and the George Washington Bridge. The Cloisters, which houses part of the Metropolitan Museum's medieval collection, is located there.

ALFRED CORN
Author and educator

14.12 The Cloisters, The Metropolitan Museum of Art
1939, Allen, Collens & Willis
In Fort Tryon Park
99 Margaret Corbin Drive
☎ 212 923 3700; www.metmuseum.org
Closed Mondays.

The Cloisters, an extraordinary branch of the Metropolitan Museum at Fort Tryon Park, is a time machine that takes us back to medieval days. It is rich in its collection of tapestries, windows, statues, and icons from before the Renaissance, and the music playing softly throughout is authentic and reverent.

HUGH MARTIN
The late Hugh Martin was a songwriter. He wrote the score for Meet Me in St. Louis, in which Judy Garland sings "The Trolley Song" and "Have Yourself a Merry Little Christmas."

Unicorn Tapestries
c. 1500
Unicorn Tapestries Room

The Cloisters houses the celebrated Unicorn Tapestries, a series of late medieval tapestries depicting The Hunt of the Unicorn. The medieval legend, an allegory of both human love and the Incarnation of Christ, relates that only a virgin can tame the swift and powerful unicorn. An ivory tusk from a narwhal, once thought to be that of a unicorn, stands in one corner of the tapestry room.

KIM DRAMER
Art historian

The Cloisters' Gardens
1938, Margaret Freeman and James J. Rorimer

In the spring and summer visit the outdoor, early-fouteenth-century-style herb garden, located in the Bonnefont Cloister. The enchanting smells of two hundred and fifty species of flowers, plants, and herbs include those used for medicinal purposes, for painting illuminated manuscripts, for poison, and for cooking.

CHRISTINE MOOG
Graphic designer

There are three different gardens: the Trie Cloister and the Bonnefont Cloister Herb Garden are located on the lower level; the Cuxa Cloister is located near the entrance on the upper level.

Three cloisters in the building have gardens planted according to horticultural information gathered from medieval art and literature. This place is relatively tourist-free and there are magnificent views of the Hudson from the terraces. All this, along with the smell of the flowers and herbs, makes you feel as if you're in an old palazzo in Tuscany, even though the building itself is constructed from various buildings from France.

KATHARINE RISTICH
Editor, Theheart.org and Femina.com

14

14.13 Arts for Transit: *At the Start . . . At Long Last . . .*
1999, Sheila Levrant de Bretteville
www.mta.info

Traveling north to Fort Tryon Park or the Cloisters at the last (or first) stop on the A train in Inwood, one passes through Sheila Levrant de Bretteville's multifaceted oral history project at 207th Street and Broadway. *At the Start . . . At Long Last . . .* includes on the walls of the mezzanines scores of reminiscences about the neighborhood by community members past and present, representing several waves of immigration. The words and notes of the jazz classic "Take the A Train" are etched into the railings, and long, leggy mosaic Caribbean festival dancers descend or ascend the elevator with you from the street to the station.

JOYCE KOZLOFF
Artist

14.14   Inwood Hill Park

Entrance on West 215th Street and Indian Road
www.nycgovparks.org

Take the A train to 207th Street and walk a few blocks west
to Inwood Hill Park. The park, bounded on the west by the
Hudson River, on the north by the Harlem River and on the
south by Dyckman Street, occupies the northernmost tip of
Manhattan Island. From the entrance on Seaman Avenue,
wide paths wind along the edge of acres of ballfields. The
fields descend to a broad tidal marsh tucked into a cove of
the Harlem River. Covered by mud and reeds at low tide,
and shallow water at high tide, the marsh attracts legions of
birds. On the south side of the open fields are dense woods
and soaring ridges of stone, and at the opening of a narrow
valley between two ridges is a small boulder bearing a bronze
plaque that reads: *Shorakkopoch.*

According to legend, on this site of the principal Manhattan Indian village, Peter Minuit in 1626 purchased
Manhattan Island for trinkets and beads worth about sixty
guilders. This boulder also marks the spot where a tulip tree
(*Liriodendron tulipifera*) grew to a height of a hundred and
sixty-five feet and a girth of twenty feet. It was until its death
in 1933, at the age of two hundred and eighty years, the
last living link to the Reckgawawanc Indians who lived here.

Beyond the boulder, paths snake through thick woods
up the face of the western ridge. The trails pass alongside
tall cliffs and through groves of ancient, towering tulip-
poplar trees, perhaps the last vestige of primeval forest on
the island. At the summit of the ridge, the foliage opens to
reveal panoramic views of the Hudson. There are expansive vistas across to the New Jersey Palisades, south to the
George Washington Bridge, and many miles upriver to the
Tappan Zee. The serenity of the spot is only slightly

undercut by the sounds of traffic on the West Side Highway far below.

Peter Minuit's meeting with Native Americans at their village may be apocryphal. Historians have proposed other locations for the exchange, or suggested that an official purchase never took place. Native people had no conception of the private ownership of land, so even if the "purchase" occurred, it had little meaning for them. Still, there is a palpable sense of history here. It is easy to imagine Indians living in this valley. Fish and small game would have been abundant in the tidal marsh, and patches of corn or squash would have grown nicely in the low fields. A scout could run quickly up the western ridge, and from its peak observe anyone approaching from the Hudson. The proximity of two rivers made the village easily accessible, yet the high ridge hid and protected the valley behind it. Stone caves in the cliffs provided convenient shelter, as confirmed by Indian artifacts discovered there and removed in 1909.

The undisturbed landscape of Inwood Hill Park and the presence of a Native American past join to convey an impression of what Manhattan was like before being reshaped by Europeans.

DAVID L. REESE
Director, Gunster Hall, Virginia

Inwood Hill Park is virgin forest, not chopped down since the days of the Dutch.
PETE SEEGER
Songwriter

INDEX OF CONTRIBUTORS

Committee in the EPA's Harbor Estuary Program, a member of the Harbor Roundtable and Nature Network, and a council member of the Linnaean Society of New York. He has received the Wildlife Management Trust's prestigious Presidential Award and the New York State Department of Environmental Conservation Commissioner's Award, among others. pp. 17, 261

The Honorable JAMES J. BRUCIA is a justice, now retired, of the New York State Supreme Court. pp. 43, 152

The late MARGARET BRUCIA was a schoolteacher in Roslyn Heights, New York. p. 152

MARGARET A. BRUCIA is a Latin teacher. pp. 118, 203

JOHN BRYANT received a grant from the National Endowment for the Humanities to launch Melville Electronic Library, a digital "critical archive" of the works of Herman Melville. He is the author of *Melville and Repose* and *The Fluid Text*, and the editor of *Leviathan: A Journal of Melville Studies*. He is a professor of English at Hofstra University. p. 15

MARIO BUATTA, also known as the "Prince of Chintz," is one of America's foremost decorators. His high-profile clients include Henry Ford II, Malcolm Forbes, and Barbara Walters. p. 279

MELVIN JULES BUKIET is a novelist and literary critic. He is the author of six books of fiction, including *Strange Fire*, *Signs and Wonders*, and *A Faker's Dozen*. p. 298

The late PETER BURCHARD was an author, designer, and illustrator. His book *One Gallant Rush* was a major historical source for the motion picture *Glory*, which won three Academy Awards. He also wrote several children's books about slavery, abolitionism, and the American Civil War. He was a Guggenheim Fellow. p. 96, 100

CHRISTOPHER CAHILL is the author of *Perfection*. He has edited the essays of Thomas Flanagan under the title *There You Are: Writings on Irish and American Literature and History* as well as an anthology of Irish popular poetry, *Gather Round Me*. He is the executive director of The American Irish Historical Society and editor of its journal, *The Recorder*. p. 130

GEORGE CAMPBELL JR. recently retired as president of the Cooper Union for the Advancement of Science and Art. A physicist, he is a director of Con Edison, Inc., and Barnes & Noble, Inc., and a trustee of Rensselaer Polytechnic Institute. A recipient of the 1993 George Arents Pioneer Medal in Physics, he is a Fellow of the American Association for the Advancement of Science and the New York Academy of Sciences. p. 97

SARAH CAPLAN is a graphic designer and author of the Pratique shopping guides to SoHo, Nolita, the Meatpacking District, and the West Village. She is also the designer of paper dresses made of Tyvek, which have been sold around the world, and are in the permanent collection of the Museum at the Fashion Institute of Technology in New York. pp. 62, 212

CAROLYN CARTWRIGHT is an interior decorator and set designer for films. pp. 35, 96

The late GIORGIO CAVAGLIERI, a renowned architect, won the Gold Medal of the Architectural League of New York; the Medal of Honor of the New York Chapter of the American Institute of Architects; the Presidential Citation of the National American Institute of Architects; and fellowships from the American Institute of Architects and the NIAE, among other honors. p. 269

ARTnews executive editor ROBIN CEMBALEST is an award-winning investigative reporter who has published articles in *The New York Times*, *The Wall Street Journal*, and *El Pais*, in addition to many other newspapers and magazines in the United States and Europe. p. 316

WALTER CHATHAM is an architect based in New York City. He is a fellow of the American Academy in Rome and has served as president of the Architectural League of New York. pp. 31, 265

DAVID CHILDS is a consulting design partner at Skidmore, Owings & Merrill. He serves on the board of the American Academy in Rome, the Museum of Modern Art, the Municipal Art Society, the New York City Partnership, and the National Building Museum. pp. 19, 25

MARY CLARKE is a writer, editor, and native New Yorker. She was beauty director at *Modern Bride* and *Elegant Bride*, founding beauty editor of *Sassy Magazine*, and editor at magazines such as *Seventeen* and *Redbook*. p. 130

ROBIN CLEMENTS teaches at St. Bernard's School in New York City. p. 34

STACY COCHRAN has written and directed three feature films: *Drop Back Ten*, *Boys*, and *My New Gun*. She produced and directed *Richard Lester!*, a documentary about the director. p. 92

JIM CODDINGTON is chief conservator at the Museum of Modern Art in New York. p. 203

The artist PIER CONSAGRA has taught at Bard College, the Rhode Island School of Design, Pratt Institute, Columbia University, and Bennington College. He has had numerous shows. In 2005, he started a drawing program at the Metropolitan Museum of Art Education Department. p. 226

ROBERT COOK is an attorney at Anderson Kill & Olick, where he specializes in land-use matters in New York City. He is the author of *Zoning for Downtown Urban Design*, chairman of the Zoning Committee of Citizens Housing and Planning Council, and former chairman of the Committee on Land Use Planning and Zoning of the Association of the Bar of the City of New York. p. 30

THERESA CRAIG is the author of *Edith Wharton: A House Full of Rooms—Architecture, Interiors and Gardens*. She has taught literature at City University of New York and humanities at the New School University. pp. 29, 170

MICHAEL CUNNINGHAM is the author of the novels *A Home at the End of the World*, *Flesh and Blood*, *Specimen Days*, and *The Hours*, which was awarded a Pen/Faulkner Award and a Pulitzer Prize. p. 83

The late PHILLIP DANZIG was a muralist and an architect. He worked with the Cityarts Workshop project to design and implement *Rolling Bench*, a mosaic tile bench around Grant's Tomb in upper Manhattan. p. 306

GLORIA DEÁK is a scholar of American art and cultural affairs. She is the author of many books about American cultural history, including *Picturing America* and *Picturing New York*. p. 79

LISA DENNISON is an executive at Sotheby's auction house. She was formerly the deputy director and chief curator at the Solomon R. Guggenheim Museum. p. 243

LORRAINE B. DIEHL is the author of *The Late, Great Pennsylvania Station*; *Subways: The Tracks That Built New York City*; and *The Automat: The History, Recipes, and Allure of Horn & Hardart's Masterpiece*. She has contributed to *New York* magazine, *The New York Times*, *Travel & Leisure*, *American Heritage*, and the *New York Daily News*. p. 270

The painter SIMON DINNERSTEIN has had numerous one-man exhibitions, and two monographs of his work have been published. He is the recipient of the Rome Prize from the American Academy in Rome and a Fulbright grant. p. 217

KIM DRAMER is a specialist in the art and archaeology of early China. She is the author of numerous books on China for the young adult audience, and lectures extensively on Chinese culture. She is an assistant professor in humanities and social sciences at the Cooper Union. pp. 318, 326

LAURIE DUCHOVNY is a teacher and a writer. She has taught at Saint Ann's School, a private school in Brooklyn, for many years. p. 120

ALEXANDER DUFF is a restaurateur in Miami and New York whose endeavors have included A Fish Called Avalon, Rebar, Pacific Time, Pacific East, Groovejet, Gigi Bistro, and Top of the Strand. p. 188

KATE HARTNICK ELLIOTT is president and founder of Hartnick Consulting, a marketing strategy, communications, and executive search firm in New York City. On the weekend, she is an avid urban explorer. pp. 115, 291

LOUISA ERMELINO's novels celebrate the power of women, her Italian American ancestry, and her New York City neighborhood. She is the author of *Joey Dee Gets Wise*, *The Black Madonna*, and *The Sisters Mallone*. She is chief of reporters at *InStyle* magazine. p. 63

MATTHEW FIELD has edited more than fifty books on magic and is the video reviewer for *Genii*, the international conjurer's magazine. He is the editor of the *Magic Circular* magazine. p. 119

JANE FISHER is a consultant in publishing and direct marketing whose career has included stints at such companies as Oxford University Press, Macmillan, Condé Nast, and Scholastic. pp. 38, 45, 177

DAVID FISHMAN is an architectural historian at Robert A. M. Stern Architects. He is co-author, with Robert A. M. Stern and Thomas Mellins, of *New York 1880* and *New York 1960*, and co-author, with Robert A. M. Stern and Jacob Tilove, of *New York 2000*. pp. 201, 204

Since 1989, CHRISTOPHER FORBES has been vice chairman of Forbes, Inc., which publishes *Forbes Magazine* and Forbes.com. He is the chairman of the American Friends of the Louvre, and he sits on the boards of the Friends of New Jersey State Museum, the New York Academy of Art, and the Prince Wales Foundation. In 2003, he was appointed a Chevalier of the Legion of Honor by the French Government. p. 76

BRUCE S. FOWLE co-founded FXFOWLE Architects in 1978. His work has been widely published and includes numerous award-winning projects. He is a member of the American Institute of Architects' College of Fellows and Academician of the National Academy of Design. In 2010, he received the Harry B. Rutkins Award for Service to the AIA New York Chapter. He is a founder of the New York chapter of Architects, Designers, and Planners for Social Responsibility. p. 179

ALEX FRENCH is a writer and journalist. His work has appeared in numerous publications, including *GQ*, *New York* magazine, the *Los Angeles Times Magazine*. p. 53

M. PAUL FRIEDBERG is a landscape architect, planner, product designer, and author. Principal in charge of design at M. Paul Friedman & Partners since founding the firm in 1958, he is best known for his work in urban landscape, including urban playgrounds, plazas, malls, and parks. He received the ASLA Design Medal, the highest honor of the American Society of Landscape Architects, and the AIA Medal in recognition of his influence on the architectural profession. He is Professor Emeritus at City College New York. p. 306

The late MARGOT GAYLE was an eminent preservationist, and co-founder, in 1966, of the Victorian Society in America. She was also the founder of the Friends of Cast Iron Architecture and is credited with raising public awareness nationwide of the significance of iron-fronted buildings of the Victorian era. Her preservation efforts extended from the 1960s when she successfully campaigned to save the Jefferson Market Courthouse in Greenwich Village, to a drive in the 1990s to restore the Yorkville sidewalk clock on Third Avenue near 85th Street.

Among her books are *Cast-Iron Architecture in America: The Significance of James Bogardus* and *Cast-Iron Architecture in New York.* p. 247

LEE GELBER, a born and bred New Yorker, is an urban historian and tour guide. He gives architecture walking tours, as well as tours of neighborhoods such as the Lower East Side, Harlem, and the Financial District. He was dubbed the "Dean of Guides" by *The New York Times.* p. 192, 294

ESTELLE GILSON is a writer, journalist, and translator. She is the translator of works by Umberto Saba, Massimo Bontempelli, and Giacomo Debenedetti, and (from Hebrew) of poet Gabriel Preil. She is the recipient of numerous awards for journalism and translation, including the PEN Renato Poggioli Translation Award. p. 323

KENNETH SEEMAN GINIGER is a publisher, an editor, and the author of ten books. p. 168

SCOTT GLASS is a founding principal of Guerin Glass Architects, a full-service firm with a focus on architecture, interior design, and planning. Previously, he was a founder of BDDW, Inc., a design and manufacturing firm. p. 222

MARYELLEN GORDON is the director of the Magazine/Digital Program at the Summer Publishing Institute at New York University. She is the founder of Stable of Content, consultants to lifestyle and fashion brands, helping to create an editorial vision for their websites and published content. Previously, she was the deputy editor at *Glamour* magazine. p. 23

ALEXANDER GORLIN is principal and founder of Alexander Gorlin Architects in New York City. The firm has won numerous awards, most notably AIA Design Awards for the Ruskin Place town house, House in the Rocky Mountains, North Shore Hebrew Academy, and the Southampton House. p. 158

JOHN GUARE was awarded the Gold Medal in Drama by the American Academy of Arts and Letters for his Obie-, New York Drama Critics' Circle–, and Tony-winning plays, including *House of Blue Leaves*, *Six Degrees of Separation*, and *A Few Stout Individuals*. He teaches playwriting at the Yale School of Drama. pp. 85, 135, 213, 259

AGNES GUND is President Emerita of the Museum of Modern Art and chairman of its International Council. She is currently chairman of the Mayor's Cultural Affairs Advisory Commission of New York City. In 1977, she founded the Studio in a School Association in response to budget cuts that virtually eliminated arts classes from New York City public schools. A philanthropist and collector of modern and contemporary art, she has served on the boards of numerous arts organizations, including the Barnes Foundation and the Menil Collection, and currently serves on the boards of Chess in the Schools, Contemporary Art Center, P.S. 1, the Frick Collection, and Socrates Sculpture Park, among others. p. 216

JUDITH MARA GUTMAN is a writer, lecturer, and academic. She is the author of seven books, including a biography. She is a member of PEN and its Freedom-to-Write committee, and the Authors' Guild. p. 26

Born in New York City and raised by two architects, SEBASTIAN HARDY has been exploring New York City without supervision since he was old enough to unlock the front door. pp. 111, 127, 305

ANGELA HEDERMAN is editor and publisher at The Little Bookroom. pp. 56, 181

STEVEN HELLER is an art director, author, and the co-founder and co-chair of the MFA Design Department and co-founder of the MFA Design Criticism Department at the School of Visual Arts in New York. He is the author, co-author, or editor of over a hundred books on graphic design, illustration, and political art, and a columnist for The New York Times Book Review. He was an art director at The New York Times for thirty-three years. pp. 93, 175

DAVID J. HELLERSTEIN is the director of Medical Communications at the Columbia University Department of Psychiatry and associate professor of Clinical Psychiatry at the Columbia University College of Physicians and Surgeons. He has also received national recognition for his literary writing, and has been awarded the Pushcart Prize and several MacDowell Colony Fellowships. His books include Battles of Life and Death, Loving Touches, and the memoir Family of

Doctors. His journalism has been published in magazines including Harper's and The New York Times Magazine. A Distinguished Fellow of the American Psychiatric Association, he has served as President of the New York County District Branch of the American Psychiatric Association. p. 186

SCOTT HESS is a screenwriter, an award-winning writer/performer, and author. He is a regular contributor to several national magazines, as well as the gay/lesbian section editor of Harper Collins' Access Guide New York City. p. 84

SAM HOFFMAN has produced, directed, and assistant-directed movies such as The Royal Tenenbaums, School of Rock, Dead Man Walking, Groundhog Day, and Curse of the Jade Scorpion. He is the founder, with Eric Speigelman and Tim Williams, of the website Old Jews Telling Jokes. p. 142

PETER J. HOLLIDAY is a professor of the history of art and classical archaeology at California State University, Long Beach. He has written extensively on Greek and Roman art. pp. 225, 275, 301

RACHAEL HOROVITZ's feature-film producing credits include About Schmidt, State and Main, and Next Stop, and she was the executive producer of HBO's Grey Gardens. She recently returned to independent producing after a decade as a senior production executive at Revolution Studios and New Line Cinema. She co-founded, with Joe Hall, the Cinema School, a public high school in the Bronx. p. 90

received fellowships from the Guggenheim Foundation and the National Endowment for the Arts. He is on the faculty of the creative writing program at the University of Arizona. p. 242

The late PHILIP JOHNSON came to prominence in the 1930s as the first director of the Department of Architecture at the Museum of Modern Art. He had a long and influential career as an architect, curator, and critic. He was awarded the American Institute of Architects Gold Medal and received the first Pritzker Prize in 1979. p. 200

CELEDONIA JONES is Manhattan Borough Historian Emeritus. In 1998, he was recognized as one of New York City's Centennial Historians. p. 318

FIONA KAHN is managing editor of City Secrets and co-founder of Fang Duff Kahn Publishers. p. 175

LAWRENCE KAHN is a Professor Emeritus of Pediatrics at Washington University in St. Louis. Currently, one of his main activities is leading a group from the Lifelong Learning Institute in reading and interpreting all of Shakespeare's plays. He takes great pleasure in the practical application of his son's City Secrets guides. p. 243

ROBERT KAHN, editor of the City Secrets series, is founding principal of the award-winning firm, Robert Kahn Architect, based in New York City. A recipient of the Rome Prize in Architecture from the American Academy in Rome, he has received numerous awards from the NY chapter of the American Institute of Architects. He has taught at Columbia University, Ohio State University, and Yale University, where he held a Davenport Chair Professorship. He is co-founder, with his wife Fiona Kahn, of Fang Duff Kahn Publishers. pp. 37, 68, 71, 156, 161, 213

PAUL KANE is a professor of English and co-associate chair of English at Vassar College. He has published four collections of poems. He has been poetry editor of *Antipodes* since 1987 and has served as artistic director of the annual Mildura Writers Festival. He was a Fulbright scholar to Australia in 1984–1985. Other awards include fellowships from the National Endowment for the Humanities and the John Simon Guggenheim Memorial Foundation. p. 134

DAVID BAR KATZ is a writer and director in every medium other than comic books, though he hopes to break into them soon. p. 105

ROBERT KAUFELT is the proprietor of Murray's Cheese Shop, one of Greenwich Village's oldest continuously running businesses. He writes and teaches about food and lives in Greenwich Village with his wife, Patricia, an artist. p. 54

EDMUND KEELEY is a novelist, translator, critic, and the author of thirty-two books. He is a prize-winning novelist and a noted expert on Greek poets and on post-Second World War Greek history. A former president of the PEN American Center, he received the Rome Prize from the American Academy in Rome, the Academy Award in Literature from the American Academy of Arts and Letters, and the Ralph Manheim Medal for Translation. In 2001, he was awarded with Commander of the Order of the Phoenix by the Greek government. He is the Charles Barnwell Straut English Professor Emeritus at Princeton University. p. 56

BETTY KEIM is an editor, writer, and musicologist. She is the founder of Keim Publishing, which provides editorial, production, and design services to publishers, nonprofit organizations, and other companies. She has written scripts for documentary films on American architecture. p. 205

BINNIE KIRSHENBAUM is the author of two story collections and six novels, the most recent of which is *The Scenic Route*. She is the chair of the M.F.A. program at Columbia University. p. 146

HOWARD KISSEL, who blogs as the Cultural Tourist for the *Huffington Post*, has written about the arts in New York for four decades. He was the chief theater critic of the *New York Daily News* for twenty years. Before that he was the arts editor of *Women's Wear Daily* and *W*. He is the only person to have been the chairman of both the New York Film Critics Circle and the New York Drama Critics Circle. He is the author of several books, including *The Abominable Showman*, a

biography of producer David Merrick, and *The Art of Acting*. He has also written for *The Wall Street Journal*, *Vogue*, *Playbill*, and *Interview*. p. 290

EDWARD I. KOCH served in the United States House of Representatives from 1969 to 1977 and three terms as the mayor of New York from 1978 to 1989. He was born and raised in the Bronx. p. 224

BILL KOMOSKI is a painter and native New Yorker. He teaches at the School of Visual Arts. p. 132

JOYCE KOZLOFF is an artist. She lives in New York City. pp. 144, 274, 327

GAIL KRIEGEL is a playwright, librettist, and composer. Her plays include *On the Home Front* and *Sweetie*. The film *Fragments*, adapted from her play and for which she wrote the screenplay, won top awards at five film festivals. She was a visiting artist at the American Academy in Rome and is the recipient of a Rockefeller Foundation Fellowship. pp. 28, 30

EVELYN and PETER KRAUS are the owners of Ursus Books and Prints, specializing in art books, rare books of all kinds, and decorative master prints. p. 111

ALISA LaGAMMA is an art historian and a curator in the Department of the Arts of Africa, Oceania, and the Americas at the Metropolitan Museum of Art. p. 232

ANNE LANDSMAN is the author of *Rowing Lessons*, for which she won the Sunday Times Fiction Prize, and

for the New York Public Library's Schomburg Center for Research in Black Culture. He is author and co-author of several works including *The Black New Yorkers* and *Slavery In New York*. He wrote and co-produced the History Channel's award-winning series *The African Burial Ground: An American Discovery*. He is commissioner of the NYC Landmarks Preservation Commission and the New York City Archival Review Board. In 2008, he received the U.S. Congressional Black Caucus's Veterans' Braintrust Award. He founded Teaching America, a historic walking-tour program for educators and students. He is a twelfth-generation descendant of Manhattan's first African, Dutch, and Native American community. pp. 20, 43, 308, 312

GREGORY MOSHER is a director and producer of nearly two hundred stage productions and has received every major American theater award, including two Tony Awards and a Drama Desk Special Award. He was the director of Lincoln Center Theater from 1985 to 1992 and created the Arts Initiative at Columbia University in 2004. He is also a film and television director, producer, and writer, as well as an adjunct professor at the School of the Arts at Columbia University. pp. 62, 169, 274

ANTONI MUNTADAS is a multidisci-plinary media artist. His work has been exhibited widely, including at the Museum of Modern Art, the Venice Biennale, Documenta VI, and Documenta X. He was a Research Fellow at the Center for Advanced Visual Studies at MIT from 1977 to 1984, and is currently visiting professor at the MIT Visual Arts Program. p. 162

GERALDINE NAGER-GRIFFIN is a senior vice president at Sotheby's New York. p. 252

VICTORIA NEWHOUSE is an architec-tural historian. She is the author of *Towards a New Museum and Art* and *Art and the Power of Place-ment*, two studies of museums and their relationships with collectors, trustees, artists, and the public. She lectures internationally on museums and architecture, and has published on the subject in *The New York Times*, *Architectural Record*, and *ARTNews*. p. 317

KATHRYN NOCERINO is a writer. Her fiction appears in *Growing up Ethnic in America* and *Identity Lessons*. Her books of poetry include *Death of the Plankton Bar and Grill*, *Candles in the Daylight*, and *Wax Lips*. p. 281

STARR OCKENGA is a garden photographer, writer, and lecturer. Her books include *Eden on Their Minds: American Gardeners with Bold Visions* and *Earth on Her Hands: The American Woman in Her Garden*, which received an American Horticultural Society Book Award. Her work has

collections of neurological case histories, including *The Man Who Mistook His Wife for a Hat*, *Musicophilia*, and *The Mind's Eye*. *Awakenings*, his book about a group of patients who survived the great encephalitis lethargica epidemic of the early twentieth century, inspired the Academy Award–nominated feature film starring Robert De Niro and Robin Williams. He is a frequent contributor to *The New Yorker* and the *New York Review of Books*, and a Fellow of the American Academy of Arts and Letters and the American Academy of Arts and Sciences. p. 313

The late ARTHUR SAINER was a playwright, teacher, and critic. His plays were honored with awards from the Ford and Rockefeller Foundations, and the National Foundation for Jewish Culture. His books include *Zero Dances*, a biography of Zero Mostel, and *The New Radical Theatre Notebook*. p. 312

BARNET SCHECTER is a historian and the author of *George Washington's America*, *The Devil's Own Work*, and *The Battle for New York*. He was an advisor for the New-York Historical Society's exhibit *Lincoln and New York*, and a contributor to the companion volume. A contributing editor of the three-volume *Encyclopedia of the American Revolution* and *Landmarks of the American Revolution*, he is also a contributor to the *Encyclopedia of New York City*. He is a Fellow of the New York Academy of History. p. 280

MARTHA SCHULMAN, a native New Yorker, is a writer and teacher whose short stories have appeared in *Gulfstream* and *The Seattle Review*. She is a Writing Associate and Writing Fellow at the Cooper Union Center for Writing. pp. 57, 113, 289

MICHAEL SCHWARTING is an architect, urban designer, and professor. He is a professor of architecture, and director of the graduate program in Urban and Regional Design at New York Institute of Technology, where he has also served as chair at the Central Islip Campus. He has taught at Columbia University, the Cooper Union, University of Pennsylvania, Yale University, and Cornell University. He received a Rome Prize Fellowship from the American Academy in Rome, for which he is a Trustee Emeritus. p. 40

FREDERIC SCHWARTZ is an award-winning architect and planner with particular expertise in affordable, sustainable housing. He was recently selected by the citizens of New Orleans and the New Orleans City Planning Commission to replan one-third of the city for forty percent of its post-Katrina population. As winner of an international competition, he designed the Staten Island Ferry Terminal in Manhattan. He is a Fellow of the American Academy in Rome, and was selected by the Architecture League of New York for both the Young Architect's Award and the Emerging Voice in Architecture Award. He has taught at Princeton, Columbia, Harvard,

Her other novels are *Cranberry Queen*, *The Difference Between You and Me*, and *Drizzle*. She has been a consultant for NYU's Tisch School of the Arts M.F.A. dramatic writing program, as well as for Tisch's undergraduate dramatic writing candidates. She is a senior lecturer in Cinema Studies at the University of Pennsylvania. pp. 16, 37, 38, 52, 68, 294

JANE TUCKER VASILIOU has held various positions at Wall Street firms, including five years as vice president of Institutional Corporate Bonds at Paine Webber Jackson and Curtis. Currently she is with Vasiliou & Co., Inc., an investment management firm. She is on the board of trustees of the Graduate Center Foundation, City University of New York. p. 278

ANITA VELEZ-MITCHELL is a poet, short-story writer, essayist, actress, and dancer. She has received four Ibero-American Writers Awards. p. 250

THOMAS VON ESSEN was appointed the thirtieth FDNY Commissioner of the City of New York in 1996, and served in that position until 2001, nearly four months after the September 11, 2001, attacks. In 2002 he was made an Honorary Commander of the Order of the British Empire. p. 293

BASIL WALTER is the founding partner of Basil Walter Architects (BWA), an international architecture and design firm with offices in New York City and Beijing, China.

Recent projects include the preservation and reinvention of the former IRT Powerhouse and the re-design of the Monkey Bar restaurant, both in New York. He is the architecture and design advisor for *Vanity Fair*. p. 182

GERALD WEALES is an Emeritus Professor of English at the University of Pennsylvania. A former drama critic for *The Reporter* and *Commonweal*, he is the author of many books on theater and film, as well as a novel and several children's books. p. 306

The late GEORGE WEISSMAN was a former president of Philip Morris Companies, board chairman of the Lincoln Center for the Performing Arts, founding board member of Jazz at Lincoln Center, a trustee of the Whitney Museum, and a director of the New York Chamber of Commerce and Industry. Baruch College's Weissman School of Arts and Sciences is named after him and his wife. p. 274

MARJORIE WELISH is a poet, artist, and art critic. She is the author of *Signifying Art: Essays on Art after 1960* and *The Annotated "Here" and Selected Poems*, which was a finalist for the Lenore Marshall Prize from the Academy of American Poets. Her writing on art has appeared in *Art in America*, *Art International*, *ARTNews*, *Bomb*, and *Salmagundi*. She has received grants and fellowships from the Gottlieb Foundation, the Djerassi Foundation, the International Studio

ROBERT KAHN, creator and editor of the City Secrets series, is founding principal of Robert Kahn Architect, based in New York City. A recipient of the Rome Prize in Architecture from the American Academy in Rome, he has received numerous awards from the New York chapter of the American Institute of Architects. His work has been featured in *The New York Times Magazine*, *The New York Times*, and *Architectural Digest*, among other publications. He has taught design at Ohio State University, Columbia University, and Yale University, where he held a Davenport Chair Professorship.

A portion of the proceeds of the sale of this book will be donated to the Municipal Art Society of New York and The New York Times Neediest Cases Fund.

THE MUNICIPAL ART SOCIETY OF NEW YORK is a private not-for-profit membership organization whose mission is to promote a more livable city. Since 1893, the society has worked to enrich the culture, neighborhoods, and physical design of New York City. The Municipal Arts Society advocates for excellence in urban planning, contemporary architecture, historic preservation, and public art. (www.mas.org)

THE NEW YORK TIMES NEEDIEST CASES FUND was founded in 1912 by Adolph S. Ochs, then publisher of *The New York Times*. Each year, the Foundation administers a fundraising campaign during the holiday season, with daily stories describing the hardships of many of the city's neediest children, disabled, and elderly. The campaign draws contributions from thousands of readers, totaling about $6 million each year. Assistance by the fund is rendered through seven large multi-service agencies that serve New Yorkers of all denominations in the metropolitan area. Over the years the Fund has raised $250 million. (www.nytco.com)

I am deeply grateful to all the contributors who have so generously and eloquently shared their insights, expertise, and love of New York. It has been a privilege and an honor to receive each one of your essays.

NOTES

NOTES